ENGLISH AND ITS TEACHERS

English and Its Teachers offers a historical overview of the development of secondary English teaching in schools over the past 50 years. Initially charting the rise of a new progressive approach in the 1960s, the book then considers the implications for the subject and its teachers of three decades of central policy intervention. Throughout, document and interview data are combined to construct a narrative that details the fascinating and, at times, turbulent history.

The book is divided into two main parts – 'The age of invention' and 'The age of intervention'. The first of these sections details how innovative English teachers and academics helped to develop a new model. The second section explores how successive governments have sought to shape English through policy. A final part draws comparisons with the teaching of the subject in other major English-speaking nations and considers what the future might hold.

English and Its Teachers is a valuable resource for those interested in the teaching of English in secondary schools, from new entrants to the profession, to experienced teachers and academics working in the sector.

Simon Gibbons is the director of teacher education at King's College London.

NATIONAL ASSOCIATION FOR THE TEACHING OF ENGLISH (NATE)

NATE

The National Association for the Teaching of English (NATE), founded in 1963, is the professional body for all teachers of English from primary to Post-16. Through its regions, committees and conferences, the association draws on the work of classroom practitioners, advisers, consultants, teacher trainers, academics and researchers to promote dynamic and progressive approaches to the subject by means of debate, training and publications. NATE is a charity reliant on membership subscriptions. If you teach English in any capacity, please visit www.nate.org.uk and consider joining NATE, so the association can continue its work and give teachers of English and the subject a strong voice nationally.

This series of books co-published with NATE reflects the organisation's dedication to promoting standards of excellence in the teaching of English, from early years through to university level. Titles in this series promote innovative and original ideas that have practical classroom outcomes and support teachers' own professional development.

Books in the NATE series include both pupil and classroom resources and academic research aimed at English teachers, students on PGCE/ITT courses and NQTs.

Titles in this series include:

International Perspectives on Teaching English in a Globalised World
Andrew Goodwyn, Louann Reid and Cal Durrant

Sharing not Staring, 2nd Edition
Trevor Millum and Chris Warren

Teaching Grammar Structure and Meaning
Marcello Giovanelli

Researching and Teaching Reading
Gabrielle Cliff Hodges

Introducing Teachers' Writing Groups
Jenifer Smith and Simon Wrigley

Creative Approaches to Teaching Grammar
Martin Illingworth and Nick Hall

Knowing about Language
Marcello Giovanelli and Dan Clayton

ENGLISH AND ITS TEACHERS

A History of Policy, Pedagogy and Practice

Simon Gibbons

LONDON AND NEW YORK

First published 2017
by Routledge
2 Park Square, Milton Park, Abingdon, Oxon OX14 4RN

and by Routledge
711 Third Avenue, New York, NY 10017

Routledge is an imprint of the Taylor & Francis Group, an informa business

© 2017 Simon Gibbons

The right of Simon Gibbons to be identified as author of this work has been asserted by him in accordance with sections 77 and 78 of the Copyright, Designs and Patents Act 1988.

British Library Cataloguing in Publication Data
A catalogue record for this book is available from the British Library

Library of Congress Cataloging in Publication Data
Names: Gibbons, Simon, author.
Title: English and its teachers : a history of policy, pedagogy and practice / Simon Gibbons.
Description: Abingdon, Oxon ; New York, NY : Routledge, [2017]
Identifiers: LCCN 2016041429 | ISBN 9781138948921 (hbk) | ISBN 9781138948938 (pbk) | ISBN 9781315669366 (ebk)
Subjects: LCSH: English philology--Study and teaching--England--History. | English language--Study and teaching--England--History.
Classification: LCC PE68.G5 G53 2017 | DDC 428.0071/242--dc23
LC record available at https://lccn.loc.gov/2016041429

ISBN: 978-1-138-94892-1 (hbk)
ISBN: 978-1-138-94893-8 (pbk)
ISBN: 978-1-315-66936-6 (ebk)

Typeset in Bembo
by Taylor & Francis Books

MIX
Paper from
responsible sources
FSC
www.fsc.org   FSC® C013056

Printed and bound in Great Britain by
TJ International Ltd, Padstow, Cornwall

Dedicated to Leanne and Ruby

CONTENTS

Acknowledgements   *viii*

1   Introduction   1

PART I
The age of invention   **13**

2   A new progressivism: English in the 1960s and into the 1970s   15

3   The calm before the storm? English from the 1970s into the
    1980s   40

PART II
The age of intervention   **59**

4   Standardisation? The National Curriculum and assessment   61

5   New Labour, new policies: the focus on literacy   84

6   To coalition and beyond: back to the future?   109

PART III
Abroad and beyond   **137**

7   An English subject abroad   139

8   Conclusion   158

Index   *167*

ACKNOWLEDGEMENTS

No text, even one that appears to be the work of a single author, is an individual enterprise, and thus thanks are rightly due to a number of individuals and groups without whose support this book would not have progressed beyond the stage of a nebulous idea. I'd like to thank Gary Snapper and the NATE/Routledge editorial group for encouraging me to pursue this work at the proposal stage and for making helpful suggestions, along with Ken Jones, for improvements in content and structure. Thanks are also due to those colleagues who generously gave their time to be interviewed as part of the research for this book; they did this freely and in a spirit of honesty and openness. It was a privilege to listen to their knowledge and expertise as they shared their memories.

As the writing of this book progressed, the conversations with my colleague Bethan Marshall were crucially important in helping me to organise my thinking and, in acting as a critical friend, Viv Ellis' comments on various drafts were of enormous assistance. My wife, Leanne, too, deserves huge acknowledgement for supporting me during the writing process and all the stresses and strains that can bring.

Finally, to the many, many English teachers who have been an inspiration to me throughout my career – those I have worked alongside, helped to train, met at conferences, socialised with. They are too numerous to name, but they are the inspiration for this book. I firmly believe English teachers are a special breed – optimistic, positive and unflinching in their desire to improve young people's lives and futures. Their collective history should be remembered.

1

INTRODUCTION

I would argue that this book is long overdue. In terms of subjects taught in England's schools, perhaps the focus of the most intense argument, debate and dispute over the last fifty years has been the content and nature of secondary English, its curriculum, its teaching and its assessment. After a period of such argument, debate and dispute the time is right for a retrospective reflection – an evaluation of where we've been, where we are and where we might be going.

Reasons for the arguments around the nature of English are obvious. Even those who would reduce an English curriculum to something they might call the basics of learning to read (or at least decode) fluently, use grammar correctly in speech and writing and spell and punctuate accurately would find it hard to defend a position that claims that the role of the subject in the education and development of children is not only profoundly important on an individual level but also in the way society itself evolves. A basic skills curriculum in itself works to reinforce and reproduce certain societal norms – in fact it could easily be argued that it seeks to reverse or at least stem the tide of inevitable changes in the way the world functions. This is not a neutral enterprise.

A broader English curriculum that embraces the seemingly ever-increasing varieties of language and dialect, explores how language changes over time, introduces children to the breadth of ways in which they can speak and write in the increasing forms of media available to them, and exposes them to literature from across times and continents and cultures has the potential to do so much more. The links between language development and thought attest to the significance of English in the way it can enable the growth of character, and how in developing linguistics resources children are internalising culture and society. Literature, in revealing the worlds, minds, sensibilities and beliefs of writers, allows children to deepen understanding of the way they and others live, and pursue fundamental moral, ethical and political questions. A schooling in English is powerful, or it is dangerous – or both, depending on one's own perspective. Sophisticated users of language in all its forms are able to question, to criticise, to challenge. Little wonder battles have been fought, won and lost over what English should look like for children. Though the arguments may not be new, the battles have been at their most intense in England over the last five decades.

If we can generalise – as indeed one inevitably must to an extent when writing a history – it might be fair to characterise these last fifty years of subject English as being represented by three periods. The first, from the mid-1960s to the mid-1980s, was a period when English as a subject was rapidly expanding – with teachers looking beyond its traditional boundaries to draw in new technologies, media and moving image, multicultural literature and new teenage fiction that reflected the challenges of an ever more diverse culture. The period saw the rapid expansion of comprehensive schooling in England. This was a time when significant numbers of English teachers, individually and collectively, were fighting for something; an English curriculum that would best serve the needs of children in changing contexts – both socially and educationally. It was, too, a time when increasing attention to ideas about cognitive development and psychology, and concerns about class, race and gender, were harnessed in efforts to articulate an overarching theory for the teaching and learning of the subject. This was the time of the growth of a new progressive pedagogy for the teaching of English in the secondary school.

The second period, which we can perhaps roughly date from the advent of the National Curriculum in the late 1980s to the early years of the new millennium, was a time of unprecedented central intervention in schools in terms of curriculum, assessment and pedagogy, symptomatic of a standards-based reform agenda in education that was taking hold in many parts of the globe. The period saw increased marketisation of education, and a move away from aspirations for a comprehensive system administered by strong local authorities towards a more fragmented school landscape, ultimately in the form of mass academisation.

English was always at the head of the queue when the latest policy intervention was to be delivered. During this period, many English teachers were fighting against central impositions, endeavouring to ensure the curriculum retained many of the progressive elements that had become part of orthodox practice, resisting assessment regimes that threatened to narrow the curriculum and constrain teaching, and trying to retain methods that came under threat from new, apparently evidence-based teaching strategies that did not always even seem to be English – at least not as many teachers knew it – and that intended the subject to serve ends that, for many teachers, were at least at odds with, if not anathema to, their own visions. New models of English, or attempts to return to more traditional models, more neatly fed the standards reform agenda so that, whether policymakers actually believed in them or not, they were promoted at the expense of progressive models of the subject.

The third and final period, dating from the mid-2000s and existing as the status quo today, is perhaps one where it is tempting to say that the fight has disappeared, perhaps because it is difficult to see where the fight is, how to fight it and to sustain any belief that it can be won. Even if, to an extent, central intervention has become less overtly direct, and even if the landscape now purports to offer schools and teachers more freedom, the legacy of nearly thirty years of top-down reform has been profound deprofessionalisation – leaving English teachers with the underlying sense that the critical decisions about what to teach and how to teach are no longer theirs to make. So hegemonic seems the discourse around standards, accountability, performance and attainment that it can appear that this is just the way things are. In such a context it is critical for English teachers to review how this came to be.

This division into three periods is, as I say, to generalise, and it is, further, my perspective. Reality, of course, is not so straightforward. I know I am not alone, however, in taking the view that the introduction of the National Curriculum was a watershed moment in the story of government intervention into the teaching and learning of English. Whether widely shared or not, this perspective is a critical starting point, and a foundation for my claim about the importance of this book. Many of those engaged in the researching and writing of educational history have made claims for the importance of history. As McCulloch has shown (McCulloch, 2011) there have been competing rationales within the study of the history of education, and in most recent decades, in the United Kingdom at least, the importance of research in the field seems to have been largely overlooked, certainly by policymakers – despite their claims to favour evidence-based policy reform. McCulloch argued for a reassertion of the value of historical research and its significance for the present and the future. If we consider the specific case of English in schools, the contested history of its development demands that those who genuinely want to make sense of current curriculum and assessment regimes appreciate how we got here.

I would argue that to be a genuinely effective teacher of English, one needs more than the ability to implement the most recently recommended teaching strategy or to download the latest inspection-proof lesson or unit of work. One needs to have a clear sense of what English is, what its purpose in the education of children should be, and the ways in which this is best effected in a given classroom, at a given time, with a particular group of pupils. For want of a more satisfactory term, it is about having an underpinning foundation – a philosophy – of the subject and how it is best learnt and taught. To establish this, and I am perfectly content to live with the ambiguity that different teachers of English have different, firmly held, philosophies, it seems self-evident that a knowledge of history is critical. To be able to evaluate the ideas that have emerged about the subject, how these have found favour – or not – in the minds of policymakers and how this has contributed to the current state seems unavoidable if one is going to learn from the past, embracing values and ideas that if not timeless are at least still valuable, and uncovering the blind alleys in the various directions that have been travelled. With this knowledge as foundation, an English teacher can, with some confidence, negotiate the future, assimilating in whatever sensible way they can the latest incarnations of curriculum and assessment policy. Without such a foundation, it is not that a philosophy or an ideology is not being played out in an English teacher's lessons, it is that it is someone else's philosophy or ideology, it is merely enacted rather than understood, and in the worst cases it is confused, incoherent and damaging for both teachers and learners.

I am not subscribing to a golden age theory that there was a time when English teaching was at its best and we should simply re-enact that period. I am simply arguing that the profession, as it seeks to continually redefine itself for new times, should have knowledge of the past and use that to inform and build a better future. History for me is about the present and the future as much as it is about the past; in the words of Brian Simon, the value of an understanding of history is to know that 'things have not always been as they are and need not remain so' (1991, p. 92).

So, why this book and why now? The principal answer is that no similar text exists that considers the development of English teaching policy and practice over the period from 1965 to the present day. That is not to say that there are not books, chapters and articles that contribute to our knowledge of the development of English in schools; there are many, and it has been claimed that there is 'a rich archive that we now have available to us in English education and English curriculum studies' (Green, 2004, p. 293).

What might be considered to be the seminal history of English is that by David Shayer, *The Teaching of English in Schools, 1900–1970* (1972). This fascinating work carefully detailed developments in English over the period, drawing evidence primarily from text and method books, policy documents, inspection reports and examination papers. The timing of Shayer's book was interesting, in that its publication came at a moment when what might be termed the new English, a progressive pupil-centred model emerging from the work of James Britton, Harold Rosen, Nancy Martin, John Dixon and others connected with both the National and London Associations for the Teaching of English, was beginning to develop as an orthodox method – both in England and more widely – in the aftermath of the seminal Dartmouth Seminar in 1966. Shayer's book concluded with questions about the future of English; in some ways he was optimistic, suggesting that 'English teaching priorities are now (theoretically) more thoughtful, humane, far-sighted, imaginative and worthwhile than they have ever been before' (pp. 185–186), yet he warned against potential dangers of a theory he described as 'pupil-centred, self-expressive, anti-examination, anti-grammar, common culture, "relevant" literature' (pp. 184–185). That description, an unfair – but familiar – caricature of the progressive model of the subject gaining ground in England, would be employed by other harsher critics of the new method, particularly those seeking a return to a more traditional curriculum. Shayer, again optimistically, suggested that 'We have reached a point where there is substantial agreement among teachers that the best – the only – way to approach English is by establishing a "philosophy" or total view first' (p. 184) and he imagined that the subject would continue 'to be pushed outwards in the next seventy years' (p. 184).

Implicit in Shayer's concluding thoughts was an invitation for a similar historical review to be conducted in 2040 to see how far English had indeed come. In some ways this book attempts to take up that invitation, albeit some years earlier than Shayer implied – a fact in part justified by the rapidity of change in the last 50 years and in part by a view that the current state of English teaching demands it. I'm unconvinced that the substantial agreement about the need for a philosophy remains; changes in curriculum and assessment policy and in the way teachers are trained and educated in service point, to many, to a deprofessionalisation of teachers that threatens to obscure the perceived need for a personal philosophy. Increasingly the rhetoric from policymakers has been about teachers drawing on what works. Even if what works is in some way evidence based, or research informed, the suggestion has been that effective teachers merely employ these strategies, rather than developing their own philosophies and ideas and basing their choices of strategy on these foundations. In such a climate, it becomes even more important that English teachers do establish a 'total view first'; a knowledge of the past is critical to this.

This book is not an attempt to imitate Shayer, but the pace of change in the last 50 years means a similar historical consideration of how we have got here is necessary for English teachers to take stock of the ways in which there has genuinely been progress, and to consider what, if any, underpinning principles lay beneath the recommended approaches and downloadable lesson plans that are so freely available. Shayer acknowledged that changes in society, culture, the class system and so on would mean changes would be necessary to English, suggesting that the 'new' ideas of 1970 would seem 'quaint at best, antediluvian at worst' (p. 184) but it's doubtful he could have ever imagined the massive shift to central intervention from the period of the National Curriculum onwards, and the ways in which elements of this would impact on progress in English. Nor is it likely that Shayer could have predicted the seismic shift in technology, particularly the internet. This advancement provides the space for any (often self-appointed) expert on English to blog their opinions on the right way to teach the subject and reach audiences that book and journal writers, whose work may well be rooted in well researched philosophies, may only dream of. The aim of this book is not to preach the right philosophy on the way to teach English; its aims are to tell the story of how we have reached the point we are at and invite all those involved in the teaching of English to consider their own practice in the light of this and to see to what extent these practices are rooted in a coherent vision of the subject in the way that they would like to see it taught. One would hope the result would be a reconsideration of one's own practice from a standpoint of increased knowledge.

Aside from Shayer, the other much referred-to history of the subject is Margaret Mathieson's *The Preachers of Culture: A Study of English and its Teachers* (1975). Although the title of this book has echoes of Mathieson's work that is in no way intended to evoke a direct comparison. Whereas Shayer's book is in some ways a relatively straightforward narrative of English in schools, Mathieson's work is arguably more far reaching and philosophical. It deals with important landmarks in the development of English teaching in schools – like the Newbolt Report – but it has, too, a very distinct focus on the teachers themselves, particularly in its third section 'The Ideology and The Teachers'.

Mathieson's work, like Shayer's, should be recommended reading for anyone entering the profession for it must be the case that in building one's own philosophy and approach to English a knowledge of the past is a hugely valuable prerequisite. Interestingly, Shayer and Mathieson's stories of English appear, in many senses, to portray the subject and its teachers as existing in a non-existent, or at least benign, policy context. They of course reference key governmental reports into the subject, but the authors wrote in a time that it is now almost impossible for English teachers to imagine, when the decisions about how and what to teach were taken far from the offices of policymakers and civil servants. Their stories have an enviable purity in that they tell of the development of a subject in the hands of the experts – experts that may have disagreed on what English should be, but who were all developing and advocating models of the subject from the basis of a set of beliefs and a stock of professional experience, all driven by visions of what English should be, and what it should do, for children and young people. Certainly *War Words: Language, History and the Disciplining of English* (Clark, 2001) much more clearly sets the debates about the development of the subject within the context of political intervention, written as it was at the turn of the twenty-first century. Yet the publication of this book predated the single most expensive central intervention into the teaching and learning of secondary English; as such it too, though still eminently readable, could not provide the deeply important perspective that this book can.

In dealing with the development of the subject over the last 30 years, this book has no choice but to focus on the impact and effect that centralisation has had on English teaching. Centralisation has almost invariably not been in the hands of subject experts, nor have policymakers often appeared to have a vision of the subject beyond the way in which it can contribute to the overall economic health and competitiveness of the nation, or to the way it might help to construct some notion of Britishness. Of course, the nation is made up of individuals and curriculum documents may be expressed in terms of what individuals should learn and be able to do, but it is a benevolent or naïve reader of these documents that doesn't believe that for policymakers, whatever their rhetoric, the central function of schooling in the world today is the production of a competitive nation. A consideration of English and its teachers post-Shayer and post-Mathieson must in some ways be the reality of how the subject has fared at the hands of the policymakers. It is unavoidable.

International perspectives on the teaching of English have been relatively few and far between, with notable examples including the texts edited by Britton, Shafer and Watson (1990), Peel, Patterson and Gerlach (2000), Doecke, Homer and Nixon (2003) and Goodwyn, Reid and Durrant (2013). Whilst each of these has some historical perspective – the first in particular – they are essentially edited volumes that draw together researchers and authors from the major English-speaking nations of the world who contribute a view from their unique perspective on an aspect of English teaching. The aim of this text cannot be to provide a deep and extended comparative analysis of English overseas; its aim in exploring the subject in a selection of major English-speaking nations is to capture key developments in policy around the subject from those nations over the period under consideration, drawing comparisons with the development of English in England where relevant. In doing so the spread and influence of developments in English can be considered, and the nature of the treatment of the subject in the context of each country's own education reforms can be reflected upon. I would hope that readers involved in the teaching of English in other jurisdictions will be encouraged to reflect on their own experience in the light of the story of English in England, whilst in offering snapshots of English overseas readers in this jurisdiction will be encouraged to see that we are not alone with our problems, but also, on a positive front, there may well be alternatives.

The structure and content of the book

Michael Barber, a key figure at the centre of the New Labour project to improve education in the late 1990s, famously divided the past 50 years into four categories: 'uninformed professionalism' covered the period of the 1970s when teachers were essentially allowed autonomy, 'uninformed prescription' described the 1980s and the introduction of the National Curriculum, 'informed prescription' the 1990s and the advent of the National Strategies, and 'informed professionalism' describes the way forward for the profession (see, for example, Street and Temperley, 2005, p. 14). There are many issues to take with this kind of analysis of the past 50 years, particularly the notion that prior to the introduction of central curriculum and assessment policy teachers were uninformed – that does a huge disservice to many of the English teachers who will feature in the early chapters of this book. However, the temptation to impose a structure on the history of education is powerfully tempting, and in succumbing to that temptation in telling the story of English this book has, essentially, two parts, covering the time period 1966–2016. The starting point for the history was the year of the hugely significant Dartmouth Seminar of 1966, an event that helped to shape the subsequent development of English as a discipline in the secondary school. The end point marks the end of the first year in the United Kingdom of a majority conservative government, when, liberated from constraints of coalition, the new administration were arguably freed to unveil their vision for education, and for subject English within that.

For the purposes of framing, the two parts of this text are titled 'The age of invention' and 'The age of intervention', and in a sense correspond to the earlier description of the time of 'fighting for' and 'fighting against'. Though of course things are never this simple – there has always been intervention to some degree, and the major shifts to centralisation in the last 30 years have not eradicated inventiveness – the intention is to highlight the undoubted watershed moment of 1988 and the Education Reform Act and the impact of this and subsequent layer on layer of central policy intervention on curriculum and assessment. In no other subject is the divide between pre- and post-1988 so marked as it is in English; the last 50 years, it has been suggested, has seen an 'absolute paradigm shift' in the teaching of English from 'the era of teacher autonomy to the time of externalised conformity' (Goodwyn, 2016, p. 17). This is a very different, but probably more accurate, description than that of a move from 'uninformed professionalism' to 'informed professionalism'.

Although there are references to the teaching of English in the primary school throughout the text, this work is intended to be sharply focused on the secondary phase. I make no apology for that. Though there are of course some shared concerns between the teaching and learning of English across the phases there are, too, fundamental differences – both in the teaching of the subject and its teachers. The focus of this text on the secondary phase will serve, I believe, to sharpen its insight rather than restrict its scope.

In 'The age of invention' the new progressive model of English, developed in the post-war years, is examined and its evolution through the late 1960s and into the 1970s is explored, as is the backlash that the model attracted from those who saw in it all that was worst about the comprehensive system with its pursuit of allegedly damaging policies in the name of child-centred teaching and progressive education. In accounts of the development of secondary English the new model has been variously described as English as language, London English or personal growth English, sometimes with these titles used interchangeably. To some extent the titles are unhelpful as in themselves they suggest self-contained, defined models. The new English that evolved did start from work in London and indeed attracted the title personal growth following the seminal 1966 Dartmouth Seminar. It did, too, prioritise a broad definition of language. However, as it evolved, it had different strands and defies a simple categorisation – for some teachers literature remained central, for others linguistics and language study assumed importance, for others personal expression, creativity and imagination were at the core, whilst still others were more explicitly political in their practice. More unites than divides these strands, however, and the division into different models creates an illusion of discrete approaches that is unhelpful in exploring the broad history of the subject. In considering the development of the subject, this text takes a broad definition of this new English as, essentially, a progressive-growth model; under this broad umbrella the unifying factor is that the child and her experience is the starting point for the work of the English teacher.

In examining the years leading up to 1988, the ways in which the new English grew through national teacher-led projects and expanded to encompass areas such as gender, multiculturalism, the media and new technologies are considered. This was a hugely creative time for many in the profession, when the scope of the subject came to appear almost limitless and there was undoubtedly a feeling amongst many English teachers of a sense of control over their own destinies and those of the subject and its learners. The new progressive English, whilst obviously not practised to the exclusion of other versions of the subject, can rightly be seen as a dominant orthodoxy by the time of the introduction of the National Curriculum, certainly in the state education sector.

In 'The age of intervention' the focus shifts to the increasing central policy intervention and the effects of this, from the introduction of the National

Curriculum and national testing, through the literacy-focused years of the New Labour administration, to the back-to-basics approach of the coalition – later conservative majority – governments as they sought to impose a version of English that many saw as reminiscent of a stereotypical grammar school education in the subject dating back many decades. There is, of course, overlap; it is interesting to see how it was that some of the most important teacher-led initiatives into the development of English coincided almost exactly with the imposition of central curriculum and assessment. If there was an inverse to the cliché that it is always darkest before the dawn (something like lightest before the night) it would be tempting to describe the period in English teaching spanning the end of the 1980s and the beginning of the 1990s in this way. In two concluding chapters, comparison is made with key developments in curriculum and assessment in the subject in major English-speaking nations of the world before some concluding thoughts consider what future or futures might lie ahead for the subject, given that the only guaranteed constant is further change.

Material for the book comes primarily from document sources: contemporary writing on the subject, text books, government documents, media material and some unpublished archive material. These documents are put alongside oral testimony from some of the key individuals involved – both teachers and those involved in writing and implementing policy – to construct a history of the development of secondary English pedagogy, curriculum and assessment covering the past half century in England. Oral testimony is drawn from interviews with the following individuals: Douglas Barnes, Dorothy Barnes, John Dixon, Peter Medway, Simon Clements, Tony Burgess, Roxy Harris, Joan Goody, Elizabeth Grugeon, David Grugeon, John Richmond, Sue Horner, Sue Hackman, Jane Ogborn, Debra Myhill, Simon Wrigley, John Wilks and John Hickman. Some of these individuals will need little or no introduction to an English teaching community, but endnotes will give brief biographical details for information and context.

Interviews ranged in length from an hour to nearer five hours and a semi-structured approach was taken. Clearly there were bespoke questions asked when exploring an interviewee's involvement with a particular policy initiative or project, but across the interviews there was the attempt to create open conversations where colleagues would share their views across areas important to them in the context of the period under consideration and in the light of their own professional lives. I hope, at best, these conversations became what Goodson and Sikes have described as 'grounded conversations' (2001, p. 28). My own position in the sphere of English teaching and pre-existing relationships with some of the interviewees may of course give rise to questions about objectivity. I prefer to believe, however, that these factors led to more open conversations and that – to a degree – questions of objectivity can be resolved through the method of comparing different oral accounts of events and putting these accounts alongside material from documents – what might be termed a process of triangulation. All interviews were transcribed and coded, to an extent, using categories based both on questions and responses so that comments on key themes – the Dartmouth seminar, the National Curriculum, political intervention, and so on – emerged across the transcripts. Each transcript was individually explored for particularly significant comments. In considering the extensive literature review alongside the interview data, the central events, projects and policies of the past 50 years were identified and the structure of the book created. Using 1988 as the dividing moment was an obvious choice from the material; chapter divisions in the second half of the book most sensibly followed the changes in central administration, whilst in the first half *The Bullock Report* emerged as a logical staging post.

The interrelation of document and oral history is a historical research method that is intended to bring a depth and richness to an account that document or oral history alone could not do. When interpreting the importance, for example, of a curriculum document, the history is enriched when the memories of those present at its writing share their memories. What was written and what is remembered can have the potential to reveal contradictions, but this is not a failing of the method. Rather it reminds us that history is not truth, but an attempt to reconstruct a narrative of the past that reconciles sometimes conflicting points of view. When document and oral data reveal contradiction it does not mean one is right where the other is wrong; both are linguistic representations and thus both carry the potential for misrepresentation. Exploring such contradictions is one of the advantages of this historical research method, and it is employed by others (see, for example, Cunningham and Gardner, 2004; Medway, Hardcastle, Brewis and Crook, 2014). In *Hermeneutics, History and Memory* (Gardner, 2010) the author claimed that 'the data of oral history and of document history may undoubtedly be put to work together constructively' (ibid., p. 97). I think this is beyond question.

A history of 50 years in 80,000 words inevitably involves more than a degree of selection; the aim is here to chart the major developments in policy, pedagogy and practice in English teaching through the selection of events – some headline grabbing, others not – that seem to me to shed the most illuminating light on the subject's progress over the last half century. Other writers would no doubt make other selections and contest my omissions; history is a construction and if a response to this text is the urge to challenge this construction or offer an alternative one then that can only add to the richness of the debate around the subject – the teaching of which, for so many of us involved in it, is more a passion and a way of life than it has ever been a mere career choice.

References

Britton, J., Shafer, R. and Watson, K. (Eds) (1990). *Teaching and Learning English Worldwide*. Philadelphia: Multilingual Matters Ltd.

Clark, U. (2001). *War Words: Language, History and the Disciplining of English*. Amsterdam: Elsevier Science Ltd.

Cunningham, P. and Gardner, P. (2004). *Becoming Teachers: Texts and Testimonies 1907–1950*. London: Woburn Press.

Doecke, B., Homer, D. and Nixon, H. (Eds) (2003). *English Teachers at Work: Narratives, Counter Narratives and Arguments*. South Australia: Wakefield Press.

Gardner, P. (2010). *Hermeneutics, History and Memory*. London: Routledge.

Goodson, I. and Sikes, P. (2001). *Life History Research in Educational Settings: Learning from Lives*. Buckingham: Open University Press.

Goodwyn, A. (2016). Still Growing After All These Years? The Resilience of the Personal Growth Model of English in England and Also Internationally. *English Teaching Practice and Critique*, 15(1), pp. 7–21.

Goodwyn, A., Reid, L. and Durrant, C. (2013). *International Perspectives on Teaching English in a Globalised World*. Oxford: Routledge.

Green, B. (2004). Curriculum, 'English' and Cultural Studies: Or, Changing the Scene of English Teaching. *Changing English*, 11(2), pp. 291–305.

Mathieson, M. (1975). *The Preachers of Culture: A Study of English and Its Teachers*. Oxford: George Allen and Unwin.

McCulloch, G. (2011). *The Struggle for the History of Education*. London: Routledge.

Medway, P., Hardcastle, J., Brewis, G. and Crook, D. (2014). *English Teachers in a Postwar Democracy: Emerging Choice in London Schools, 1945–1965*. New York: Palgrave Macmillan.

Peel, R., Patterson, A. and Gerlach, J. (2000). *Questions of English: Ethics, Aesthetics, Rhetoric and the Formation of the Subject in England, Australia and the United States*. Oxford: Routledge.

Shayer, D. (1972). *The Teaching of English in Schools 1900–1970*. London: Routledge and Keegan Paul.

Simon, B. (1991). *Education and the Social Order*. London: Lawrence and Wishart.

Street, S. and Temperley, J. (2005). *Improving Schools through Collaborative Enquiry*. London: Continuum.

PART I

The age of invention

2

A NEW PROGRESSIVISM: ENGLISH IN THE 1960S AND INTO THE 1970S

It is easy to view the 1960s as a defining decade in the development of English teaching. Although the Education Act of 1944, often referred to as the Butler Act,[1] had cleared the ground for non-selective secondary education in the form of the comprehensive school, and some local education authorities – notably London[2] – had been early adopters of this system, it was not until the Labour government issued its circular 10/65 (Department for Education and Science, 1965) in the middle of the decade that the requirement was made for all local authorities to submit plans for a fully comprehensive schooling system. The comprehensive ideal was never truly realised, of course, with even some areas of the capital retaining selective schools, but the move towards that ideal had profound influence on the nature of schooling and on the particular nature of English as a school subject.

English in the comprehensive school – the beginning of the new progressive English

In London, the dual impact of the Butler Act bringing many thousands of new children into secondary schooling and the move towards comprehensivisation cata-lysed shifts in the nature of English pedagogy and practice that had begun in the wake of World War 2 with the formation of the London Association for the Teaching of English (LATE). A full account of the early history of this remarkably influential subject network (Gibbons, 2014) demonstrated how – through the bottom-up collaborative work of teachers and academics – a new model of English teaching developed in the two decades following the end of the Second World War. With the changing nature of schooling and the schooled at the time, 'a changed map of English as a subject … was the immediate task' (Burgess, 1988, p. 158). This view was echoed by John Dixon, who taught in experimental London comprehensives Holloway and Walworth and went on to write the seminal English method book *Growth through English* (1967), the direct product of the 1966 Dartmouth Seminar. Dixon claimed that 'the immediate problem was what you should do in a comprehensive school about curriculum, and particularly with an English curriculum'.[3]

The old-style grammar school curriculum, devised for the relatively few so-called academic children, would simply not serve the many, and both established and newly trained English teachers lacked the tools with which to cope with the pupils now in front of them. Many of these new teachers had been rapidly trained to alleviate the teacher shortage in the immediate post-war years, and they simply weren't equipped for the challenges of the teaching of English to the full ability range. This much was obvious to those who stood in front of the children in London, where comprehensive classrooms were a reality as early as the late 1940s,[4] and it was here that the nature of English in schools began to change in the post-war years. However, the way in which a new model of English spread – increasingly through the late 1960s and into the early 1970s – across much of the rest of the country demonstrated a much wider rejection of the traditional model of grammar school English as one no longer fit for purpose.

In general terms the new model was progressive; it was child centred, had a focus on pupils' own uses of language, emphasised the expression of personal experience and, though it valued literature, it did so in very different ways to the reverential appreciation of the canon that characterised the Leavisite-inspired Cambridge school of English that was at the heart of the bulk of traditional English teaching in the grammar school. The growth English, or English as language, model that evolved from the work of James Britton, Nancy Martin, Harold Rosen, Douglas Barnes and others working under the umbrella of LATE has been caricatured as neglecting the importance of literature, or for valuing only that literature that might be seen as relevant to the lives of children – with the term relevant being taken in hugely simplistic, and often pejorative, ways. It was true that the advocates of this model of English did seek to find texts which reflected, for example, the lives of the working class or those from different ethnic and cultural backgrounds, the sort of literature that had failed to find its place in classrooms before, but they still wanted children to take ownership of the canon. Speaking of his father Harold, who spearheaded the changes in English through the late 1950s and 1960s, Michael Rosen recalled that literature was the most important thing for him, and that the first text he studied with children when taking up post at Walworth School, one of the first experimental comprehensives in south London, was Shakespeare's *Anthony and Cleopatra*.[5] Similarly, when teaching at Walworth, John Dixon recalled the kinds of dramatic productions the pupils produced when working with him and his colleagues: 'Val Avery and I did scenes from *A Midsummer Night's Dream*. In the first year I was there we did *The Devil's Disciples*. Later on, Charlie Jervis, who was in the department, did *Le Bourgeois Gentleman*.' Shakespeare, Bernard Shaw and Moliere were hardly the playwrights one might assume were particularly relevant to the lives of working-class pupils. Part of the new English, for those like Harold Rosen and John Dixon with their overtly political stance, was to ensure that the kind of cultural capital attached to the canon was not denied to working-class children; this view of English was about acknowledgement and vindication of children and their backgrounds, but it was, too, about empowerment and challenge.

The model of English emerging from London was not, however, a formulated theory that was converted into practice; the work of LATE was diverse with research projects on comprehension and composition, efforts to reshape O-level examinations and conferences on comprehensives and the education of working-class children. English embraced drama and media education, in an embryonic form, genuinely for the first time, with popular culture not treated as the corrupting influence on character and language as it had been previously when more traditional models of the subject barred it from the classroom. There were strands of LATE work that addressed child psychology, and others that addressed socio-economic factors and their influence on education. There was, too, a strong emphasis on teachers as professionals, with evening programmes of poetry study and conferences involving music and drama helping to develop subject knowledge far beyond that directly useful for the classroom. This helped to contribute to a broader notion of the teacher as both person and professional. LATE, too, from its outset was a campaigning organisation that pledged to champion the causes of English teachers; this was enshrined in its constitution (LATE, 1947).

The version of English that was shaped emerged from these diverse activities, activities that were prompted by the professional concerns of teachers and rooted in the challenges they identified in their own classrooms. This was the Association's strength. LATE was never a top-down policy-making body that decided on some theoretical or ideological sense of the best way to teach English; its approaches evolved from the projects of its study groups, and these study groups published reports and convened conference workshops that enabled new practices to be disseminated more widely. LATE supported the setting up of similar regional networks across the country. Always the individual and collective drive was not to promote a particular view of the subject, but to seek practical ways by which to improve the quality of teaching and learning for children. Theoretical ideas were harnessed when these shed light on the practical challenges faced and the solutions proposed. Academics and practitioners worked together in ways that appeared to have cut across any perceived hierarchies; theory and practice seemed genuinely to be in dialogue. The diverse nature of activities and practices meant that a simple definition or title for this model of English was difficult to ascribe with any real accuracy. It can be called growth English, or English as language, or London English; no single title accurately encompasses the range of ideas contained therein nor recognises that for different teachers different areas of work were more important than others. It was a new, broad progressive English, the boundaries of which continued to expand.

Although the growth or language model of English that was emerging from the work of LATE was not fully formed or published in some kind of manifesto, there were interesting examples of where the description of the model was first synthesised or crystallised. The most striking example of this was a document titled *The Aims of*

English Teaching (LATE, 1956). Although this document was circulated to LATE members, its originally intended audience was very different. In fact, LATE had been approached by the British Council to produce the document which was to be sent, accompanied by examples of children's written work and spoken work on tapes, to schools and colleges in India. It would describe 'the aims that lie behind current practice in teaching the mother tongue' (LATE, 1955, p. 2). Whilst the document in itself acknowledged a plurality of views about what English teaching looked like, and that it represented the view of only one group, there was something significant in such an influential body as the British Council seeking to gain an authoritative view on English from LATE. If nothing else this pointed to the status that the organisation had already gained within the English teaching community nationally, and more than that it may have suggested that this new model of English was already establishing itself as an accepted version of the subject well before that is perceived to have happened by many commentators. It also said something about the time that a teacher-dominated subject association should be approached to provide material such as this to inform English teaching overseas – it was a time when the judgment of the profession was respected.

An account of *The Aims of English Teaching* and its contemporary and historical significance (Gibbons, 2013) clearly demonstrated how it very effectively articulated the new progressive English; it forefronted language and experience as the critical building blocks for the subject, highlighted the importance of the relevance of English to children's lives, stressed the need for personal response and engagement with poetry rather than traditional literary critical analysis and emphasised the need to talk about language in context rather than promoting the teaching of formal grammar. Quite how it was received and used in schools and colleges in India is difficult to know, but it was an important step in the exporting of growth English from its developing roots in London.

If the progressive, growth model became articulated as a formed philosophy at any point for the wider teaching community in England, then this probably first happened in 1963, in embryonic sense at least, with the publication of the students' and teachers' text book *Reflections* (Clements, Dixon and Stratta, 1963a, 1963b), essentially a course book and supporting material for a fourth year syllabus that had been devised at Walworth School by three English teachers working there and facing the challenges associated with a comprehensive cohort. *Reflections* was an attempt to articulate a version of English that would be relevant for youngsters and which would provide some motivation and inspiration for learners not destined for further or higher education. It was the first mass commercially produced concrete and practical embodiment of the English that has been variously termed London English, English as language or personal growth English, although with its topics including things like the mass media and the world of work it perhaps had a more sociological or cultural studies leaning tone than the earlier *The Aims of English Teaching*. In a sense the story of the 1960s is the story of the ways in which this model of English – distributed to the profession in these two early texts – expanded and rose to dominance in state-maintained schools and classrooms across the country and indeed spread beyond these shores to gain prominence, sometimes even official endorsement, in places such as the United States and Australia.

The growth of growth English

In part the spread of this new progressive model of English, or English as language, was facilitated by the formation of the National Association for the Teaching of English in 1963, and the early debates over the form and constitution of that new body. Although the English Association (similarly a subject association) had been in existence since 1906, this organisation could not really be said to have been representative of the English teachers in state-funded secondary schools, and certainly not those in the rapidly increasing number of comprehensives. Its membership was, and remains to this day, predominantly from the independent sector and higher education English departments. NATE was to be the association for all English teachers, perhaps particularly those teaching in the new comprehensives and secondary modern schools. In its embryonic stages (a full account of the development of NATE can be read in Gibbons, 2014) there was undeniably a struggle between English teachers and academics coming from the Cambridge tradition and those emerging from London. In simplistic terms, the argument was won by the London representatives, although in real terms the initial arguments were not so much about the view of English teaching that the new association ought to promote, but about the way in which a body of teachers ought best to function – as a top-down policy-making body involved in discussions with governments, examination boards and the like, seeking to influence policy, or as a bottom-up organisation driven by members' concerns and local groups, seeking to develop the teaching of the subject through collaborative classroom-based activity and representing the concerns of the profession. The latter of these two visions – championed by those in the new association that had been active in LATE and various other local groups (many of which LATE had advised or supported) – won the day. LATE members had been steadfast in insisting that this vision would drive the new national association. According to Douglas Barnes,

> It's a bit like going into the European Union. LATE felt that they were going to be taken over, rules were going to be made and they were going to become part of it. LATE was an evangelical movement at that time, they didn't want these other people telling them what to do.[6]

The fact that the earliest chairs of NATE – Boris Ford and Frank Whitehead – emerged from the Cambridge tradition was perhaps part of the settlement or compromise that was reached, but in terms of the new association's working practice, the London model was adopted. The fact that the organisational structures of LATE, with its working and researching groups leading the direction of the association as a whole, had been enshrined in NATE's constitution probably played a significant role in the way that the Association in time came to be led by those from the new emerging progressive English group – Douglas Barnes succeeded Whitehead as chair, before Bill Mittins and James Britton then assumed the role. As time passed, NATE itself seemed to pursue a vision of English very much more in line with the English as language model.

Although there is no evidence of a battle of contrasting philosophies of the subject at the time of NATE's establishment, retrospective accounts (notably, for example, Whitehead (1976)) certainly point to a division between Cambridge and London views of English which began in the earliest days of NATE. Ultimately this led to those holding predominantly Cambridge views realigning within the English Association, and with the journal *The Use of English*. In NATE's early years, however, Cambridge and London views of English co-existed within the Association, and even if there were tensions there was certainly productive collaboration too. The contributions of those most associated with Cambridge English to NATE's new journal, *English in Education*, and the corresponding contributions from apparently London English teachers and academics to *The Use of English*, is evidence enough that these were not, initially at least, two warring factions battling to establish their own view of the subject as dominant.

It's true to say, however, that the English-as-language model was by the mid-1960s already assuming a central place in policy forums for the subject and in public rhetoric. In one of the earliest Working Papers of the new Schools Council,[7] a description of good English teaching talked of 'the enormous importance of increasing command of language for personal development and intellectual growth' of the fact that 'pupils should talk and write about subjects which matter to them' and that 'material can be drawn from the whole of the environment (home, school, other subjects)' (Schools Council, 1965, p 3). A growth view of English was clearly being articulated, but debates about what effective English teaching should be were still very real, and when it came, in 1966, to the members of the British delegation to the seminal Dartmouth Seminar, figures associated with both Cambridge and London positions were strongly represented. It was at Dartmouth, however, that the new progressive English moved firmly into the ascendancy.

The 1966 Dartmouth Seminar

It was perhaps the Dartmouth Seminar that proved to be the most significant single event in establishing the personal growth, English-as-language, model as what might be termed the accepted orthodoxy, in one form or another, for the teaching of English from the mid-1960s until – still for many – the current day, not only in England, but across countries such as the United States, Canada and Australia. However, it is probably more accurate to say it is one account of the Dartmouth Seminar – John Dixon's *Growth through English* (1967) – rather than the seminar itself that was most critical in helping to achieve this outcome.

The seminar itself appears now as an almost unbelievable historical phenomenon; it is unfeasible it could be repeated in the current context, and almost impossible to imagine a future educational policy context (or financial environment) that would allow it. Funded by the Carnegie charity, around 50 teachers and academics involved in English teaching – half from the United Kingdom and the remainder from North America – met over a six week period at Dartmouth College in New Hampshire in a series of seminars with the express purpose of coming to some conclusions about the role of English in the curriculum and what the subject ought to look like. It was an unprecedented event, and will probably always remain unique. The contingent from the British Isles included around a dozen members of NATE and among these were key figures who had spearheaded the development of London English, including John Dixon, James Britton and Douglas Barnes. A joint venture between NATE and its American sister association, the National Council of Teachers of English (NCTE), there had been, even in the planning stages according to Douglas Barnes, a difference of opinion, with the British contingent seeing the seminar as primarily to be of use to classroom teachers, while NCTE saw it as an event for academics.[8]

Interpretations of proceedings at the Dartmouth conference differ, but it is clear from various accounts (e.g. Smagorinsky, 2002; Gibbons, 2014) that there were very different starting points for the Americans and the British. The American education system at the time was undergoing some quite radical changes – what might be most easily described as a move to a more structured curriculum focusing on the development of skills. Government funding had already significantly changed the science and maths curriculum in the States, and similar moves were planned for English, such that – according to John Dixon – the NCTE contingent viewed the ideas coming from Britain as an 'outmoded progressivism' (LATE, 1966, p. 1). Politically, the Cold War and the fear of the Russians moving ahead in the space race were factors exerting influence on United States education policy, prompting an overhaul of the curriculum that would ultimately, it was hoped, lead to the country being more competitive on the global scale. In a sense this was an early incarnation of the standards-based reform agenda that would not really take hold globally until at least two decades later. There was already a federally funded Project English underway in the United States, the aim of which was 'to define a sequenced curriculum for the study of language and literature from kindergarten to college' (Harris, 1991, p. 635). At Dartmouth, the Americans were apparently drawing on this in proposing a structured curriculum which would specify 'certain literary works and genres to be studied based on the tripod of language, literature and composition' (Shafer, 1986, p. 22). The English delegates, on the other hand, were advocating 'a shift in attention from the subject matter of English to the learners in English classes' (Smagorinsky, 2002, p. 24). This shift from the subject to the learner was a core principle oft repeated in arguments LATE had made in the decades before, particularly in attempting to reshape assessment in English, when James Britton had described what he saw emerging in new approaches to English as highlighting for teachers 'the conflict of loyalties – to the subject they teach or the child who is taught' (Britton, 1955, p. 178).

In his post-seminar memo to NCTE, the organisation's executive director, James Squires, regarded the event as 'stimulating, often stunning' (Squires, 1966) and claimed the group did reach 'much general agreement'. Whether or not the 40 days of debate at Dartmouth resulted in a consensus, however, is unclear. Apparently, 'arguments rose to fever pitch every day and in virtually every gathering' (Simmons, Shafer and Shadiow, 1990, p. 108). Certainly one British delegate, Frank Whitehead, writing some ten years later, thought there had been 'very little meeting of minds' and that there had been a 'bemused intellectual climate' (Whitehead, 1976, p. 13). Whitehead's criticism should, however, be considered in the knowledge that he was a strong proponent of Cambridge English and by the time he published these thoughts on Dartmouth the growth view of English had certainly risen to the status of perceived orthodoxy for the teaching of the subject.

Whatever the reality of proceedings at Dartmouth, 11 points of agreement were published following the seminar. These (see Simmons et al., 1990, p. 109) were student centred, prioritised speaking and listening, argued against setting and streaming and put a high value on creativity and imaginative writing. In many ways, however, in terms of the importance of Dartmouth to the development of English on this side of the Atlantic and in fact beyond, it was not so much what happened at the seminar but the means by which it was represented and communicated to the wider teaching community that mattered. John Dixon was given the task of writing up the proceedings at Dartmouth and the conclusions that were reached, and did so in such a way that a vision of English that established enduring significance was firmly encapsulated.

Although there were other published outcomes from Dartmouth – a series of papers including Douglas Barnes' *Drama in the English Classroom* (Barnes, 1968) and Geoffrey Summerfield's *Creativity in English* (Summerfield, 1968), for example – *Growth through English*, Dixon's account of the Dartmouth proceedings, remains for many the definitive account of the event, to the extent that the alternative version commissioned to be written by the American delegate Herbert Muller, *The Uses of English* (Muller, 1967), has been largely forgotten, certainly on the British side of the Atlantic. Although Dixon has claimed that he preferred the title 'Language in Operation'[9] for the book and that *Growth through English* was preferred by the Americans, it is hard to avoid the conclusion that the title has had enormous significance; it is from this title – whether they know it or not – that most English teachers' definition of the personal growth model of the subject comes, and it formed the basis of one of Brian Cox's five models of English when he came to write the first National Curriculum for English in the late 1980s.

The view of English in the text has been seen (by, for example, Gibbons (2014)) to be an articulation of the vision of English that grew through Dixon's work in London – a neat summation of the 20 years' work of LATE in collaboration with the Institute of Education and schools like Walworth. In its opening pages, *Growth through English* offered a powerful critique of two established models of the subject – what Dixon called the skills and cultural heritage models. Dixon attacked the Cambridge, cultural heritage model of the subject as having 'a fatal inattention to the processes involved in such everyday activities as talking and thinking things over, writing a diary or a letter home, even enjoying a TV play' (Dixon, 1967,

p. 4). The new model Dixon presented, and which he claimed emerged from the consensus of Dartmouth, was termed 'language and personal growth' (ibid., p. 4). This model would have a strong respect for children's own language and dialect, and children's own attempts at writing were to be placed on the same language continuum as the work of the literary greats; even children's gossip should exist on the very same continuum – something that received particular criticism from Frank Whitehead a decade later (Whitehead, 1976). The links to Dixon's work in London were obvious – even to the point that examples of children's writing were taken from LATE's published anthology of pupils' work, *And When You Are Young*[10] (LATE, 1960), and an extract of children's speech was printed that was lifted from the reported proceedings of a LATE conference.

Certainly *Growth through English* had clear echoes of *Reflections* detectable throughout, too. It seemed to be little affected by an American viewpoint, certainly rejecting strongly any notion of a structured skills-based curriculum, and cynics may suggest that Dixon could have written the book without Dartmouth having happened at all, so in tune with his own thinking the content of the book seemed to be. When talking of Dartmouth, Douglas Barnes said 'all sorts of other things went on there besides what John reported' but that, significantly, 'many of them not so much to our taste'. NCTE, according to Barnes, 'weren't unwilling to accept that [*Growth through English*] as a version of what happened' however he confessed that 'You still meet American teachers who know the truth is very different'.

In his critical evaluation of Dartmouth and its legacy, Harris (1991) claimed that Dixon's report of Dartmouth was 'highly skewed' (p. 631). It's hard not to agree that Dixon – a powerful, passionate and committed English teacher with a strongly held philosophy about the nature of the subject – chose to present views that emerged from the seminar that were in line with his own ideas – omitting those ideas that, to echo Barnes' words, were not to his taste. In doing so Dixon undoubtedly gave the impression of a consensus that was very likely never there – in later writing Dixon himself conceded that the synthesis reached at Dartmouth, although powerful, was not 'all-inclusive' (Dixon, 2015, p. 432) – probably something of an understatement. In reality, there were most certainly differences of opinion even within the British contingent on the interpretation of growth in itself – it meant something very different to Leavis-inspired Cambridge English teachers, who would have more closely aligned growth with great literature and the power of such material to nurture and develop young minds than it did to those teachers from the NATE representation who were advocates of what is now commonly accepted to be personal growth English.

The other key question, of course, is to what extent Dartmouth, and more particularly *Growth through English,* changed the reality of what happened in classrooms in both the immediate and longer term. Again, opinion is divided and certainly in the final decades of the twentieth century in England, when heavy central intervention, standardised assessments and a strangling accountability framework increasingly took hold, these factors worked to limit the space in English for the growth model of the subject as Dixon defined it. There is, however, a sense in which the events changed the discourse around the teaching of English – the 'Copernican shift', as Harris termed it, 'from a view of English as something one *learns about* to a sense of it as something one *does*' (Harris, 1991, p. 631). Surveys of English teachers (see, for example, research carried out by Goodwyn and Findlay (1999) and Marshall (2000)) have repeatedly shown that personal growth is the model the largest proportion of the English teaching community point to as being central to their motivation and to their practice, and the very fact that this version of the subject attracted such subsequent negative attention from advocates of the Cambridge view of the subject – in addition to Whitehead, Allen's book *English Teaching since 1965: How Much Growth?* (1980) was highly critical of the impact of the growth model – would suggest that it had major significance in real classrooms. The reaction from Whitehead and Allen, emerging from the Leavisite tradition, gave perhaps the strongest indication that, in the decade following Dartmouth, Cambridge English had lost its pre-eminent place as the most often-enacted version of the subject in classrooms, certainly in state schools. Whitehead's assessment of the lack of consensus at Dartmouth is particularly ironic when considered in the light of Dixon's view in the immediate aftermath of the seminar that it was in fact Whitehead who had 'brilliantly demolished the Americans' case for a structured curriculum', arguing instead for an English that 'took into account such basic principles of child psychology as individual differences, readiness for learning, play activity, and interest' (LATE, 1966, p. 1). These principles hardly seem to be indicative of the Leavisite approach, but taken at face value, Dixon's recollection throws into further doubt those accounts of historians of English that have made the Cambridge/London English divide so straightforward and who have dated that divide to 1963 and the formation of NATE.

Whatever the effect in classrooms, it is tempting to view Dartmouth as the moment that effectively marked out the divisions that many see as separating the Cambridge/English as literature and London/English as language positions. This division has been used as a matter of convenience by some writers (see, for example, Ball (1985)) in attempts to construct neat accounts of the development of English in the curriculum. In one account the description is made of 'polarisation of the English subject community between the London and Cambridge positions' (Ball, Kenny and Gardiner, 1990, p. 57). The evidence from Dartmouth doesn't support such an easy reading, and indeed the significant amount of cross-fertilisation between the two models and the champions of each, and incidences like Dixon's recollection of Whitehead's significance at Dartmouth, also undermine this neat binary construction. As Martin Lightfoot pointed out, a simple contrast of English as language and English as literature is to 'make no allowances for shifts in views and emphasis over time, for temporary alliances and genuine syntheses which cross classificatory lines' (Lightfoot, 1988, p. 244). However, in championing the growth model as the consensus of Dartmouth, *Growth through English* effectively established an English orthodoxy that – as time passed, and as its advocates increasingly took leading positions in NATE, engaged with government bodies as representatives of the English teaching community and played prominent roles in nationally funded projects – was seen to stand in opposition to the traditional Leavisite model of the subject and which undoubtedly held a prominent position in a majority of secondary English teachers' hearts and minds. This new progressive English was certainly not merely personal growth, it was a broader notion of a progressive English that continued to develop and embrace new strands of thinking. Tony Burgess felt that personal growth became 'much too convenient a label' and one that was 'an unfortunate way of labelling English'.[11] In fact, 'Dixon's proposal for a new growth model for English teaching was never intended as the naming of a movement, a status that has sometimes been attributed to it by later commentators' (Burgess and Hardcastle, 2000, p. 12). Whatever the intention, this new progressive English certainly rose to prominence from the mid-1960s and into the 1970s; if it hadn't, then it would not have been the target of the backlash it later received from right-wing commentators and educationalists.

The theorising of English

That the new progressive English assumed a dominance in the hearts and minds of many English teachers may be, in part, accounted for by the fact that perhaps what set it aside from the Leavisite model was that there appeared to be a genuine attempt to construct an overarching philosophy of the subject and to articulate a vision of English that could be underpinned by theoretical ideas. Whereas English in the Leavisite tradition may well have had clear motives – the development of morality and proper use of language through the study of the fine literature of the canon – and clear approaches – the employment of close practical criticism in the mode of I.A. Richards – it is difficult to suggest that there was any genuine underpinning theory that supported the ideas or could offer supporting argument to show how these lofty ideas related, in practice, to children's learning. Leavis' assertions about the importance and power of literature were instrumental in making English a serious subject – in fact it's fair to say that without his work it's unlikely that teachers would even have debates about contrasting models. However, Leavis' ideas remained assertions, and they were not concerned with the ways in which children might engage with the subject or assimilate what they were told would be good for them to consume.

Within the progressive model of English that grew in the post-war years from the work going on in the London Institute of Education and LATE, there was, in the view of Tony Burgess, 'the commitment to an underlying rationale for the teaching of English that could go on developing as a body of ideas … to try and build a sort of framework, or ongoing knowledge and theory'. Interestingly, Burgess felt that often, rather than seek to build this framework, others interested in ideas about English teaching tended to 'resist the notion of a synthesis. It sounds too grand. They resist the idea of trying to coordinate different bodies of thought – they prefer to take intellectual positions that are not about the whole of English teaching.'

This commitment to build an overarching framework for the whole of English teaching was essentially what inspired the Dartmouth Seminar and, whether or not there was consensus among delegates over a progressive growth pedagogy, this was the enduring legacy, and in the late 1960s and early 1970s – particularly in the work of James Britton – that attempt to construct a theory of English was perhaps most nearly realised.

James Britton's *Language and Learning*

No account of the development of subject English would be complete without extended reference to the work of James Britton. A founding member of LATE, Britton was highly influential in the development of the new English in the decades following the Second World War from his position within the London Institute of Education. He was a driving force behind many of LATE's most influential research projects and prominent in their campaigns around assessment of English language and literature at O level. Of all those associated with the development of London English it was Britton who most forcefully sought to develop the over-arching philosophy for the subject. He did this, in part, by drawing on his back-ground in psychology, using this to help him to articulate ideas that would offer an account of the learning and development of children through their development and uses of language. It was this that formed his view of what the subject English ought to look like. He was, according to Simon Clements, 'the iconic English teacher/scholar'.[12] Though Britton published widely, *Language and Learning* (Britton, 1970) is generally accepted to be his foremost contribution to the field of English education – indeed education more widely.

It would be inaccurate to describe Britton's *Language and Learning* as a method book for the teaching of English – indeed the author stated his intended reader was 'anybody who for any reason wants to listen with more understanding to children and adolescents and who has for any reason a concern for what becomes of them' (ibid., p. 7). However, the text was in many ways an articulation of growth pedagogy or the English as language model in its most overtly theoretical form, and as such it was a text that provided what might be termed a philosophical underpinning or foundation for English teachers who, in the wake of Dartmouth and *Growth through English,* were helping to establish the new child-centred version of English as the dominant pedagogy in England's schools. In constructing the text, Britton drew on the language of children – both from the classroom and from his own home through his observations and recordings of his own children's speech development – to develop overarching ideas about the role of language in learning and development. To support his ideas he also drew widely from distinct fields of thinking – delving into the worlds of cognitive science, psychology, sociology, linguistics and literary theory. For Tony Burgess, 'Jimmy's way of theorising was probably fundamentally psychological', and as an intellectual he 'was very idiosyncratic, he picked from all over and created his own synthesis'. The works of Jerome Bruner, I.A. Richards, Jean Piaget, George Kelly, Ernst Cassier, Edward Sapir and Basil Bernstein were among those mined by Britton in what was certainly his most significant output as a writer – one that remains a core reading on many primary and secondary teacher training courses to this day. Perhaps most notably, it was *Language and Learning* that played a significant role in bringing the ideas of Vygotsky to the contemporary reader. In drawing particularly on Vygotsky's *Thought and Language* (1962), a work that like all Vygotsky's writing had been unknown in the West due to its suppression under Stalin's regime until its translation at the Massachusetts Institute of Technology in the early 1960s, Britton was a pioneer, forging a path that subsequent educationalists preoccupied with ideas about speech and thinking would continue to tread.[13] Vygotsky's ideas about the relationship between thought and language, the development of inner speech and the role of language in the formation of concepts featured explicitly in *Language and Learning*, and their direct significance for the teacher was summed up by Britton some years later (Britton, 1987), some time after Vygotsky's other seminal work – *Mind in Society* (1978) – had too become available in the West. Though Vygotsky's work had begun to feature before *Language and Learning* – Dixon referred to him briefly, for example, in *Growth through English* – it was Britton's work that was critical in this regard.

In themselves, Vygotsky's ideas gave a powerful backing for teachers who perhaps instinctively felt the value of oracy in the classroom, but *Language and Learning* went beyond being a justification for speaking and listening. Britton incorporated what by then for him were long-standing ideas about the notion of language use in the spectator and participant roles, in doing so making the argument for the importance of literature in children's education and experience. Although his colleague, Douglas Barnes, has confessed to misgivings and in some ways viewed the ideas of participant and observer as a distinction that didn't really work,[14] these notions were eventually given what might be termed official backing in the Bullock Report, *A Language for Life,* some years later and were central to the Schools Council project which led to the publication of *The Development of Writing Abilities 11–18* (Britton, Burgess, Martin, McLeod and Rosen, 1975).

In forefronting the importance of language in development, highlighting the value of oracy, emphasising the absolute need for children to be encouraged to bring their own language and experience into their learning and placing literature as an integral part of learning, and eclectically drawing on a breadth of key thinkers to shed light on examples of real children's language use, *Language and Learning* was the book that to a large extent theorised the new progressive growth English. As such it sits as a powerful companion to *Growth through English* – Dixon's work a model of what English should look like, Britton's the theoretical underpinning to add weight to the method. However, the new English had other, equally important, and complementary strands that meant it was more than a narrow growth model in the way some critics have maligned it. One notable strand was that emerging from the field of linguistics in the form of the *Language in Use* project.

The *Language in Use* project

As English as language developed as a model for the subject, aided and abetted by the continued rise of NATE as the major subject association and its journal *English in Education*, the work of those such as Barnes, Britton and Rosen was complemented by a parallel, and in many ways related, strand of work looking more explicitly at language and linguistics. The Schools Council Programme in Linguistics and English Teaching began life as the Nuffield Programme in Linguistics and English Teaching in 1964, with Michael Halliday as its director. Halliday was to become critical in the development of systemic functional grammar, work that would later have great influence on English curriculum policy as it was harnessed in Australia at the end of the twentieth century by educators developing a genre model for the teaching of English. This, in turn, would be highly influential in the development of the National Literacy Strategy and Key Stage 3 Framework that were introduced to transform the teaching of reading and writing in England around the turn of the millennium; later still, it would be at the core of heavily funded research around the teaching of grammar and its impact on writing.

The Nuffield Programme in Linguistics and English Teaching was taken on by the Schools Council in 1967 for its development stage, with the secondary work being led by Peter Doughty. Doughty had been an active member of LATE, involved in various study groups (not only those related to language; according to John Dixon he worked with Doughty on a LATE poetry anthology group), so very much came from the emerging progressive tradition of an English teaching focused on the child. This focus came through his more explicitly linguistic work and culminated with *Language in Use* (Doughty, Pearce and Thornton, 1971), the publication of the Schools Council Programme. The title – reminiscent of Dixon's preferred choice of 'Language in Operation' for *Growth through English* – placed the stress of the work on an exploration of the functions of language in society, but insisted that the starting point for this exploration should be the child's own language use.

Language in Use comprised 110 units of work, each made up of a sequence of lessons. The material had been extensively trialled in schools and, although its authors claimed its approach to language was new, they admitted that there would be familiarity with the material given that 'they draw upon all that has been achieved in the field of English teaching over the last two decades' (ibid., p. 8). With activities employing discussion, group work, scripted and improvised drama and the use of tape recordings of real language in use, the heritage of the work was clearly the post-war London model of English. And whilst the focus of the activities was linguistic, there was no oppressive focus on grammatical terminology – the whole thrust of the material was for pupils to 'understand much more fully than before the nature of their own experience as users of language' with the level of explicit terminology expected to be left to 'the judgement of those who teach them' (ibid., p. 9). The aim, ultimately, was to develop pupils' own competence as users of language themselves, but the text acknowledged that the link between developed understanding and increased competence was not straightforward. It was, again, work set against the traditional model of grammar teaching that supposed – without any strong evidence – that learning about language as a set of rules or facts would somehow automatically lead to improved language use in speech and writing.

In some senses *Language in Use* can be seen as a direct antecedent to the later work of the Language in the National Curriculum project in the early 1990s. The linguistic focus of *Language in Use* was directed more explicitly at the teacher, rather than suggesting pupils should learn terminology, and it offered a further underpinning theory to support effective practice. For the teacher of English interested in developing pupils' own intuitive use of language through explorations of their own and others' usage, in different contexts, *Language in Use* offered a way to link back worthwhile classroom activities to the discoveries of linguistic science. Thus, in effect, the work contributed further to a sense of a progressive model of the subject being underpinned by theory. *Language in Use* was translated into many languages, and on the event of Doughty's death, one obituary made the claim that it is 'still widely used around the world' (*The Guardian*, 2013). Although it's unlikely that the specific materials in *Language and Use* have stood the test of time, the approach embodied in the publication – exploring language in use and seeking to understand how language does its work in different real situations and contexts, the whole 'exploratory' approach to language study – has most certainly retained its currency in the work of English teachers across the world. The value of the Schools Council linguistic programme was not, in effect, the units and lesson plans – when reflecting on the work, Peter Medway thought that 'All that strand got nowhere in English really, which I regretted in a way as there was some good stuff.'[15] The success of the programme was in making this kind of language study in the classroom a serious pursuit, rooted in evidence and research from linguistic experts. It supported this approach to language work in a way that has always been blatantly missing for advocates of formal grammar teaching with explicit forefronting of facts and rules about correct usage.

Growth through English, Language and Learning and *Language in Use* all in different ways contributed to the development of a model of English, offering theoretical support to the way that the teaching of English was evolving in many state secondary schools across England. The unifying factor was the idea of English being about the child, and seeing it as a subject that began with the learner and her language and experience and considered that this should be used as the building block for developing as a powerful user and interpreter of language in all its forms. These publications, as much as contributing to the English teachers' repertoire, brought support to the progressive model of English by offering underpinning theories from linguistics, psychology and child development to strengthen those teachers who sought to articulate a notion of a progressive English being central to their work. Though personal growth may have been a common title, this description was not an accurate reflection of the breadth of work going on.

A head of English seeking to establish ways of working and a curriculum that might include mixed ability teaching, a focus on writing from experience, the importance of talk in the classroom, the celebration of linguistic diversity and the embracing of popular culture had, by the beginning of the 1970s, some strong theoretical backing to support her approach. An advocate of a traditional curriculum might be able to appeal to some misguided notion of common sense to support, for example, a decision to subject pupils to explicit grammatical instruction, but the powerful arguments about how children learn, and how language and experience are fundamental to that learning, were in the hands of those advocating progressive English methods. The rise of the progressive growth, language model of English had its roots in the practicalities of the classroom, with teachers – like those in the early years of LATE – seeking to find things that worked with children. It was disseminated through the work of the largest subject association, NATE, through conferences and publications and by the involvement of teachers advocating these methods in things like Schools Council projects. By the 1970s, the theory was in place to show why these things worked and to vindicate the approach. It was an approach that could draw on common sense too – of course children would like to write about themselves, of course they would like to read things that reflected their own lives – but the theory was showing why this common sense was in fact meaningful. It made this notion of English powerful.

Progressive growth English: increasingly political

Perhaps attempts to articulate a fully formed theory to underpin the emerging progressive orthodoxy of English were not ultimately realised. This is not surprising; since English had historically been the umbrella for both the study of language and literature, there was difficulty enough in finding a single unifying theory. That complexity was further underlined in the 1960s and into the 1970s as the subject began to expand its boundaries further and as the politics of English teaching became more pronounced. If there had ever been a time when teaching English was apolitical, then it had passed. The focus of work on pupils' own language use inevitably brought politics into the classroom as it would be impossible not to consider issues of gender, class and – increasingly in multicultural environments – ethnicity in English lessons.

One prime example of the increasingly political nature of English came at NATE's annual conference in 1971. This conference was the first to build directly from Dartmouth and the first in an eventual series of four yearly conferences held under the banner of the International Federation for the Teaching of English (IFTE), a body that was formally constituted in 1983 and is formed by the Australian Association for the Teaching of English (AATE), NATE, NCTE and the New Zealand Association for the Teaching of English (NZATE). In the wake of Dartmouth a more informal International Steering Committee (ISC) had been set up to facilitate exchanges between the four associations and the first major conference was scheduled to coincide with NATE's annual event in York.

Although the event was planned to take up the baton from Dartmouth and featured speakers from both the United States and Australia, there was apparently a significant minority among the British delegates who felt uneasy. According to

Tony Burgess, about three days into the conference a group 'put around a sort of note to everybody saying where are the progressive ideas of English teaching? Do they have anything to do with politics and socialism?' There was then 'a tremendous flurry of people taking on different sides and the whole thing dividing up, and great pain'. Although any constitutional crisis was avoided by the staging of a meeting, with James Britton in the chair, at which there was discussion of the future role of NATE, there were reverberations. The dissatisfied group formed an alternative commission – Commission 7 – at the conference to discuss the politics of English teaching. Through Commission 7, according to Peter Medway, 'certainly race politics became an issue, and also the alternative schooling movement'; it was 'a liberation sort of politics'. Employing biblical language, Britton reflected 'In six commissions NATE created a new heaven and a new earth for English teachers – but in the seventh commission all hell broke loose' (Britton, 1973, p. 7).

This impetus of Commission 7 was taken further the following year when LATE held a conference on Teaching London Kids. A direct result of this was the publication of the same name that emerged from the Inner London Education Authority English Centre (later the English and Media Centre). Short lived though this publication was, it was influential in giving voice to the strong left-wing agenda that significant numbers of English teachers felt was influential in their practice. Commission 7 and what followed pointed towards a more explicitly political strand in the development of English – one that much more explicitly focused on race, class, gender and ethnicity and championed the advancement of equal opportunities as a major role for the subject and its teachers. In essence, there was a form of progressive politics that formed an umbrella for growth English, under which colleagues with differing views could congregate. For Tony Burgess this 'tried to include both socialist and progressive dimensions and that would occasionally run into difficulties'. Roxy Harris thought:

> People had a political commitment. I don't think it was ever just to do with English … people came with a sort of left to liberal political commitment first which they wanted to enact partly through their English teaching.[16]

Politics and pupil voice

As English expanded, and for some became more overtly political, and as an increasingly child-centred progressive pedagogy appeared to hold sway, one notable incident demonstrated the shifting culture. The event that captured the spirit of the potential of the new progressive English for the development of pupils' own voice was the famous – or perhaps infamous – case of the pupil strike in East London of 1971. Chris Searle, a 24-year-old probationary English teacher at the Sir John Cass Foundation and Redcoat Church of England school in Stepney, East London, in the best spirit of a progressive model of English teaching, validating children's experience and bringing authentic pupil voice into the classroom, published – with the support of the local bishop but apparently against the wishes of the school's governing body – an anthology of his children's poetry under the title *Stepney Words*. As a consequence, Searle was dismissed from his post, the result of which was a seemingly unchoreographed walkout by 600 pupils, who refused to return to school until their English teacher was reinstated. The story made the front page of the biggest-selling tabloid newspaper of the day under the banner headline 'Please Don't Sack Sir' (*The Sun*, 1971). It took two years for Searle to be reinstated, thanks in part to the intervention of the secretary of state, Margaret Thatcher.

According to Searle, speaking at an event in East London to mark the 40 year anniversary of the strike, the publication of the children's poems was the answer to a strikingly simple question:

> I used to do play readings but I found they responded better to poetry, and I was reading William Blake and Isaac Rosenberg to them, both London poets who took inspiration from the streets. So I took the pupils out onto the street and asked them to write about what they saw, and the poems these eleven-year-olds wrote were so beautiful, I was stunned and I thought they should be published. Blake and Rosenberg were published, why not these young writers?
>
> (*Spitalfields Life*, 2011)

That sense of placing the work of pupils if not on a par with then at least in the same sentence as great poets from the Romantic and World War 1 periods was directly in the spirit of the progressive growth model of English and aligned with the messages from *Growth through English*.

The new progressive growth English: the backlash

Incidences like that of the pupil strike in Stepney, whilst for some a triumph of the ability of progressive English teaching to empower young people, were viewed differently by those not in tune with the left-leaning politics ascribed to the progressives. By the beginning of the 1970s it was certainly the view of noted right-wing educational thinkers that the new progressive model of English was firmly rooted within what they saw as a failing progressive system more widely. The arguments about what an effective education system should do, and what effective English teaching should be within it, were in many ways an argument between the left and right on the political spectrum, or at least this is the way they were represented publicly.

Progressive, growth English was perceived as coming from the left; John Dixon and Harold Rosen would have been comfortable with this – Dixon was a member of various political groups, including Labour Teachers, and Rosen had been a member of the Communist party – they fitted the description of radicals who were upfront about their views and how it impacted on their teaching (see Gibbons (2016) for a perspective on these two significant figures and the ways in which their politics influenced their teaching). Douglas Barnes and James Britton, however, were far from overtly political; progressive or growth English was anything but a single, monolithic conception – it was a broad umbrella of a term and even if there was a pursuit of a single overarching theory it would have within it teachers with different personal motivations and with consequent different priorities for the way they went about the business of teaching and learning the subject.

Politically, however, it was certainly convenient for certain parties to caricature progressive English as left wing and include it as part of a wider problem with what was seen to be the failure of the educational experiment that was the comprehensive system, which had seen standards slipping. For English this meant that children taught the subject in the comprehensive system were taught a curriculum that was slack on grammar and the use of so-called correct English, by teachers who had eschewed the traditional teaching of grammar and literature for the new-found child-centred methods. The critique of progressive education was most strongly seen in *The Black Papers*, a series of publications that spanned the end of the 1960s and the early years of the decade.

Although five *Black Papers* amounted to a wide-ranging attack on all areas of what its authors considered to be the failings of left-wing education policy, particularly the move towards the comprehensive system, they included particular contributions that showed the contempt in which progressive English teaching in particular was held. Arthur Pollard, for example, an English professor from the University of Hull, claimed that 'free expression ('creativity') is all the vogue, not least in my own subject, English' (1969, p. 72–73) before going on to suggest that 'most of the pupils have little enough to be creative about. They would be far better occupied with some good old-fashioned teaching of grammar, spelling and punctuation' (ibid., p. 73). Referencing the work of Halliday as part of the problem, Pollard insisted that the suggestion of teaching such things as the basic skills would 'send our so-called "progressives" berserk. They would deny the existence of correct English' (ibid., p. 73). Pollard went on to claim that this view of English had been taken on by the establishment in the form of the London GCE O level examination board whose paper apparently revealed:

> the extraordinarily limited view it takes of the candidates it is supposed to be testing: they are all presumed to be 'teenagers' in a very self-conscious sort of way, to be from urban working-class backgrounds, and to be devoting their energies to 'protest'.
>
> *(ibid., p. 73)*

Pollard's criticisms of progressive English were somewhat bizarre; advocates of this notion of English would indeed have denied the existence of correct English and would prefer to speak of appropriate language for the particular context. Pollard simply took as read that there is such a thing as correct English, itself a highly questionable assertion as Halliday's work illustrated. The tone of the piece, which was not uncharacteristic of many of the pieces in the five *Black Papers*, illustrated the feelings of some of those on the right about the teaching of English and indeed the comprehensive project as a whole, which they associated with such dire practices as mixed-ability groupings, child-centred approaches and discovery learning. The *Black Papers* were influential in that they attracted much attention from sections of the media and from some policymakers and they were significant in marking the beginning of the kind of right-wing, traditionalist assault on progressive English that would be seen time and time again over subsequent decades. There is irony, of course, in the fact that one of the co-editors of the *Black Papers*, Professor Brian Cox, himself became the target of such an assault after he authored the first National Curriculum for English, which was – for traditionalists predominantly of the right – far too influenced by the thinking of the 'so called progressives'.

Conclusion

Whilst the *Black Papers* did provide a backlash to progressive teaching and to the new English in the comprehensives, the period from Dartmouth to the mid-1970s was a pivotal one for the development of subject English. The advent of an alternative model for the teaching of English was driven by English teachers working individually and collectively to investigate their own practice and develop the subject in new ways. Strengthened by the creation of NATE, it was offered legitimacy from the foremost thinkers in the field at the Dartmouth conference and with the subsequent publication of *Growth through English*. The work of Britton, Halliday, Doughty, Rosen and Barnes combined to offer underpinning foundations from psychology, child development, linguistics, philosophy and sociology. Reflecting on the development of this new English on the event of NATE's tenth anniversary, Britton concluded:

> Our concerns have burst the bonds of English as traditionally defined. It is important, I believe, that we have not only broadened by this means our conception of our subject but that we have – constantly and by many diverse undertakings – deepened it. We have moved towards a definition of our responsibilities that does justice to language – the language of every child – and to literature, not as a double-bill, but as inseparable parts of one process.
>
> *(Britton, 1973, p. 6)*

It is entirely fair to say that it was not then, nor has ever been, a coherently, neatly defined model; if growth English is taken as an overarching definition then this has always meant different things to different teachers. Equally, even in characterising this period as one in which the model assumed the place of an English teaching orthodoxy in the secondary school, this implies a form of consensus that did not exist; English was during the period a highly contested subject. However, it is difficult to avoid the conclusion that by the earlier 1970s there had been 'significant, even radical changes in the teaching of the subject in secondary schools, and the methods teachers are using in their classrooms' (Stratta, Dixon and Wilkinson, 1973).

There was a radical paradigm shift, but it was far from the convenient victory for English as language over English as literature as, it has been asserted (Ball, 1985), was the direct result of Dartmouth; nor was there the 'polarisation of the English subject community between the London and Cambridge positions' (Ball et al., 1990, p. 57). The continued publication of the *Use of English* journal, with its Leavisite heritage, and the writing of those such as Whitehead and Allen, demonstrated that the Cambridge, English as Literature model was still at the forefront of a significant number of English teachers' thinking and the cross-fertilisation of work of individuals conveniently placed within one or other of the two groups belies any serious attempt to suggest that an outmoded practice had simply been wiped away by a new improved version. Even at the 1971 NATE Conference, whilst those seeking a more radical approach which would build a version of growth English to embrace politics and society were convening Commission 7, counter arguments remained. Speaking at that conference, Fred Inglis, for example, took issue with both *Growth through English* and *Language in Use*, although even in doing so he acknowledged that such a critique would be labelled as 'Luddite, Leavisite, irrationalist' (Hilliard, 2012, p. 138).

Inglis' comments at the 1971 NATE conference and Allen's and Whitehead's withering attacks on the growth pedagogy of course do, in effect, testify to the fact that, in the years following Dartmouth, this model of English – whether informed in individual teachers' perspectives by thinking from psychology, cognitive development, sociology or linguistics – had assumed a prominent position within English departments and that this was being reflected in both curricula and examinations in a decisive shift 'from a Scrutiny conception of English in schools' (Hilliard, 2012). Hilliard, whose book, *English as a Vocation: The Scrutiny Movement*, is in some ways a lament to the loss of the Leavisite approach to English in schools, attributed the rise of the new English and the subsequent demise of the Cambridge approach to the advent of the comprehensive system, and to the theoretical support taken from social science – acknowledging that the Leavisite approach was one that was moral and artistic. In reality, Leavisite approaches to the study of literature were so integral to the majority of English teachers' own education, particularly their higher-education experience, that they probably persisted even if unacknowledged or employed for different ends by those adopting new progressive approaches. Indeed, the literary critic Terry Eagleton once reflected that 'there is no more need to be a card-carrying Leavisite today then there is to be a card-carrying Copernican: that current has entered the bloodstream of English studies in England as Copernicus reshaped our astronomical beliefs' (Eagleton, 1983, p. 27). True or not, for many of the young people in state secondary comprehensive schools by the mid-1970s, the influence of Leavis and the Cambridge school of English had largely been supplanted by the seemingly irresistible growth of the new English.

Notes

1 As is often the case with government acts that are perceived to have particular significance, they historically bear the name of the relevant Secretary of State – in this case

Rab Butler. It is clear that the Butler Act, written as it was in the dying days of World War 2 when victory for the Allies was assured, was a deliberate attempt to radically reshape education in Britain in an attempt to rebuild and to create a better future.

2 The London County Council published its London Plan in 1944. Designed to facilitate the regeneration of London in the post-war years, the education element of the plan made a commitment to a comprehensive system. This bold move was made on social as much as education grounds, as part of a bid to create a more socially cohesive community (Rubinstein and Simon, 1973).

3 Comments from John Dixon taken from an interview with the author. Dixon, perhaps most famous as the author of *Growth through English* (1967), taught English in London schools including the experimental comprehensives Holloway and Walworth. He later worked in higher education at Bretton Hall College.

4 Eight experimental comprehensive schools were established in London between 1946 and 1949. The first custom-built comprehensive, Kidbrooke School, was opened in 1954.

5 Michael Rosen made these comments in an interview with the author filmed for the organisation Local Schools Network, a group that advocates good-quality, local state schooling. The film can be viewed via the Local Schools Network website at http://www.localschoolsnetwork.org.uk/2015/12/harold-rosens-5-radical-commitments-to-e ducation accessed on 1st May, 2016.

6 Comments taken from an interview between the author and Douglas Barnes. Barnes had been head of English in Minchenden School and was an important early member of LATE and instrumental in the establishment of NATE. He was later involved in many Schools Council projects and has published widely. He is perhaps best known for his contributions to work on oracy.

7 The Schools Council had been set up in 1964 by the education minister Edward Boyle. The work of the body was to lead research and projects on curriculum and assessment reform and it was predominantly made up of teachers, with teaching unions and professional organisations heavily represented. It was not, according to Tony Burgess, unanimously supported, since 'teachers thought it was airy fairy and politicians thought it was a waste of time'. Its demise was announced in 1982 by the Secretary of State for Education, Keith Joseph, in what was one of the first significant centralising moves of Margaret Thatcher's Conservative government. The abolition of the Schools Council began a process that saw the influence of the profession on curriculum and assessment reform steadily dwindle.

8 Barnes recalled participating in the planning committee for Dartmouth: 'NCTE saw it as a seminar for education academics, we saw it as a conference for teachers so it was quite a battle to get them to see we wanted teachers there and that on our side it would be more education ... that the university people would be educationalists not English specialists.'

9 Dixon claimed that he felt the title *Growth through English* was too 'Holbrookian', a reference to the work of David Holbrook whose books *English for Maturity* (1961) and *English for the Rejected* (1964) were influential in the English classroom. Holbrook himself is typically described as coming from the Cambridge tradition, and he was indeed a student of Leavis whilst at university. However, his experiences as a secondary school teacher meant that his view of English was more complex than the traditional English-as-Literature model. According to Dixon it was one of the 'most reactionary North Americans' who had suggested *Growth through English* as a title, and Dixon felt he had to agree.

10 The publication of children's writing gained popularity from the 1970s; LATE's anthology of children's compositions – both poetic and narrative – was a very early, perhaps the earliest, example of this trend.

11 Comments taken from an interview with Tony Burgess. Tony Burgess is a hugely influential figure in English teaching who worked alongside James Britton and Nancy Martin at the London Institute of Education.

12 Comment made by Simon Clements in an interview with the author. Clements, one of the writers of *Reflections*, worked in a number of London schools, including Walworth, before later becoming a member of Her Majesty's Inspectorate (H.M.I.).

13 A good example would be Neil Mercer, whose extensive work on language and thought (for example *Words and Minds* (2000)) draws on the work of Vygotsky and Britton.

14 Barnes said, 'I think observer/participant distinction doesn't work. That both poetic language and engaged political language can be both and I wanted a different definition of the distinction as I didn't think his [Britton's] definition worked. A lot of scientific language actually stands back and doesn't try to influence, just as a lot of poetic language engages fiercely with the world. He'd picked this up from … it wasn't Jimmy's idea originally. Wasn't it from one of the Scrutiny people? I think it was Dennis Harding's distinction originally. I think it was one of these cases where you read something and internalise it so much that it eventually pops out as your idea. I felt there was a distinction to be made but not that one.' Barnes' views on Britton's ideas about participant and spectator illustrate again how, not only was the Cambridge/London divide far from straightforward, but also how London or growth English itself was far from one coherent, uncontested model of the subject.

15 Peter Medway taught at Walworth Comprehensive school in London and later became a teacher educator at King's College London. He wrote extensively throughout his professional career on the development of subject English.

16 Roxy Harris began teaching in the early 1970s and worked within the West Indian Supplementary Service in the London Borough of Walthamstow, supporting students from the Caribbean within a London school English department. His interests in language and ethnicity eventually led him to work in higher education.

References

Allen, D. (1980). *English Teaching Since 1965: How Much Growth?* London: Heinemann.

Ball, S. (1985). English for the English Since 1906. In Goodson, I. (Ed), *Social Histories of the Secondary Curriculum*. Sussex: Falmer Press.

Ball, S., Kenny, A., and Gardiner, D. (1990). Literacy Politics and the Teaching of English. In Goodson, I. and Medway, P. (Eds), *Bringing English to Order*. Sussex: Falmer Press.

Barnes, D. (1968). *Drama in the English Classroom*. Illinois: NCTE.

Britton, J. (1955). The Paper in English Language at Ordinary Level. *The Use of English*, 6(3), pp. 178–184.

Britton, J. (1970). *Language and Learning*. Harmondsworth: Penguin.

Britton, J. (1973). Ten Years of NATE. *English in Education*, 7(2), pp. 5–9.

Britton, J. (1987). Vygotsky's Contribution to Pedagogical Theory. *English in Education*, 21(3), pp. 22–26.

Britton, J., Burgess, T., Martin, M., McLeod, A. and Rosen, H. (1975). *The Development of Writing Abilities (11–18)*. Aylesbury: Macmillan.

Burgess, T. (1988). Cultural and Linguistic Diversity and English Teaching. In Lightfoot, M. and Martin, N. (Eds), *The Word for Teaching is Learning: Essays for James Britton*. Oxford: Heinemann.

Burgess, T. and Hardcastle, J. (2000). Englishes and English: Schooling and the Making of the School Subject. In Kent, A. (Ed), *School Subject Teaching: The History and Future of the Curriculum*. Oxford: Routledge.

Clements, S., Dixon, J. and Stratta, L. (1963a). *Reflections*. Oxford: Oxford University Press.

Clements, S., Dixon, J. and Stratta, L. (1963b). *Reflections – Teacher's Book*. Oxford: Oxford University Press.

Department of Education and Science. (1965). *The Organisation of Secondary Education*. London: Her Majesty's Stationery Office.

Dixon, J. (1967). *Growth through English*. London: Penguin.

Dixon, J. (2015). Developing English. *English Teaching Practice and Critique*, 14(3), pp. 427–434.

Doughty, P., Pearce, J. and Thornton, G. (1971). *Language in Use*. London: Schools Council Publications.

Eagleton, T. (1983). *Literary Theory: An Introduction*. Oxford: Blackwell.

Gibbons, S. (2013). The Aims of English Teaching: A View from History. *Changing English*, 20(2), pp. 138–147.

Gibbons, S. (2014). *The London Association for the Teaching of English 1947–67: A History*. London: Institute of Education/Trentham Press.

Gibbons, S. (2016). W(h)ither the Radicals? The Depoliticization of English Teaching. *English in Education*, 50(1), pp. 35–43.

Goodwyn, A. and Findlay, K. (1999). The Cox Models Revisited: English Teachers' Views of Their Subject and the National Curriculum. *English in Education*, 33(2), pp. 19–31.

Harris, J. (1991). After Dartmouth Growth and Conflict in English. *College English*, 53(6), pp. 631–646.

Hilliard, C. (2012). *English as a Vocation: The Scrutiny Movement*. Oxford: Oxford University Press.

Holbrook, D. (1961). *English for Maturity*. Cambridge: Cambridge University Press.

Holbrook, D. (1964). *English for the Rejected*. Cambridge: Cambridge University Press.

LATE. (1947). London Association for the Teaching of English Constitution. LATE Archive Folder 8, Item Number 1, held in the University College London Institute of Education Library archive.

LATE. (1955). Report of autumn term meeting. LATE Archive, Folder 11, item 8 held in the University College London Institute of Education Library archive.

LATE. (1956). The Aims of English Teaching: A Pamphlet prepared for British Council Study Boxes to be used in India. LATE Archive Folder 11, Item Number 4, held in the University College London Institute of Education Library archive.

LATE. (1960). *And When You Are Young: Prose and Verse by Young Writers, 5–18* London: The Joint Council for Education through Art.

LATE. (1966). Report to LATE of the Dartmouth Conference, 1st December 1966. LATE Archive Folder 16, Item Number 33, held in the University College London Institute of Education archive.

Lightfoot, M. (1988). Teaching English as a Rehearsal of Politics. In Lightfoot, M. and Martin, N. (Eds), *The Word for Teaching is Learning: Essays for James Britton*. Oxford: Heinemann.

Marshall, B. (2000). A Rough Guide to English Teachers. *English in Education*, 34(1), pp. 24–41.

Mercer, N. (2000). *Words and Minds: How We Use Language to Think Together*. Oxford: Routledge.

Muller, H. (1967). *The Uses of English*. New York: Holt, Reinhart and Winston.

Pollard, A. (1969). O and A Level: Keeping up the Standards. In Cox, C.B. and Dyson, A. E. (Eds), *Black Paper 2: The Crisis in Education*. London: The Critical Quarterly Society.

Rubinstein, D. and Simon, B. (1973). *The Evolution of the Comprehensive School 1926–1972*. London: Routledge and Kegan Paul.

Schools Council. (1965). *Working Paper No.3: English – A Programme for Research and Development in English Teaching*. London: Her Majesty's Stationery Office.

Shafer, R. (1986). Dartmouth and Beyond. *The English Journal*, 75(3), pp. 22–26.

Simmons, J., Shafer, R. and Shadiow, L. (1990). The Swinging Pendulum: Teaching English in the USA, 1945–1987. In Britton, J., Shafer, R., and Watson, K. (Eds), *Teaching and Learning English Worldwide*. Philadelphia: Multilingual Matters Ltd.

Smagorinsky, P. (2002). Growth through English Revisited. *The English Journal*, 91(6), pp. 23–29.

Spitalfields Life. (2011, 16th August). Available at http://spitalfieldslife.com/2011/08/16/the-stepney-school-strike-of-1971/ (accessed on 19th February 2016).

Squires, J. (1966). Post Dartmouth Memorandum. Available at http://archives.library.illinois.edu/ncte/about/about_images/dartmouth/memorandum01.jpg (accessed on 1st June 2016).

Stratta, L., Dixon, J. and Wilkinson, A. (1973). *Patterns of Language: Explorations of the Teaching of English*. London: Heinemann.

Summerfield, G. (1968). *Creativity in English*. Illinois: NCTE.

The Guardian. (2013, 28th July). Peter Doughty Obituary. Available at http://www.theguardian.com/theguardian/2013/jul/28/peter-doughty-obituary (accessed on 31st March 2016).

The Sun. (1971, 28th May). Please Don't Sack Sir. Available at http://spitalfieldslife.com/2011/08/16/the-stepney-school-strike-of-1971/ (accessed on 1st March 2016).

Vygotsky, L. (1962). *Thought and Language*. Cambridge, Massachusetts: Massachusetts Institute of Technology Press.

Vygotsky, L. (1978). *Mind in Society: The Development of Higher Psychological Processes*. Cambridge, Massachusetts: Harvard University Press.

Whitehead, F. (1976). The Present State of English Teaching: Stunting the Growth. *The Use of English*, 28(1), pp. 11–17.

3

THE CALM BEFORE THE STORM? ENGLISH FROM THE 1970S INTO THE 1980S

Although the backlash against progressive English teaching was clearly growing from the beginning of the 1970s – both from those adherents to a Leavisite perspective who perhaps feared for the future of their own model of English and from a wider community that sought to expose the apparent failures of the comprehensive system and progressive education more generally – it would still be many years before central policy would attempt to directly intervene to change the nature of what happened in English classrooms. In the meantime, from the mid-1970s to the introduction of the National Curriculum at the end of the 1980s, developments in secondary English teaching continued apace.

This was, or certainly seems to be with the benefit of hindsight, a time when the direction of English and the approaches its teachers took were occurring in a relatively benign political context. Though thinkers and politicians of the right, in particular, may have grumbled and published their pamphlets, how English was taught, and how children experienced it, was still very much in the hands of teachers themselves – teachers who were able to try new initiatives, work in collaboration with their departments, experiment and push boundaries, without the pressure exerted by direct state intervention into curriculum and pedagogy. Nor was there the pressure of a stringent accountability framework that would make English teachers – or if not them then their senior managers in school – risk averse. Projects that emerged through bodies like the Schools Council were often, essentially, teacher led. Innovation was – even where not actively encouraged – then not suppressed. English teachers felt they had a measure of control, and that even if certain voices questioned their ideas and methods, this was a challenge to respond to, not to be becalmed by. The period from the 1970s into the 1980s has been described as one when, for an English teacher, it was easy to teach and to innovate.[1]

Expanding the progressive English curriculum: media, race and gender

English as a subject in many classrooms expanded to embrace more enthusiastically media, moving image and new technologies. In this area the courses, publications and system of teacher secondments of the Inner London Education Authority English Centre (later to become the independent English and Media Centre following the disbanding of ILEA in 1990) were important. Here the leadership of Michael Simons – who was involved with Commission 7 – was critical. Roxy Harris remembered that:

> Back in the day, they got hold of the most advanced technology, really really early. So they always had these high production values, doing committed stuff within English teaching but it wasn't to do with what the official agenda was.

The English Centre helped to make the study of television, newspapers and magazines part of mainstream English work. Additionally, the educational work of the British Film Institute, building on the foundations laid by Paddy Whannel in the 1960s, was important in helping to establish a place in many English classrooms for the study of film. The architects of growth English had long advocated the exploration of popular culture within English – John Dixon recalled his co-writer on *Reflections*, Leslie Stratta, without the benefit of video recording technology, 'got the idea of taking a programme like Top of the Pops and discussing that because it's a regular weekly thing'. The other *Reflections* writer, Simon Clements, remembered Stratta saying to his class,

> Next Thursday we're going to have our own Top of the Pops – you're all to bring in a record, a 45, LPs, you're all to bring in a record, choose a bit to play and tell us why you like it. They thought this was wonderful, so we all did it.

In the late 1950s and early 1960s such practice was unusual and experimental; the 1970s and 1980s saw newspapers, television and film increasingly as part of mainstream English teaching.

In part this serious approach to media and popular culture within English had developed through the 1960s alongside the broader cultural studies movement, led by Richard Hoggart and Stuart Hall at the Centre for Contemporary Cultural Studies at Birmingham University. The work of Raymond Williams was also important. Hall, who collaborated with Paddy Whannel in publishing *The Popular Arts* (1964), had worked in the late 1950s in a London secondary modern school and the links between English and the developing study of culture were referred to by John Dixon, who knew Hall through the journal *Universities and Left Review*. According to Dixon, 'on the whole the left had not been interested in culture' but 'Stuart Hall, as a principal pioneer, introduced this notion that cultural issues were important'. Dixon remembered Hall leading a mini-project involving Holloway

Boys' school that focused on students discussing their relationship and response to the media. Reflecting on the development of the English curriculum, Dixon said:

> We also had the advantage that Richard Hoggart had produced the book, *Uses of Literacy*, which was a very important book for us, and Raymond Williams' *The Long Revolution* was important. I probably heard both of them speak and they probably both wrote for the *Universities and Left Review* early on. So it was quite important that you had people interested in cultural studies and English in the periphery. I kept contact with Richard and Stuart when they went to Birmingham. That notion that there was money available and that we had to do something to change English meant we had a lot of minor projects that were very useful in the Schools Council.

The work, often through NATE, of English teachers like Joan Goody was increasingly expanding the profession's knowledge of multicultural texts and world literature that would reflect the experiences and backgrounds of classrooms that – in urban centres especially – were becoming increasingly multiethnic, multicultural and multilingual through the 1970s and 1980s. Goody, who led the English department at Clissold Park School in Hackney, set up the Caribbean Teachers' Exchange, which linked teachers in London to their counterparts in Jamaica, Barbados and Trinidad. Through her links with John and Sarah La Rose, who had founded the independent publishers New Beacon Books in 1966,[2] and by leading NATE's multicultural committee for many years, Goody was highly influential in the growth of literature from other cultures in the English classroom. She was a 'quiet revolutionary who detested the hierarchies in education', who struggled to ensure the 'reading and teaching of Caribbean and world literature that few then knew' (*The Guardian*, 2008). By the time the National Curriculum was written in 1989 it was officially accepted that literature from other cultures should be a statutory part of all young people's reading experience.

As English teachers' interest and knowledge of multicultural concerns was growing, there was, too, a developing interest in gender. More and more English teachers began explicitly challenging gender stereotyping in their work, through topic-based work, exploration of sexism in language and through choices of literature – novels like *The Turbulent Term of Tyke Tiler*[3] (Kemp, 1977) became typical class readers in lower secondary age schooling. Although issues of class were already important to pioneers of the new English in the 1960s, race, ethnicity and gender were now also prominent in a child-centred view of the subject.[4] English was a political subject in the way it was framed by progressive thinkers, and as such it reflected the evolving politics of gender, race and class where arguments were becoming more sensitive and more intense as the 1970s progressed. The freedom to create curriculums that would respond to the needs of changing classrooms, and which would engage and motivate the increased number of young people in schools following the raising of the school leaving age to 16 in 1973, was supported by the assessment system with CSE Mode 3 allowing English departments high levels of autonomy.[5]

As this progressive model of English evolved and its influence continued to spread, increasingly a surge of voices, echoing the *Black Papers*, could be heard bemoaning the failure of English teachers to address the basics of spelling, punctuation and grammar. It wasn't a difficult argument to make; surely if the subject was driven by a child-centred, mixed-ability ethos, and was purporting to address issues of class, culture, society, gender, race and ethnicity, how could it possibly be paying proper attention to basic skills? And what was happening to the traditional canon of English literature? The caricature of the 1970s English teacher – liberal minded, eschewing grammar and great literature in favour of expression, personal response and relevant texts, was one that those on the right wing of educational thinking were quick to portray.[6] The Conservative administration of the day made its attempt to address the state of English and expose the failings of the progressives by establishing a committee of enquiry into the teaching of the subject across all age ranges, under the leadership of Sir Alan Bullock.

The Bullock Report

Without question the writing of the Bullock Report represented the largest investigation into the teaching of English since 1921's *The Teaching of English in England* (Departmental Committee of the Board of Education, 1921, commonly known as The Newbolt Report). According to one obituary on his death aged 89, Sir Alan Bullock was 'one of the most versatile and engaging public figures produced by Britain in the second half of the twentieth century' (*The Guardian*, 2004). A historian by trade, and author of biographies of Hitler and Ernest Bevin, Bullock was apparently also a skilled committee chair, and it was this, one assumes, rather than any particular knowledge or specialism in the field, that led Margaret Thatcher as Secretary of State for Education to appoint him to lead the committee of enquiry into English that lasted from 1972 to 1974. By the time of the Committee's report in 1974, a Labour government was in power and Thatcher's successor, Reg Prentice, was the minister of state; given the report's content it is unlikely it would have been particularly well received by his predecessor.

The scope of the Committee's report was incredibly wide ranging, reflected in a report running to over 600 pages, thereby justifying its somewhat lofty title of *A Language for Life*. Sections of the report covered all ages from early years to adult literacy, institutions addressed included not only schools but teacher training colleges and local education authorities, and there was comparative analysis, notably of the teaching of the subject in the United States. The enquiry was motivated by the kinds of sentiments expressed in the *Black Papers* over the supposed fall in standards in English, particularly in the context of comprehensive schooling, but if there was a political desire for a report that would lambast the state of progressive English teaching and its concurrent detrimental effects on the basic standards of reading, writing and spoken English, this was not fulfilled, as indeed it would not be when future Conservative administrations formed committees in the hope that a back-to-basics version of English would be recommended. On reviewing the available evidence on the teaching of formal grammar, for example, the report stated that 'What has been shown is that the teaching of traditional analytic grammar does not appear to improve performance in writing' (Department for Education and Science, 1975, p. 172). On the study of language, the committee's view was that children should learn about language by 'experiencing it and experimenting with its use' (ibid., p. 173). It was the kind of reluctance to endorse formal grammar teaching that would frustrate future Conservative education secretaries – a reluctance supported by the research evidence but at odds with what, for many, is common-sense, self-evident truth that if you know more about grammar you must be able to use it more effectively.

In fact, even if accepting that standards should be higher, the Bullock Report found no evidence of falling standards, and even noted that this same kind of rhetoric around standards appeared in the earlier Newbolt Report. The golden age syndrome, that dictates that there was a time in the not-too-distant past when children could write and speak grammatically correct Standard English and could spell with impeccable accuracy, is one that has dogged the profession for many decades; it plays well to the galleries.

Neither did the report find any evidence of the fact that in some way creative and progressive teaching methods were threatening the basic skills, as the rhetoric of the *Black Papers* had it. What Bullock's committee produced was, in the event, a wide-ranging and thoughtful exploration of the subject and one that retains power for English teachers today, and not just those of an age to remember its initial publication. It powerfully made the case for better resourcing for English departments and more specialist English teachers to be employed in schools, and came down on the side of mixed-ability teaching (whilst acknowledging the complexities of this type of pupil organisation). Interestingly, the report did include a 'Note of Dissent' written by Stuart Froome – a member of the Committee and head teacher of a junior school – in which the author took issues with the overall findings of the report around areas such as standards in reading, the effects of 'creative' teaching and pupil grouping. These concerns echoed those of the *Black Paper* authors, and it says something of the time that a government report was willing to publish opposing views within its pages. However, the overall impression was that *A Language for Life* fully endorsed and vindicated the progressive approach to the teaching of English that had developed through the work of LATE and NATE to the Dartmouth conference and into the 1970s.

Among the Report's numerous and wide-ranging recommendations were the call for additional funding and resources for English departments, the appointment of an English adviser in each local education authority and better transfer and transition work to support children as they move from one phase of education to the next. Also recommended was more support to combat the problem of adult illiteracy and additional professional development for all teachers on language.

The voice of one key committee member is apparent to an experienced English teacher throughout – James Britton. In the section on written language in the middle and secondary school, the report drew on the work of the Schools Council

Writing Research Unit explicitly referencing the concepts of 'language in the role of the participant' and 'language in the role of the spectator' (ibid., p. 164) and used the three categories of writing – 'transactional, expressive and poetic' (ibid., p. 165) – that were the basis of Britton's theories on the development of writing. These were ideas Britton had, in some ways, derived from the work of the English teacher turned psychologist D.W. Harding (see, for example, Harding (1937)), but which he had fashioned to develop a distinctive account of the development of writing in children and had articulated in *Language and Learning* (1970). The bold statement in the recommendations section that 'children learn as certainly by talking and writing as by listening and reading' (Department for Education and Science, 1975, p. 520) was quintessentially Britton-esque. Douglas Barnes' work, too, was of critical importance in terms of the content of *A Language for Life*, particularly in the area of talk and learning.

Britton's ideas, and those that represented the work that the National and London Associations for the Teaching of English had been engaged in from the late 1960s and into the 1970s, were strikingly clear in the section of the report on 'Language Across the Curriculum'. In this chapter, *Language, the Learner and the School*[7] was directly referenced, and the NATE Conference of 1971 was given as an example of good practice – an event at which teachers across all curriculum areas were invited to discuss and develop ideas about language use across the school. The Committee's clear recommendation that 'every school should develop a policy for language across the curriculum' (ibid., p. 529) was one that led to many interesting developments, as schools set up language and learning, or language across the curriculum, working groups. According to Harold Rosen, 'although the Bullock Report gave a mere five pages of its 600 to language across the curriculum ... the impact of that short chapter was enormous' (Hickman and Kimberley, 1988, p. 4). It's likely that, in many institutions where policies were produced, they remained simply as paper exercises, and probably impacted little on practice; secondary schools are often graveyards for cross-curricular initiatives given such institutions' size, complexity and very nature. In the revised version of *Language, the Learner and the School* (Barnes, Britton and Rosen, 1971) Rosen had made clear that a working language across the curriculum policy would need to evolve and be shaped within the specific circumstances of an individual school – there was never a view that there could be a one-size-fits-all approach. In schools where the policy was written, to tick the language-across-the-curriculum box, but not developed by teachers through their own practice there would have been little effect on children's experience.

There were, however, striking examples of projects that took off in the wake of Bullock, and which saw the expertise of English teachers genuinely begin to influence and enhance the work of teachers across a diverse range of subject areas.

The Vauxhall Manor Talk Workshop

One such example of work inspired by the Bullock Report was that which took place in Vauxhall Manor School in South London and led to the publication of the influential *Becoming Our Own Experts* (Eyers and Richmond, 1982). In the wake of Bullock, Dr Birchenough, the Chief Inspector for the Inner London Education Authority, did indeed ask that all schools develop a language-across-the-curriculum policy. According to John Richmond, who had joined the teaching staff at Vauxhall Manor in 1974, 'for very many schools, once the policy had been written it disappeared into a filing cabinet.'[8] Teachers at Richmond's school, however, did far more than pay lip service to the demand to address language issues across the curriculum. Here, a working group was formed which included teachers of English, modern foreign languages, commerce and maths, The group met on Tuesday afternoons to consider the importance of oracy on the development of children's learning, aided by recordings made on 'ancient tape recorders and black and white reel to reel video'. It was work inspired and supported, according to Richmond, by Rachael Farrar, the leader of the oracy project within ILEA, and that centred on 'speculation and observation about how talk had enhanced the learning of children in the classroom'.

Over the course of two years, the group assumed the name of The Talk Workshop Project and produced a series of papers, which ultimately were published together – with a loan of £6000 from the Schools Council – through the labours of Richmond, under the title of *Becoming Our Own Experts*. More than 4,000 copies were sold and the loan repaid in full. Over the lifespan of the project there was involvement from the ILEA English Centre and from the University of London Institute of Education in the shape of Alex McLeod.[9] It was, however, essentially a project led by teachers. The project certainly drew on LATE traditions and on the *Language, the Learner and the School*, and if it did not have an explicit methodology it has been viewed as a clear example of action research in practice; Charles Sarland, who conducted historical research into action research in schools claimed that the Vauxhall Project shared 'many of the markers of action research' and had 'the strongest claim to be the most teacher directed' (Sarland, 2001, p. 179).

Schools Council English projects

The work at Vauxhall Manor was certainly inspired by the Bullock Report, so it would be unfair to say that *A Language for Life* had no concrete impact. And though many of its recommendations went either unheeded or unimplemented, it had a powerful effect in that it endorsed a humane, child-centred, progressive model of English. In the years before and after the report, there were further Schools Council projects that ensured English teachers continued to be involved in bottom-up curriculum and assessment development, even as prime minister James Callaghan's famous Ruskin College speech in 1976 had sparked the great debate into education in England that would ultimately result in the closing down of teacher influence on these areas.

One particularly significant Schools Council project was that which led to the publication of *The Development of Writing Abilities (11–18)* (Britton, Burgess, Martin, McLeod and Rosen, 1975). The research for this lengthy project had in fact taken place between 1966 and 1971, and was followed by a four-year development project during which individual teachers and groups put into practice some of the research team's key findings. The project itself was cross-curricular, with the research team analysing over 2,000 pieces of writing from students across over 60 schools, with the ultimate aims being to reconceptualise how school writing was categorised and to propose a new model that would describe writing and its development. Though cross-curricular, the research team were, essentially, the English department of the London Institute of Education, and all active members of LATE. As a cross-curricular project, however, and published at the same time as the Bullock report, *The Development of Writing Abilities* was a critical resource for any teacher or school seeking to harness ideas about both spoken and oral language in an overarching approach to language across the curriculum.

The Development of Writing Abilities approached the analysis of the sample of school writing using a conceptual framework which came from Britton's work and which would be familiar to readers of *Language and Learning*. Writing was described in terms of its function – transactional, expressive or poetic – with the writer of a given piece taking up the participant or spectator role. The continuum constructed as a frame for analysis placed transactional writing/participant role at one end, passing through expressive writing to poetic writing/spectator role at the opposing end (Britton et al., 1975, p. 81). Project team members analysed samples of writing, categorising them by function and by audience, and tables reproduced in the text show how instances of function and audience were distributed across year groups, subjects and school types. The results enabled the project team to come to judgements about the sorts of writing demands made of students, how their writing skills were enabled to develop by different types of task and what opportunities were afforded to write in different forms, in different subjects and at different ages.

Although *The Development of Writing Abilities* ended with nearly as many questions as it began, these were markers for future research and development and don't detract from the project's importance. The painstaking approach to the collection of data and the analysis of scripts was symptomatic of perhaps the most serious attempt to throw light on school writing that had hitherto taken place. Read in conjunction with *Language, Learner and the School*, *Language and Learning* and *Understanding Children Writing* (Burgess et al., 1973), which emerged from the 1971 NATE conference, and put in the context of the Bullock report recommendations, it can be seen that many of the central ideas around growth English and its pedagogy and practice were perfectly placed to affect oral and written work across the curriculum.

Another particularly interesting area of Schools Council work was in the area of post-16 teaching. In the rapid developments that had been taking place in English teaching across the compulsory school age, A-level English literature had remained largely unchanged. In fact, if the new progressive English was becoming the orthodox model across the compulsory years of comprehensive schooling, as the contents of Bullock certainly suggested, literature in the sixth form remained stubbornly Leavisite in form and approach. Interestingly, given developments to study of English in higher education, this not only left sixth form teaching in some ways at odds with the rest of secondary schooling, so that 'it found itself uncomfortably sandwiched between the modern student-centred, language-led school English curriculum and the radically re-focused, theory inspired literature-led university discipline' (Snapper, 2013, p. 54).

The Schools Council English 16–19 Project ran from 1975–1978, led by John Dixon. It essentially reviewed provision in post-compulsory schooling and considered, in the light of changing educational contexts, changing demands of society and the world of work and changing cohorts of students, what developments were needed in terms of curriculum and assessment to ensure that the experience for young people was fit for the purposes it needed to fulfil. The key findings appeared in *Education 16–19: The Role of English and Communication* (Dixon, Brown and Barnes, 1979). The most significant impact of the 16–19 project was probably the introduction of A-level courses in English language, media and communications. Its impact on literature teaching has been viewed as minimal as 'only a limited liberalisation of approaches took place' (Snapper, 2013, p. 54). However, in the focusing on this age of schooling the project had a legacy in the future work and publications of NATE's 16–19 committee.

English into the 1980s

The Schools Council's English projects then, often strongly influenced by NATE members, further rooted a broad notion of a progressive, growth English as the established approach in many secondary classrooms. The late 1970s into the 1980s saw a burgeoning of the subject as the range of literature available to teachers expanded and diversified and published classroom resources were made available that were a world away from traditional text books. A leading organisation in this development was the English and Media Centre, under the stewardship of Michael Simons. Classroom resources like *School Under Siege* (English and Media Centre, 1979) and *The Island* (English and Media Centre, 1985a) promoted creative, project-based English work with students inhabiting imaginative worlds in which they would talk and write for different purposes and audiences. *Changing Stories* (English and Media Centre, 1984a) and *Making Stories* (English and Media Centre, 1984b) enabled children to play with familiar narratives, subvert them and write their own fiction. Their *Materials for Discussion* series included *The English Curriculum: Gender, The English Curriculum: Media* and *The English Curriculum: Poetry* (English and Media Centre, 1985a, 1985b, 1987). These were resources that encouraged teachers to address both new and traditional areas of the curriculum through new approaches. Such texts as these were common to large numbers of English departments; English teachers felt that they worked, and that was due in no small part to the process of their production.

The English and Media Centre's approach, when part of ILEA, was to work with seconded teachers to develop materials, trial the materials with teachers on courses at the centre and only publish when it was felt the resources had been proven to work in the eyes of those who would ultimately put them to use. John Wilks, who became a central figure in protests around English assessment in the 1990s, remembered:

> The English Centre courses might have three days but they'd be spread out. You'd be in the English Centre, you'd look at something – how mixed ability works or narrative or story telling – you would construct some materials and then try them out in your classroom. Then you'd have a day back at the Centre and you might rewrite some material. I think a lot of EC publications came about in that way. So teachers involved in that process were committed to those materials, they were more likely to work in our classrooms.[10]

The range and breadth of materials produced by the centre reflected a creative time for English teachers and departments, and when moves were made to radically transform the later years of secondary schooling with a revamped system of examinations, there was scope for English teachers to extend the creativity and richness of the curriculum for all students across the secondary age range.

Development of 100 per cent coursework GCSE

For many English teachers the introduction of the General Certificate of Secondary Education was a hugely positive move. With many holding a commitment to mixed-ability teaching and a belief that differentiation was best achieved through outcome, it seemed illogical that students were segregated by ability when it came to assessment in English. What's more, under the system of O levels for those that were seen as academically able and CSEs for the remainder, English literature was often viewed as a subject for those at the higher end of the ability spectrum. There were even grammar schools – already having selected the most academically able – who would stream students in the final years with those thought to be most able taking English Literature O level and others taking a qualification like Business English which was viewed as more relevant to those who were unlikely to pursue academic futures.[11] The GCSE opened up the study of literature for examination purposes to students of all abilities.

The GCSE was first taught in 1986 and first awarded two years later, but in fact it was almost ten years earlier that the Waddell committee, instigated to explore the Schools Councils' recommendation of a single examination system for all abilities, posited that:

> A common system of examining in English language is feasible and could, though it need not necessarily, take the form of a common examination provided that this is carefully and skilfully designed and makes provision for suitable choice for candidates to show their respective capabilities.
>
> *(Department for Education and Science, 1978, p. 12)*

The election of the Conservative government of 1979 meant any immediate developments on this front were put on hold and it was not until 1984 that the then education secretary Sir Keith Joseph made the move to a common exam system that would finally unite GCE O level and CSE and attempt to end the divisive effects of the two-tier system.

It was not long before a 100 per cent coursework GCSE in English Language and Literature became available, and this was a natural choice for English teachers, perhaps used to working with Mode 3 CSE, for whom a negotiated curriculum, child-centred approaches and appropriate choice and selection of texts and tasks was central to their thinking about the subject. The 100 per cent coursework GCSE genuinely offered the opportunity to create an experience for students from 14–16 that enabled them to develop their abilities in English and be assessed in a way that rewarded their true potential. John Wilks felt that for working-class children in particular this form of assessment was critical in the context of a perspective that such students need clear, short-term goals:

> I think that made sense to me from a middle class perspective. Whereas middle class life … you're paid monthly, you see your way to saving up for something in the future. It seemed to me working class life was very short term, you'd be paid by the day, by the week, you don't really know what life is going to be like. It seemed to me that made sense in terms of how children were looking at their learning. Most of the kids I taught weren't really able to think 'if I work hard now in two years' time I'll succeed'.

According to a report by the exams regulator, by the late 1980s and early 1990s 'about two-thirds of 16 year olds were taking GCSE English through syllabuses that had no examinations' (Qualifications and Curriculum Authority, 2006, p. 9). It was a brief period, but one that many English teachers look back on as a golden age, recalling as they do the hours of work students would put in on redrafting pieces to include in their final folders, the rigour of the school and area moderation meetings (described in Gibbons and Marshall (2010)) and the fact that these were as much about professional development for the teachers as they were about agreeing standards. The workload for English teachers was significantly increased with 100 per cent coursework assessment, but the reality is that few complained of the burden given that what they saw was a humane assessment system which worked to the benefit of their children.

The untimely death of 100 per cent coursework

The lifespan of the 100 per cent coursework GCSE was brutally, and for the majority of English teachers, prematurely ended when in 1991 the Prime Minister, John Major, announced a cap of a maximum of 40 per cent coursework assessment; apparently he adopted this view following conversations he had with members of the right-wing think tank the Centre for Policy Studies, and initially wanted to set the cap at 20 per cent. There are also stories – perhaps apocryphal – that Major had surrendered to the demands of the right wing of his party on education in some kind of deal for support in what would be fraught internal battles over European issues in the lead up to the ratification of the Maastricht treaty. Whatever the explanation for Major's intervention on the coursework issue, the reaction of the vast majority of English teachers was unequivocal as shown by the striking response to the Save English Coursework campaign set up by Mike Lloyd, a head of English in Birmingham. A tireless campaigner for English coursework, Lloyd surveyed nearly every secondary school English department in the country – around 4,000 – to ascertain their views on coursework. The results were nothing short of unambiguous:

> Over 80% have expressed their views on the best weighting for coursework and exam. Over 95% of these schools have firmly stated that there should be a maximum weighting of 20% for any terminal exam; and many of these have been very reluctant to concede that there is any value even in the 20% exam.
>
> (Lloyd, 1994, p. 7)

Although the Save English Coursework campaign failed to achieve its aims, and the proportion of teacher-assessed work in GCSE went on to progressively shrink, there was probably something in the reaction of English teachers to the seemingly education-free policy intervention from the Conservative government that contributed to the concerted collective action that would follow very shortly afterwards in the response to the Key Stage 3 national tests.

As the end of the 1980s approached, it became clear that the age of intervention was upon schools, and the intensity of centrally driven policy was rapidly being ramped up. The Schools Council, a body that was by its nature collaborative and representative of the profession with members from subject associations and teacher unions, had been superseded by the School Curriculum Development Committee in 1984, and this was quickly replaced when the National Curriculum Council (NCC) was established following the 1988 Education Reform Act. Although members of these bodies may have been teachers at some point, and certainly those working on English groups within the NCC had this pedigree, the bodies themselves were in effect quangos, and its members essentially civil servants. Before this centralisation began to take hold, however, English teachers had what might be seen as their last real opportunity to engage in profession-wide, officially endorsed, projects that reflected the point to which progressive, growth English had come by the end of the 1980s.

The National Writing Project and the National Oracy Project

Although official control of curriculum was being steadily brought to the centre and placed in the hands of ministers and their appointed working group, there was still time for two final substantial projects in English, both rooted in the kinds of teacher-driven research which was at the heart of the best work in the development of English curriculum. These projects, the National Writing Project and the National Oracy Project, were perhaps the last centrally funded initiatives that genuinely involved teachers, and NATE as the major subject association, as genuinely active participants in the development of curriculum and pedagogy. All too soon teachers would be on the receiving end of policy, so in a sense the Writing and Oracy projects were the swansong for English teachers and for a way of working that would soon become a thing of the past.

The National Writing Project ran from 1985–1989. Although centrally funded, the project was structured to be coordinated by local education authorities, with project coordinators working with teachers in schools in networks around specific writing projects. NATE was involved, and in some cases higher-education institutions, and the project coordinators in the various LEAs involved included many familiar names including Margaret Meek, Helen Savva and Sue Horner, who would in fact go on to lead the English team in QCA as the National Curriculum evolved. John Richmond was one of the central project officers, and the central steering committee included Douglas Barnes – clearly the project involved a wealth of talent and experience. The project was designed to work with existing teacher support structures and be 'bottom up':

> Central to the National Writing Project's organisation is the belief that curriculum development should occur within existing LEA structures rather than be imposed upon authorities. Central, too, is the intention that teachers themselves determine the local projects' directions.
>
> *(Schools Curriculum Development Council, 1986, p. 2)*

Many hundreds of teachers across the country were involved in various projects focused around the learning and teaching of writing in what was described as an 'experiment in mass consultation' (National Writing Project, 1989a). Through its newsletters and occasional papers, teachers' experiences from local projects were disseminated during the Project's development phase and then, in an additional implementation year when the Project continued under the auspices of the National Curriculum Council, a range of publications were produced by publishers Thomas Nelson which drew together outcomes from the Project under thematic areas, with topics such as *Audiences for Writing, Becoming a Writer* and *Responding to and Assessing Writing* (The National Writing Project, 1989b, 1989c, 1989d). Each contained a wealth of examples of real children's writing with analysis, reflection and commentary and the hope was that the work would thereby continue to inform and inspire English teachers as they faced the reality of implementing a top-down National Curriculum.

Modelled along similar lines to the National Writing Project, the National Oracy Project began in 1987 and ran for six years. According to the Project's director, John Johnson, later a chair of NATE, the oracy work took from the writing project that 'large-scale, coordinated curriculum development was possible in the field of language, if teachers identified the changes needed and retained a personal stake in the implementation of those changes' (Johnson, 1992, p. 49). It was that 'personal stake' in the work that was central to the writing and oracy projects, and it is a dimension that has been viewed as absolutely critical if education reform and development is genuinely to have any impact; Goodson (2001), for example, suggested that key to the failure of centrally driven reform was its neglect of teachers' own 'sense of passion and purpose' (p. 49) and Friedman, Galligan, Albano and O'Connor (2009) suggested that, 'for educational reform to be effective, teachers must be enactors of reform rather than recipients' (p. 267). The National Oracy and Writing projects were predicated on the notion – as was the ethos behind the work of subject associations like LATE and NATE – that teachers should be involved in investigating and seeking solutions to problems they saw in their own day-to-day work.

As with the writing project, local authorities across England and Wales were involved and at school level teachers investigated areas of talk. The project's steering committee was chaired by Andrew Wilkinson, a former NATE chair and the man credited with coining the term oracy in the 1960s, through work with a research team at Birmingham University's School of Education who felt that the lack of any equivalent word to literacy to describe speaking and listening work was 'indicative of the unimportant part played by the "orate" skills in thinking about education' (Wilkinson, 1968, p. 743). Others in the steering group included Douglas Barnes. A range of publications helped to disseminate good practice over the six years of its lifespan: *Oracy Issues* was essentially a newsletter with short contributions submitted by teachers around the country about what had gone on in their classrooms; *Talk* was the more substantial journal of the project; *Occasional Papers* would highlight a particular area, for example *Oracy and Special Education Needs* (National Oracy Project, 1992); and at the conclusion of the project four documents entitled *Teaching Talking and Learning* essentially summarised findings relating to each of the Key Stages (National Oracy Project, 1990, 1991a, 1991b, 1993).

Both these projects represented a high point in the model of curriculum development that saw central funding being used to enable teachers, working with local authority advisers, their subject associations and higher education colleagues, to explore and investigate their own practice and develop new approaches rooted in the evaluation of their own experiences in collaboration with peers. Genuinely bottom up, these projects mirrored the ways in which associations like LATE and NATE had been working for 40 years and – irrespective of what they may have achieved in terms of changing the nature of the subject – they contributed hugely to teachers' own sense of professionalism and represented what for many is an ideal model of continuing professional development. Both projects were genuinely cross-curricular, with teachers from across the secondary subjects involved in projects in their classrooms, but it was inspired and led by English advisers and teachers and was, in effect, spreading the knowledge developed about language from the work of English teachers and associations across the school.

Conclusion

The period from the mid-1970s, and the publication of *A Language for Life*, and the end of the 1980s was an exciting time for English. From Bullock came a renewed sense – one originally captured in Newbolt – of the importance of English across the curriculum, and a period when it seemed that language, literacy and learning policies and practice would assume their rightful place at the heart of a school's work, with English teachers often leading working groups, committees and in-school action research work. The development of GCSE and the appearance of 100 per cent coursework assessment were in harmony with so many English teachers' vision of the subject that it should be child centred and offer all young people the chance to succeed. The National Writing and National Oracy Projects engaged many hundreds of English teachers in a model of professional and curriculum development that had its roots in ways that many English teachers had been inducted into through their work with subject associations, LEA English advisors, teacher training institutions and bodies like the English Centre in London. The relative freedom schools had meant that creative and innovative English departments were at liberty to devise curriculums and classroom activities that would enable students, within their studies of language and literature, to engage explicitly with issues of class, race and gender. This was a model of English that was rooted in personal growth, but which had become much more about the growth of the individual within communities and the relationship of the individual to culture and society. In fact, this was much truer to John Dixon's vision of growth English than his detractors gave him credit for.[12]

It remains a period that many experienced teachers look back on with huge fondness, particularly given what was to follow. Even as the National Writing and National Oracy Projects were in full swing, the power such initiatives gave to individuals and groups of teachers was about to be steadily wrested away. The end of the 1980s was in some ways a glorious time to be an English teacher; it was the culmination of a period of some 20 years that saw a progressive model of the subject evolve and flourish, that saw English expand its boundaries to embrace media, moving image texts and emerging technologies and witnessed the subject play a serious role in enabling pupils to tackle issues of gender, ethnicity, culture and class. It then saw the influence of that model of English, with its focus on language development, oracy and learning, increasingly impact upon the secondary school curriculum as a whole through policies on language and literacy across the curriculum to initiatives like the National Writing and Oracy Projects. For the author of *Growth through English*, this was a period of two decades of 'participant-led' change, that built on the 'great educational project of the sixties' which 'derived creative energies from the democratic aspirations that followed World War II' (Dixon, 2015, p. 429). There was a sense in the profession of confidence that had been constructed through the collaborative work of English teachers. However, the confidence English teachers may have felt in themselves and in their subject was about to be severely tested; as the decade came to an end it was clear, too, that English teachers faced the dawn of the age of intervention.

Notes

1 In interviews with the author a number of notable colleagues involved in the English teaching world have described the time in these terms. These include Douglas Barnes, Peter Medway and Jane Ogborn, a London teacher who became Chief English Inspector for Tower Hamlets and published a number of books on A-level teaching. Hindsight may well have influenced their view of the period, but the general sense of a time when new ideas and initiatives were encouraged prevailed.

2 A full account of the history of New Beacon Books, and its founders Sarah and John La Rose, can be found on the website of the George Padmore Institute at http://www.georgepadmoreinstitute.org/the-pioneering-years/new-beacon-books-early-history/beginnings-new-beacon-books. The independent publisher was critical in the expansion of multicultural literature within England and its schools.

3 *The Turbulent Term of Tyke Tyler* became a popular whole-class novel in the 1970s. The gender of the central protagonist is not revealed to the reader until the final chapter when we discover that Tyke is a girl; the actions of the character throughout the book are characteristically 'boyish' and so the ultimate reveal forces the reader to confront ideas about gender stereotyping.

4 In interviews with the author, Douglas and Dorothy Barnes, Peter Medway and Tony Burgess all confirmed that ideas about race and gender never featured prominently in English teachers' conversations until the 1970s; Medway pointed to NATE's Commission 7 as being a key starting point.

5 CSE had been set up in 1965 following the Beloe Report (Ministry of Education, 1960). Numbers taking the CSE, which was essentially a less academic parallel course to GCE O level, expanded rapidly when the school leaving age was raised to 16 in 1973. There were three CSE modes; mode 3 CSE courses were devised and assessed by teachers themselves, with examination boards providing moderation.

6 Douglas Barnes suggested that at this time there was a 'building up in the national press – a certain part of it – of anti teacher, anti education writings, which really suggested that kids were being allowed to do just what they wanted in schools, that there were communists, or socialists at the very least, indoctrinating them'.

7 *Language, the Learner and the School* (Barnes, Britton and Rosen, 1971) was a publication following a LATE conference on language across the curriculum and illustrated one particular strand of LATE work that, by the end of the 1960s, was looking beyond English to how language was used across the secondary school by students.

8 John Richmond's comments taken from an interview with the author. Richmond has had a career that has spanned secondary English teaching, advisory work and the media. He was a project officer on the National Writing Project in the 1980s, a consortium leader for the Language in the National Curriculum project and then became commissioning editor for Channel 4 schools programming. He was a senior executive of Teachers TV between 2004 and 2010.

9 Alex McLeod had been a key figure in LATE from the 1950s and he had, along with Harold Rosen, Simon Clements, John Dixon, Leslie Stratta and Peter Medway, worked at Walworth School in South London.

10 Comments taken from an interview with the author. John Wilks taught in a range of London secondary schools from the mid-1970s and was ultimately head of English at St Paul's Way Community School in Tower Hamlets. He was Chair and then General Secretary of LATE for many years, including during the period of the boycott of national testing.

11 This was certainly the case in the grammar school I attended. It says something about the grammar school system that despite admitting only the top 10 per cent academically a significant number of those students were deemed at fourteen not bright enough to pursue a qualification in English Literature.

12 When *Growth through English* was republished in 1975, it was subtitled *Set in the Perspective of the Seventies* (Dixon, 1975). In this new edition an additional chapter expressed

areas that the author felt had not been specifically addressed immediately post-Dartmouth. He pointed particularly towards 'language in the participant role', suggesting that growth English, rather than focussing on the personal and expressive, should be more concerned with interaction with society and getting things done in the world.

References

Barnes, D., Britton, J., and Rosen, H. (1971). *Language, the Learner and the School*. Harmondsworth: Penguin.

Britton, J. (1970). *Language and Learning*. Harmondsworth: Penguin.

Britton, J., Burgess, T., Martin, N., McLeod, A. and Rosen, H. (1975). *The Development of Writing Abilities (11–18)*. Aylesbury: Macmillan.

Burgess, C., Burgess, T., Cartland, L., Chambers, R., Hedgeland, J., Levine, N., … Torbe, M. (1973). *Understanding Children Writing*. Harmondsworth: Penguin.

Departmental Committee of the Board of Education. (1921). *The Teaching of English in England (The Newbolt Report)*. London: His Majesty's Stationery Office.

Department for Education and Science. (1975). *A Language for Life (The Bullock Report)*. London: Her Majesty's Stationery Office.

Department for Education and Science. (1978). *School Examinations (The Waddell Report)*. London: Her Majesty's Stationery Office.

Dixon, J. (1975). *Growth through English: Set in the Perspective of the Seventies*. London: Penguin.

Dixon, J. (2015). Developing English. *English Teaching Practice and Critique*, 14(3), pp. 427–434.

Dixon, J., Brown, J. and Barnes, D. (1979). *Education 16–19: The Role of English and Communication*. London: MacMillan.

English and Media Centre. (1979). *School Under Siege*. London: English and Media Centre.

English and Media Centre. (1984a). *Making Stories*. London: English and Media Centre.

English and Media Centre. (1984b). *Changing Stories*. London: English and Media Centre.

English and Media Centre. (1985a). *The English Curriculum: Gender – Materials for Discussion*. London: English and Media Centre.

English and Media Centre. (1985b). *The English Curriculum: Media – Materials for Discussion*. London: English and Media Centre.

English and Media Centre. (1987). *The English Curriculum: Poetry – Materials for Discussion*. London: English and Media Centre.

Eyers, S. and Richmond, J. (Eds). (1982). *Becoming Our Own Experts: Studies in Language and Learning Made by the Talk Workshop Group at Vauxhall Manor School 1974–1979*. London: Talk Workshop Group.

Friedman, A., Galligan, H., Albano, C. and O'Connor, K. (2009). Teacher Subcultures of Democratic Practice Amidst the Oppression of Educational Reform. *The Journal of Educational Reform*, (10), pp. 249–276.

Gibbons, S. and Marshall, B. (2010). Assessing English: A Trial Collaborative Standardised Marking Project. *English Teacher Practice and Critique*, 9(3), pp. 26–39.

Goodson, I. (2001). Social Histories of Education Change. *The Journal of Educational Change*, (1), pp. 46–63.

Hall, S. and Whannel, P. (1964). *The Popular Arts*. New York: Pantheon Books

Harding, D. (1937). The Role of the Onlooker. *Scrutiny*, 6(3), pp. 247–258.

Hickman, J. and Kimberley, K. (1988). *Teachers, Language and Learning*. London: Routledge.

Johnson, J. (1992). Pondering the Project. *Talk: The Journal of the National Oracy Project*, (5), pp. 48–50.

Kemp, G. (1977). *The Turbulent Term of Tyke Tiler*. London: Faber and Faber

Lloyd, M. (1994). *Saving English Coursework* (a self-published pamphlet made available by NATE to schools and teachers).

Ministry of Education. (1960). *Secondary School Examinations Other than the GCE (The Beloe Report)*. London: Her Majesty's Stationery Office.

National Oracy Project. (1990). *Teaching Talking and Learning in Key Stage One*. York: National Curriculum Council.

National Oracy Project. (1991a). *Teaching Talking and Learning in Key Stage Two*. York: National Curriculum Council.

National Oracy Project. (1991b). *Teaching Talking and Learning in Key Stage Three*. York: National Curriculum Council.

National Oracy Project. (1992). *Oracy and Special Educational Needs*. York: National Curriculum Council.

National Oracy Project. (1993). *Teaching Talking and Learning in Key Stage Four*. York: National Curriculum Council.

National Writing Project. (1989a). *About Writing. The National Writing Project Newsletter*, (10).

National Writing Project. (1989b). *Audiences for Writing*. Surrey: Thomas Nelson and sons.

National Writing Project. (1989c). *Becoming a Writer*. Surrey: Thomas Nelson and sons.

National Writing Project. (1989d). *Responding to and Assessing Writing*. Surrey: Thomas Nelson and sons.

Qualifications and Curriculum Authority. (2006). *A Review of GCSE Coursework*. London: QCA Publications.

Sarland, C. (2001). 'Becoming Our Own Experts': Lessons from the Past. *Educational Action Research*, 9(2), pp. 171–186.

Schools Curriculum Development Council. (1986). *About the National Writing Project*. Huntingdon: Mimeo.

Snapper, G. (2013). Student, Reader, Critic, Teacher: Issues and Identities in Post-16 English Literature. In Goodwyn, A., Reid, L. and Durrant, C. (Eds), *International Perspectives on Teaching English in a Globalised World*. Oxford: Routledge.

The Guardian. (2004, 3rd February). Lord Bullock of Leafield: Obituary. Available at https://www.theguardian.com/news/2004/feb/03/guardianobituaries.obituaries (accessed on 3rd May 2016).

The Guardian. (2008, 18th February). Education, Other Lives: Joan Goody. Available at http://www.theguardian.com/education/2008/feb/18/society.mainsection (accessed on 10th June 2016).

Wilkinson, A. (1968). Oracy in English Teaching. *Elementary English*, 45(6), pp. 743–747.

PART II
The age of intervention

4

STANDARDISATION? THE NATIONAL CURRICULUM AND ASSESSMENT

Without question, the hitherto most intense period of centralist intervention, into firstly curriculum and assessment and ultimately pedagogy, began in the late 1980s with the introduction of the first National Curriculum in England. The subsequent two decades would see wave after wave of new initiatives, and no subject experienced the amount and rapidity of change as did English. The subject's place at the centre of pupils' school experience was unquestioned; what that experience should be, however, was heavily contested and very frequently policymakers' views differed markedly from those of many sections of the profession. Throughout the 1990s and the first decade of the new millennium, successive governments sought to exercise control of the version of English enacted in classrooms, and, to generalise, the progressive, personal growth model of English came under attack from both wings of the political spectrum; from the right there was the familiar call for a return to a traditional, back-to-basics curriculum, from the centre-left New Labour government the moves were less obviously ideological. From both sides there came the rhetoric of driving up standards. The dual weapons of curriculum and assessment, reinforced by an increasingly oppressive accountability framework manifested in school league tables, performance targets and Ofsted inspection, threatened for many English teachers what they considered to be the good practice that had evolved through previous decades. So fiercely did many English teachers feel their subject to be under assault, that unprecedented collective action was taken to resist the worst excesses of the new national testing regime. However, the sheer might of central intervention in a world of high-stakes assessment meant that, after 20 years of relentless pressure, some fundamental changes had taken place in the way the subject was framed and taught. Those resisting change were increasingly finding themselves marginalised and seeking to operate under the radar, where once they might have stood together as a powerful force against aggressive reshapings of the subject from without the profession.

The National Curriculum for English

A new entrant to teaching – at a time when such policies are being, to some extent, withdrawn – may find it difficult to believe that it was not until the very end of the twentieth century that there was a National Curriculum in England's schools. The then Labour Prime Minister James Callaghan's Ruskin College speech in 1976 – when he had called for a great debate into education – is seen by many as the point at which the starting pistol was fired in the long race towards the first National Curriculum. Progress was not rapid; when Margaret Thatcher was elected as Conservative prime minister in 1979, education – and certainly within that areas such as curriculum and assessment – was far from top of the political agenda. The abolition of the Schools Council in 1982 was a signal of more direct central intervention into curriculum policy, and an indication of attempts to lessen the involvement of teacher unions and subject associations, but where there was a focus on education in the early years of Thatcher's administration it was predominantly on advancing policies that would serve to bring the market into education, and to lessen the influence and scope of the Local Education Authorities. Policies that were pursued certainly brought the government and teachers into conflict, and the mid-1980s were notable for industrial action by teachers over, in particular, workload. However, it was not until the 1988 Education Act – popularly known as the 'Baker Act' after the then Secretary of State for Education Kenneth Baker – that the spotlight was shone directly on curriculum.

The genesis of the National Curriculum for English can be most obviously traced to the earlier years of the Conservative administration, however. In the mid-1980s Her Majesty's Inspectorate published a series of *Curriculum Matters* papers which were in some ways the forerunners to the National Curriculum. These documents were in many ways strikingly imaginative in their approach to curriculum, certainly in comparison to what followed. The *Curriculum from 5–16: Curriculum Matters 2* had, for example, at the top of its list of the areas of learning and experience that ought to be in the school curriculum 'aesthetic and creative; human and social; linguistic and literary' (Department of Education and Science, 1988a, p. 16). In elaborating on the last of these three areas – one assumes this to be the subject we know as English – oracy was forefronted as 'through listening and talking in groups children are enabled to explore other people's experiences and to modify and extend their own' (ibid., p. 21). There was also explicit acknowledgement of the importance of the pupils' own uses of language in the statement that 'teachers should build on the language experience and skills which children possess on entry to school' (ibid., p. 21). The ideas expressed were in no way at odds with the kind of progressive, child-centred model of English that, for many, had by the mid-1980s assumed the place of an orthodox approach to the teaching of the subject. The general curriculum document was supported by a series of subject specific papers and, again, the *English from 5–16* pamphlet made for an interesting read, given that it was a thoughtful and reflective consideration of the subject which explicitly acknowledged that 'Teaching English well is a complex and demanding art' (Department of Education and Science, 1984, p. 13). Such an acknowledgement – particularly referring to the teaching of English as an 'art' – would have been welcomed. Drawing on the Bullock Report's comments on the interrelatedness of the strands of English, the document set out objectives in English for pupils at ages 7, 11 and 16. In its section on the principles of English teaching, there was a gently reasonable position stated on the teaching of grammar – i.e. that some attention should be given to it in the context of students' own language use, not that decontextualised teaching and the learning of linguistic terminology for its own sake was of value – and a view that pupils should be enabled to use Standard Spoken English when called for, but that 'the language children bring with them from their home backgrounds should not be criticised, belittled or proscribed' (ibid., p. 15). The teaching of grammar and Standard English would prove to be particularly contentious areas as the statutory curriculum came into being, and in *English from 5–16* the informed position that would cause so much consternation to those seeking a hard line on these areas was very clear.

The open and democratic tone of the paper was mirrored in the inserted forward by the then Conservative Secretary of State for Education, Keith Joseph, which stated that:

> We intend, subject to the outcome of the consultative process which the paper initiates, and in consultation with those concerned within and outside the education service, to move towards a statement of aims and objectives for English teaching in schools which can serve as a basis for policy at national and local level.
>
> *(ibid., inserted paper)*

At this point it seemed – in the rhetoric at least – that dialogue and consultation with the profession would be central to the development of any statutory curriculum; English teachers, used to the consultative nature of the Schools Council, could have been forgiven for taking the tone at face value.

In terms of the development of a National Curriculum for English, then, this was no bad starting point. The pupil was being placed at the very centre of learning in the subject, the complexity of the discipline was acknowledged and there was a strong sense of consultation and communication in the development of what might at some point become policy. As the National Curriculum became a reality, however, this democratic spirit seemed to be steadily eroded; relatively quickly policymakers seemed to realise that, in terms of English at least, dialogue with the profession would be unlikely to lead to consensus, and it would be even less likely to lead to an agreement on the kind of version of the subject that successive Conservative governments apparently wanted – a back-to-basics approach that would reverse the perceived, but never really evidenced, fall in standards which, it was alleged by those on the right of the political spectrum, accompanied the introduction of progressive methods from the 1960s and was a product of comprehensivisation.

The Kingman Report

Immediately prior to the publication of the first National Curriculum for English, another committee was established by the government, under the chairmanship of Sir John Kingman, specifically to 'recommend a model of the English language as a basis for teacher training and professional discussion, and to consider how far and in what ways that model should be made explicit to pupils at various stages of education' (Department of Education and Science, 1988b, p. 1). Kingman himself was a mathematician; at the time president of the Royal Statistical Society and vice chancellor of the University of Bristol. Whilst it might seem odd that a mathematician was chosen to chair a committee into the teaching of the English language, the precedent of the non-specialist had been set with Bullock, and perhaps the thinking was that an 'outsider' would bring a non-partisan approach to the enquiry. Perhaps it also meant, however, that Kingman was more than willing to listen to the views of the experts in the field. The Committee, as could be seen from the extensive list of organisations and individuals cited, consulted widely and made visits to a number of schools, polytechnics and universities.

Although the committee and its report were largely superseded by the work of the English group under Brian Cox that had set about the work on drafting English curriculum orders, the Kingman Report has its place in history. Its recommendations included admirable ideas such as the training of all new teachers in knowledge about language and that all newly qualified teachers should engage in a language study relevant to their subject specialism. And, as with the earlier HMI Curriculum Matters series, there is an acknowledgement of the complexity of the English language. The report's call for the establishment of a National Language Project – coordinated on similar lines to the National Writing Project – was one that would come to fruition in the Language in the National Curriculum (LINC) project, though the fate of this initiative, as we will see, was indicative of the mood of policymakers who were frustrated at the inability of commissioned bodies to recommend the kind of English language teaching – focused on grammar and Standard English – that was clearly desired. This view was evident in the Department of Education and Science's press statement on Kingman which simply called the report 'interesting' and suggested that it could contribute to discussion 'about the grammatical structure of the English language and the correct use of the spoken word' (Department of Education and Science, 1988c). Hardly a ringing endorsement, but clearly one that underlined the kind of language work that policymakers wanted to see in the eventual curriculum for English – the word 'correct' rather than something like 'appropriate' was a clear giveaway.

Responses to the Kingman Report from the English teaching community were varied. NATE's published response to the report welcomed the breadth of its conception of language but considered 'its accounts of these matters are less than adequate' (NATE, 1988, p. 2). Central to NATE's problem with Kingman's findings and recommendations was the way in which the relationship of language to meaning had, in the Association's view, been overlooked – an unsurprising critique given NATE's orthodox post-Dartmouth view of language in operation. NATE also challenged the perennial common-sense argument that explicit knowledge of language structures and terminology improves use of the language on the basis that the body of existing research gave no support to his claim. This goes to the very heart of the seemingly unending argument about the place of explicit language teaching in the curriculum. It would seem self-evident that – like a dressmaker knowing the properties of different fabrics in order to choose the best to make a particular garment – a writer with explicit knowledge about language would make better choices. However, with the exception of some very recent research (see for example Myhill, Jones and Bailey (2011)) the evidence has just not supported this view. It was certainly not there in the late 1980s, and even that which is emerging now is far from straightforward, in terms of the types of children that benefit from explicit work on grammar and which aspects of their English work such activity actually improves. And whilst NATE did concede that study of language might be valid for its own sake, they felt that, with a crowded curriculum, study of language might come at the expense of time available to develop children's competence as language users and this would be 'too high a price to pay' (NATE, 1988, p. 15). Other critics were harsher. In the *Times Educational Supplement*, Harold Rosen said the Report was 'liberal words [which are used] to disguise sinister messages of state coercion' (quoted in Stubbs (1991, p. 216)). For Rosen, one of the strongest advocates of bottom-up, teacher-led curriculum innovation from the early 1950s, the very idea of a report like Kingman was an anathema.

Given the pace of events, Rosen probably didn't need to worry too much about what he saw as the Report's covert ideology; although Kingman certainly laid the ground for the Language in the National Curriculum project, its influence beyond this was limited and it was quickly superseded by *English for Ages 5–16*, the first version of the National Curriculum for English. The statutory orders were drafted by a committee led by Professor Brian Cox (himself a member of the Kingman enquiry committee), then pro-vice chancellor of the University of Manchester, and over time became known simply as the Cox curriculum. The choice of Cox was no doubt seen by the Conservative government as a safe one; one of the key authors of the *Black Papers*, which damned the comprehensive system and lamented the fall in standards under progressive teaching methods, one would have thought it safe to assume that Cox would deliver the kind of curriculum it is suggested that many Tories wanted – a traditional curriculum, placing an emphasis on Standard English and the teaching of grammar and affording a high priority to classic, canonical literature.

The caricature of Cox constructed from a reading of the *Black Papers* was probably inaccurate; according to Marshall (2008), Cox always had some sympathy with progressive education, even if he did think it had gone too far, and he was clear that he did not personally agree with all that was contained within the publications he had co-edited. Perhaps those wishing for such a curriculum should have known better, for it seems that Cox's views were already very different, as his later comments on the Kingman Report demonstrated:

> Right wing Conservatives ... wanted a return to the traditional teaching of Latinate grammar, and the report came out firmly against this. Many politicians and journalists were ignorant about the problems in the teaching of grammar and about the status of Standard English, and simply desired to reinstate the disciplines of study typical of schoolrooms in the 1930s.
>
> *(Cox, 1991, p. 4)*

Whether or not he expressed these views before being appointed to chair the English working party, it was clear from *English for Ages 5–16* that Cox's view on English showed some real appreciation of the complexities of the subject and of varying perspectives held by the profession on the aims of English and what it should be to children. Famously, Cox encapsulated these complexities in the five 'views' of English within his report: personal growth; cross-curricular; adult needs; cultural heritage and cultural analysis. These views, known now most commonly as 'Cox's models', were, he stressed in the first proposals for English in the curriculum, neither 'sharply distinguishable' nor 'mutually exclusive' (Department of Education and Science, 1988d, p. 12), although some researchers have subsequently used them, for convenience, in seeking to establish the most popular model in the hearts and minds of English teachers.

This multi-dimensional perspective on the role of English in the curriculum was reflective of the Cox curriculum as a whole. It had its prescription of course – in it the attainment targets of speaking and listening, reading and writing were established, Shakespeare was given his statutory place (but he was, significantly, the only pre-scribed author with all other suggested authors from the literary canon being part of the non-statutory guidance) and the ten-level scale outlined performance at increasing competence. The document was, however, more descriptive in nature, and unlike subsequent versions of the curriculum it made explicit the debates that surround those key areas like grammar and Standard English. It invited English teachers to consider these debates and in doing so reassured them that there was not an attempt to simplify the complexity of the subject. On Standard English, Cox made clear that standard should not be confused with 'good', and on grammar he took on the view of the Kingman Report that there should be no return to old-fashioned, decontextualised grammar teaching. In fact, Cox considered that the ideas on teaching English from Bullock, Kingman and his own curriculum could be seen as 'an organic growth' (Cox, 1995, p. 190). If that were indeed true then Cox's curriculum would rightly be looked on as progressive and, to a large extent, in tune with the progressive ideas about English that had been evolving over the previous three decades.

In essence, and certainly with the benefit of hindsight and a consideration of what was to follow, many English teachers now view the Cox curriculum as a humane and principled attempt to set out both an inclusive rationale for English and a broad and balanced subject content, with many italicised sections of the document offering helpful guidance to support the statutory orders. Central figures involved in both the National Writing and Oracy Projects claimed that the work from these initiatives had clear influence on the new curriculum. Reflecting on the new curriculum, the NWP newsletter considered that 'The programmes of Study for the Writing element provide guidelines for setting up a writing environment which (with some reservations) reflect the classroom practices which teachers have talked and written about in the National Writing Project publications' (National Writing Project, 1989, p. 24). John Johnson, NOP Director, thought that 'the work of the Project was well represented in such documents as the English Non-Statutory guidance published by the NCC' (Johnson, 1992, p. 49) and that therefore 'NOP teachers and schools were better placed to implement the National Curriculum' (ibid.). In the minds of some, then, the Cox curriculum was not a challenge to the progressive English that had developed; it was in fact a curriculum that could probably be assimilated into the practice of those who worked in the familiar orthodoxy of growth English.

There were, of course, concerns and criticisms at the time – unsurprising given this was the first genuine attempt at prescribing the context of English teaching across the country. Harold Rosen took issue with the very top-down nature of the curriculum. Interviewed in *Teaching London Kids* – the self-confessed socialist magazine concerned with progressive teaching and working-class children's education, which had an all-too-short life span – Rosen, whilst admitting some form of national framework would be helpful, criticised the committees and lack of consultation:

> We have a fine tradition of English teachers talking to each other, advisers who know the need for participation of teachers. So the central point is that matters of the curriculum have to emerge from what is essentially a democratic process: consultation and participation. So I'm against *this* National Curriculum.
>
> *(Harold Rosen in* Teaching London Kids, *1990, p. 24)*

Working in LATE and as a teacher educator, Rosen was steeped in this 'fine tradition' of teachers engaging in dialogue, carrying out classroom-based projects to enhance their own teaching and disseminating findings through subject associations, conferences and local authority networks. Though Cox clearly had taken on the views of the profession there was no doubting that the National Curriculum was a centrally driven, top-down reform and one that Rosen would have taken objection to in these terms alone. The interventionist approach would only gain momentum over the coming years.

A very detailed response from NATE (NATE, 1989) welcomed aspects of *English 5–16* – particularly the handling of debates about Standard English – but detailed very significant concerns about the circumscribing performance in English with a linear scale of levels. The progressive view of English adopted as NATE's orthodoxy viewed the English curriculum as recursive, a spiral curriculum where children continually return to key ideas and concepts and deepening understanding. This, the Association felt, meant framing progress in a set of apparently incremental levels was fundamentally flawed – English was simply not a subject where learning took place in a set of identifiable sequential steps. Another critical view of Cox was offered in *English and the National Curriculum: Cox's Revolution* (Jones, 1992), in which a number of writers critically exposed ways in which – they felt – Cox's views on the English curriculum were not as embracing of a progressive model of the subject as was generally claimed. In a sense, that Cox's curriculum was widely welcomed by the profession may have been as much due to a sense of relief at what it wasn't as a celebration of what it was, and the affinity to Cox's view of English was no doubt heightened by subsequent events – the passing of time and future curriculum rewrites certainly influenced many English teachers' judgement of Cox and his curriculum.

The response from policymakers to Cox's curriculum was almost immediately evident in the speed at which it was proposed that the English orders should be revised. In 1992, the National Curriculum Council published advice to the Secretary of State in the form of *National Curriculum English: The Case for Revising the Order* (National Curriculum Council, 1992). This document, in which the Chair of the National Curriculum Council, David Pascall, set out why a revision of a curriculum barely out of nappies needed revision, is a curious read. Whilst seeking to maintain a conciliatory tone, acknowledging the strengths of Cox's curriculum, it gave short shrift to the arguments against a revision. These arguments – including that more evidence was needed before there was a clear case for revision, and that teacher morale might be adversely affected – were hardly insignificant, but they were brushed away in a mere few paragraphs without any seeming evidence for this. There are clear messages in the document about the areas of English Cox was deemed to have failed in properly forefronting; the teaching of initial reading and the specification of named literary figures featured, but once again attention to grammar and Standard English remained the strongest areas of criticism.

Cox himself has written extensively and damningly on the events leading up to the rewriting of this curriculum, perhaps most forcefully in *Cox on the Battle for the English Curriculum* (1995). In this book Cox detailed how, through 1991–1992, key positions within the NCC and SEAC were given by education ministers – first Kenneth Baker and then John Patten – to those who would be supporters of Conservative thinking on education, notably people like John Marenbon, Sheila Lawlor and John Marks who were associated with the right-wing think tank the Centre for Policy Studies. Cox also claimed that the review of the implementation of his curriculum led by Warwick University was misrepresented in the concerted right-wing assault on what Tories viewed as the soft-headed, progressive nature of his work that failed to adequately address the basics of teaching reading, grammar and Standard English. Cox's account was passionate, and it is hard not to be convinced by his stark assessment of just how politically motivated and manoeuvred the moves towards the curriculum rewrite were, although it should be noted of course that Cox was not an unbiased viewer of events – his writing must also be read as an attempt to salvage his own reputation and legacy, and that of his work in the construction of the 1989 Orders. At times it is tempting to feel he doth protest too much. According to Cox, civil servants advising John Patten had 'strongly urged him not to revise the English curriculum' (Cox, 1995, p. 57) with the three key reasons given being the insufficient time the curriculum had been in place, the damaging effect on teachers' morale and the threat to standards.

Pascall, who was apparently 'a chemical engineer who had nothing to do with English whatsoever' (Marshall, 2008 p. 40), oversaw the drafting of new proposed orders that appeared the following year (Department for Education, 1993). The contrast between the Pascall and the Cox curricula was stark; the earlier document highlighted the complexities and ambiguities of the subject, whereas the latter offered certainties, perhaps most wonderfully encapsulated in the heavily value-laden and deeply questionable assertion 'Standard English is characterised by the correct use of vocabulary and grammar' (ibid., p. 9). Gone was the apparently progressive view that Standard English should not be equated with good English; the inference in Pascall was clear – other versions of English are not grammatically correct. The Speaking and Listening orders in Pascall were dominated by Standard English, whilst the reading orders contained for the first time prescribed lists of pre-twentieth century and modern writers, and the writing component was fragmented and had distinct strands of composition, forms, grammar, punctuation, spelling and handwriting up to and including Key Stage 3. Although Pascall had claimed in his earlier advice that he would be drawing heavily on the successful elements of Cox's work, these were clearly not the elements – the broad notion of knowledge about language and the implied professionalism in refraining from listing writers – that were precisely the elements that the English teaching profession generally felt to be key aspects to the first curriculum. Pascall presented a view of the subject far more in tune with that of ministers, imbued with a sense of back to basics in terms of reading, writing, speaking and listening.

It is likely that had Pascall's curriculum become enshrined in legislation it would have provoked much disquiet, but in fact the document never went beyond the draft stage. By 1993, a full review of the National Curriculum had been commissioned, led by Sir Ron Dearing, and this would include revision to all subject orders. Given its short-lived existence as a potential curriculum, the Pascall version passed many English teachers by, particularly given that there were more pressing and stronger protests happening around assessment arrangements by 1993.

The instigation of the Dearing review and the subsequent re-rewrite of the English orders ushered in a curriculum that would outlast the Conservative administration before a further rewrite just before the turn of the millennium. In fact, although the Pascall curriculum was never implemented, its influence can be seen in the 1995 English orders, certainly much more so than the Cox curriculum that it replaced. In effect, in writing the new version, the National Curriculum Council worked from Pascall's version rather than returning to Cox's original orders. There was a consultation exercise conducted by the NCC which garnered around 2,500 responses, and discussions were held with both NATE and NAAE. Significantly, the consultation report (National Curriculum Council, 1993) noted that 'many teachers were content with the existing Orders and did not therefore think that any changes were needed' (p. 5). The report made the assertion, without much noticeable support, that this view merely reflected other factors impacting on stability – the Dearing review and the aftermath of the dispute around testing at Key Stage 3 among them – thereby undermining what was likely to have been a legitimate view expressed by the consultation respondents, i.e. that they were actually satisfied with Cox's curriculum and really did not want to see it replaced. Such a view, in the context of a Secretary of State fully committed to revision, was never likely to have carried much weight, thus the whole consultation exercise was essentially merely that – an exercise. The changes it generated were minimal – the most notable was probably the simplifying of the writing attainment target so that the proposed separate strands for 'grammar', 'spelling' and 'punctuation' were removed. Embedding the technical elements of written English into a broader notion of written composition was a welcome reversal, but the final draft was not so vastly different from Pascall's. However, the knowledge that things could have been worse may have muted the protests that resulted on its publication.

The 1995 version – as Dearing had recommended across the programmes of study for all subjects – was significantly slimmed down. The lengthy discussions in the Cox curriculum of the nature of English, the different models of the subject and the debates about grammar and language teaching disappeared to be replaced by, well, nothing. Uniquely in the brief history of statutory English orders, the 1995 curriculum had not even a paragraph in its opening on the purposes or aims of the subject. It began with some general requirements before laying out pared-down content for speaking and listening, reading and writing, with sections divided into range, key skills and Standard English and language study (Department for Education, 1995).

In its response to the draft of the 1995 orders, NAAE, whilst welcoming some aspects of the document (notably that it was not Pascall's curriculum), worried that there was 'too much emphasis on narrowly defined skills, on instruction and on "correctness"' (NAAE, 1994, p. 1). NAAE's strongest criticism was reserved for the inclusion in the orders for the first time of the prescribed list of authors. This was clearly a legacy from Pascall, and a prescription too far. Claiming the imposition of required reading to be 'wholly unacceptable' (ibid., p. 8), NAAE stated that 'there was no support for prescription of texts in the consultation, and the subject advisory group voted against it by a majority of ten to four' (ibid., p. 8). In this comment lies perhaps the most important message of the years of English curriculum revision from the mid-1980s to the mid-1990s; where there seemed to have been genuine consultation with the profession in the *Curriculum Matters* documents and in Cox's version of English, it now appeared that lip service was being given to consultation. Subject associations and noted names in English education had their views sought, but often these views were rejected whilst allowing policymakers to claim resulting documents as having undergone consultation with the profession. In the words of one former chair of NATE, Simon Wrigley, consultation had become a matter of being asked 'what colour axe would you like me to kill you with?'. Sue Horner, leading the English team at SCAA at the time of the curriculum rewrite, described the process as more 'closed door-ish' than future revisions would be.[1]

There had been a consultation group which met three times at SCAA's offices to consider drafts of the new curriculum. According to Cox's account (Cox, 1995, p. 139), the only practising secondary English teacher named within this consultative group was John Hickman, a teacher in an East London comprehensive, who represented NATE on the panel. Alistair West, a local authority English adviser and vice chair of NATE, was also in the group along with a number of head teachers. Professor Arthur Pollard was also in the group – an English academic, he had criticised what he called the 'so called "progressives"' in a contribution to the *Black Papers* about standards in English at O and A level (Pollard, 1969, p. 73) and was, according to at least one obituary on his death, 'a staunch defender of Victorian values' (*The Telegraph*, 2002). There was also a representative from Ofsted, and occasional visits from Chris Woodhead,[2] SCAA's chief executive,[3] to a panel chaired by Nick Tate, shortly to be Woodhead's successor. Given this collection of voices it's not hard to see why Cox asked 'How would they ever agree?' (Cox, 1995, p. 139).

Hickman's recollections confirmed Horner's view of the closed-door nature of the process of writing the new curriculum; he recalled that four key areas – grammar/ Standard English, the literary canon, Shakespeare and bilingualism – 'were givens', that is to say there would be little or no ground given by the policymakers.[4] According to Hickman only when one of these four areas was mentioned would Pollard look up from his crossword! Changes to these areas were, when they happened, arbitrary; Hickman remembered one discussion around the list of authors from the literary heritage where Keats was added simply on the assertion that he was as good as Pope – 'there was no rationale as long as it was old'. Such was the view of the educational members of the consultation group, that nine of the ten publicly disassociated themselves from the curriculum when they saw its final content. Alistair West, a local authority English adviser, declared this to the media via a front page article in the *Times Educational Supplement* in May of 1994, a letter quoted extensively by Cox (1995) to illustrate how so many of the recommendations of the panel – for instance that the list of authors should be exemplary rather than statutory – had been ignored in the final draft. Hickman appeared on the *ITN News at Ten* to declare that the list of authors from the literary canon was like a list of 'desert island books for a public schoolboy'. For Hickman, the experience marked 'the beginning of that whole thing where you make out you're consulting but take no notice of who you're consulting if they don't take the line you're taking'.

Who actually decided on the wording of the final, anonymously authored curriculum is unclear; Chris Woodhead denied there had been any ministerial influence (Cox, 1995) but the final draft was clearly more palatable to the government than it had been if the consultation group's views had been taken into account. Typically, despite the public dissociation, Hickman and West, along with other members of the panel, were written to by Nick Tate to thank them for their contribution to the process.

It seems to have taken a rather unruthless – or perhaps simply naïve – Conservative administration some time to learn the rather unsubtle political sleight of hand – involving the profession in consultation purely as a cosmetic exercise – but it was a manoeuvre that, once learned, was arguably exercised with increasing efficiency by successive administrations. The dilemma for the profession increasingly became whether or not to involve itself in the consultation – if it didn't it clearly couldn't influence outcomes, but if it did it still probably wouldn't influence the outcome but the claim would be made that they had been involved in the process and thereby in some ways endorsed the end product.

Despite the apparent lack of enthusiasm for the curriculum rewrite, and despite the many objections to the new programmes of study, there was no particular protest as the orders were phased in during the mid-1990s. This may have been because English teachers considered that they would be able to sustain good practice in spite of statutory orders, or it may have been an indication of the erosion of the profession's belief that any power it had to influence the direction of policy was being steadily eroded. By 1995 the ground that had been briefly won in the battle over assessment had, as we will see, been largely conceded again and the fate of the Language in the National Curriculum policy was clear evidence that the government were to be increasingly assertive when they wished to stamp on the innovative work of progressive English teachers working collectively for an informed and humane version of the subject.

The Language in the National Curriculum project

Even as the first version of the National Curriculum was being implemented in schools, and then being recommended for seemingly instant review, the Language in the National Curriculum Project (LINC) was in process. The story of the LINC project is perhaps the most astonishing example of the Conservative government's attempt to control the teaching of English language in schools, and a striking example of their failure to do this in the face of an English teaching community that – whilst it may not have been intentionally subversive – was not going to accept any simple approach to the teaching of grammar and Standard English.

In the wake of Kingman, the LINC project was set up. Earlier government-funded projects – like the National Writing Project and National Oracy Project – had been controlled initially by the School Curriculum Development Committee (the forerunner to the National Curriculum Council) and involved the production of material through collaborative work of teachers, local authority advisers and teacher educators exploring their own practice in the areas under investigation. Seeking to control the means of production, and one assumes the resulting content, however, the LINC project was to be under the direct control of the Department for Education and Science itself. Training materials to exemplify the Kingman model of language would be centrally produced and these would be delivered via local authority consortiums to expert trainers in the primary and secondary phases and then onto teachers themselves. John Richmond, one of the joint leaders of the North London Language Consortium of local education authorities, described this as 'a giant piece of educational pyramid selling' (Richmond, 1992, p. 13).

The grand plan, however, failed spectacularly. Richmond's article for the *English and Media Magazine,* 'Unstable Materials', offered a clear perspective on two key mistakes that led to the failure; the first was the appointment of Ron Carter to produce the materials. According to Richmond, Carter's approach was to seek the involvement of the consortia leaders in the production of the material over the course of a year rather than hole himself up and generate them in the space of a few weeks as had been requested. The second mistake was to allow local education authorities, by requiring them to part-fund the posts, to have a say in the experts appointed to lead the LINC work in the various consortia, resulting in 'a ragbag of people of the worst sort, including advisers on secondment or recently retired, college lecturers on secondment or recently retired, even heads of English straight out of classrooms' (ibid., p. 14). These were clearly not the experts the DES had in mind that would take the centrally produced material straight from the minister to the teachers.

In collaborating with the consortia leaders, and with the production of radio and TV programmes commissioned from the BBC, the LINC materials had a breadth and depth in their approach to the study of language that went so far beyond what must have been envisaged by the DES in their mind's eye when seeking some simple material to demonstrate to teachers how to enact Kingman in the classroom. The LINC materials were split into sections, covering topics such as early language, the process and repertoire of writing, accent dialogue and Standard English and multilingualism, and within these sections a diverse range of materials drawn from literature, the media and everyday language use gave teachers the chance to develop ideas for the classroom. The materials offered a comprehensive and complex view of language and its forms, and it's certain that a teacher engaging with them would have their own subject knowledge for teaching enhanced. Sadly, the majority of English teachers did not have the opportunity to access the LINC project training. Despite revisions made by Ron Carter, the government took the decision not to publish the final LINC materials, and further than that it refused to waive its copyright, thus meaning that interested commercial publishers would not be at liberty to run with the material. According to Richmond, what the government had wanted was 'a primer of grammar exercises' (ibid., p. 16) and this was most definitively not what the LINC project provided, despite the fact that in terms of grammatical context the materials are extensive. Thus, a project that it was promised would provide training material for every school was suppressed, and the apparent £21 million pounds spent on its apparatus wasted.

Predictably, the story made it to the press, with the right-wing media in particular using the scandal of such an enormous waste of public money to launch attacks on the creators on LINC and their progressive approaches to language study. In his book *Language Myths and the History of English,* Richard Watts quoted from a *Daily Telegraph* article of 1992 to highlight the contempt held by some journalists for this view of language, which he asserted was similarly held by the government of the time:

Although the DES (Department of Education and Science) will not publish the document, it will be distributed to teacher training institutions, where its voodoo theories about the nature of language will appeal to the impressionable mind of the young woman with low A-levels in 'soft' subjects who, statistically speaking, is the typical student in these establishments.

(Watts, 2011, p. 247)

John Richmond recalled being 'briefly publicly humiliated' following government briefings to the right wing press,[5] though there was some support from more sympathetic journalists writing for *The Independent* and the *Times Educational Supplement*. Richmond also claimed that an HMI report on the LINC project, which apparently was generally supportive of the work, was suppressed by the government as it failed to cast the scorn the administration desired. If this was indeed the case, that a report from the independent inspectorate was buried, then one can see the lengths ministers were prepared to go to in order to discredit LINC and the material it produced.

However, despite the government's response to LINC, it was not simple to erase the project and its work. Given that pre-publication copies of the materials had been circulating anyway, it was permitted for the work to be used for in-service training (which had been the intention anyway – there was never the suggestion from those working on the LINC project to use the material with children), and the University of Nottingham distributed at cost price many thousands of copies. Ultimately the material was reborn as a CD Rom and the approach to knowledge about language teaching embodied in the work of LINC remains highly influential to large numbers of English teachers. If there was a legacy for English teaching in the LINC project, then there was perhaps, too, a legacy for the policymakers and implementers. When New Labour launched its own version of pyramid selling in the form of the National Strategies, they appeared to draw lessons from the ways in which the politicians' intentions for LINC had so obviously failed.

Assessment battles

Although there were grumblings amongst English teachers about the National Curriculum, and its revision – and had Pascall's version made it to classrooms there would undoubtedly have been much stronger protest – it was assessment that brought English teachers and the policymakers into direct conflict in the 1990s.

At GCSE level, English teachers had generally been highly supportive of the brief window of opportunity that allowed for 100 per cent coursework assessment in English. The potential for this kind of assessment to offer students of all abilities the chance to be graded on their best English work, and the space it gave teachers to have a powerful role in the setting and marking of the qualification, were both powerful features in the attraction of the GCSE. Not that it didn't significantly impact upon teachers' workload, but the hours of drafting and redrafting gave meaning to the work students were doing across Year 10 and 11, and the marking and the intense moderation meetings at school and consortium level undoubtedly helped to enhance both teachers' assessment skill and their sense of professionalism.

When the 100% English GCSE was removed in 1994 there were protests, and Mike Lloyd led a 'Bring back 100% Coursework' campaign for many years with the support of significant numbers of English teachers, but there was nothing on the scale of the reactions of English teachers to the introduction of national testing for 14 year olds at the end of Year 9.

National testing for students in English at age 14 was due to be introduced across the country in 1993, though thinking about how the new National Curriculum would be assessed began when Kenneth Baker set up the Task Group on Assessment and Testing (TGAT) in the summer of 1987. This group was chaired by Professor Paul Black of King's College London, someone known widely in education for his work on assessment, whose later work most closely in association with Professor Dylan Wiliam would form the foundation of developments in assessment for learning.[6] The TGAT report (Centre for Educational Studies, 1987), as one might expect given the group's chair, was a detailed and well-argued document, stressing the need for national testing to be predominantly formative in nature, and emphasising that it ought to be rooted in teachers' classroom practices. It warned of the danger of using data from national testing in the publication of school league tables. Three supplementary reports followed (Centre for Educational Studies, 1988) which followed responses from stakeholders to the main report, and which further elaborated on practical areas for the implementation of the proposed assessment arrangements, including in-service training for teachers and the group, cross-school moderation of teachers' assessments.

Albeit that there was resistance from some quarters about the notion of a national assessment system like that proposed by TGAT, the group's vision of a system where teachers' own assessments and a bank of varied national assessment tasks combined to offer formative feedback to pupils and parents would not be something the majority of English teachers could not have lived with. Whether it was a matter of economics (a full implementation of TGAT proposals would undoubtedly have been very costly) or – more likely – a matter of political imperative, however, the reality was that the Key Stage 3 tests that were introduced for English bore little resemblance to what might have been in Professor Black's mind, and drew a forceful reaction from the profession.

Prior to the first national round of SATs, a series of four conferences was held by SEAC for representatives from local authorities, seemingly to garner the support of LEA personnel in the implementation of the new tests. The introductory speech given by Lord Griffiths, the chair of SEAC, was a carefully crafted sales pitch which sought to reassure the audience of the rigour of the tests and the process by which they evolved. The speech detailed how initial trials and pilots of English tests run by CATs (the Consortium for Assessment and Testing in Schools) and ELMAG (East London and Macmillan Assessment Group) had used banks of tasks taken by pupils over a period of time. The CATs team involved Terry Furlong and Anne Barnes[7] who were both prominent figures in NATE at the time and widely respected within the English teaching community for their work on assessment, and this certainly helped to bring some legitimacy to the task-based approach that was originally planned. Despite teachers' responses to these tasks being 'generally favourable' (Griffiths, 1993, p. 6), the approach had been dropped when the secretary of state Kenneth Clarke had advised that 'end of key stage tests at age 14 should take the form predominantly of written terminal examinations' (ibid., p. 7). The time-consuming nature of the tasks was given as an issue raised by teachers involved in the pilots as justification for the move away from this model, but it was clear that there was strong political will for quick pen-and-paper tests that would generate what was considered to be robust data.

CATs and ELMAG were subsequently dropped from the process and the NEAB (Northern Examinations and Assessment Board) were awarded the contract to devise these new tests, piloting them in 1992. According to Griffiths, the 1993 national tests grew from all of the work from 1989–1992, and in listing the specific elements in the new tests that had come from earlier work he declared his impatience 'with suggestions that the 1993 tests bear little relation to what went before' (ibid., p. 10). Clearly there was already a strong sense within SEAC that the tests were to receive a hostile reaction from the profession.

Ironically, within his speech, Griffiths made particular mention of the use of an anthology in the 1992 pilot which, according to NEAB, had been praised by teachers for its 'excellence' (ibid., p. 9). It was in fact the Anthology issued to schools for the first Key Stage 3 tests in 1993 that, according to one leading figure in the boycott movement, proved the final straw for a group of English teachers increasingly despairing of the ways in which it was proposed that 14 year olds' achievements in English were to be judged. Although the boycott of the SATs would be a union-led movement, and ultimately cover all Key Stages, the National Union of Teachers (NUT) and the National Association for Schoolteachers and Union for Women Teachers (NASUWT) were riding the wave whose origin was in London, specifically within LATE. As proposals for the SATs took shape over time, LATE took an oppositional stance, but – according to John Wilks, the Association's Chair at the time – the publication of the anthology, which he and others saw as a product of the then Education Secretary, John Patten, brought teachers' reactions to a head. Wilks said the Anthology was the 'biggest contention' for English teachers who met at a LATE conference in Seaford, near Brighton, in the summer of 1992 and suggested 'arrogance' on the part of the secretary of state for deciding on a range of texts for all children across the country. They were texts that 'were not going to work' for children in inner-city schools. Clearly significant numbers of English teachers felt this imposition of a hand-picked collection of texts was an affront to their own professionalism, and that it had the potential to very radically change the nature of classroom practice and the curriculum.

The Anthology for the 1993 SATs was certainly a curious selection box. An extract from Wilde's *The Importance of Being Earnest* followed a small section of *The Prologue* to Chaucer's *The Canterbury Tales*; a snippet from Samuel Johnson's *Rasselas* preceded Shakespeare's *Sonnet 73*. If one tries very hard it's possible to perhaps see some thematic links between the pieces – as it was claimed by its producers that there was – but it's difficult to see that this was anything other than what a particular type of educated conservative thought it would be good for children to read, and difficult to escape the conclusion that to prepare children for examination on the Anthology could have meant anything other than teaching to the test in a didactic way, doing whatever one could as a teacher to try to help confused 14 year olds understand why it might be useful for them to study a seemingly random page and a half from a Georgian writer's novel that in all likelihood they would never encounter again (even if they went on to study a degree in the subject). Whether it was simply a random selection of a public schoolboy's own reading history is in itself debatable – Jane Coles, herself a leading voice in the anti-SATs campaign – claimed that the Anthology was actually 'part of the ideological enterprise which has constituted Conservative education policy since the mid-eighties' (Coles, 1994, p. 26). This enterprise, whilst involving notions of Englishness, was broader – it was about bringing the market into education with league tables, school rankings and all the trappings of accountability.

The testing of Shakespeare in the SATs through the focus on a single scene and the notion of levelling children's achievement when progress in English is so complex certainly angered many English teachers, but for those who made the initial moves to boycott, this Anthology lit the fuse. For many used to working with their Key Stage 4 students on a 100 per cent coursework mode of assessment with the possibilities this offered for choice and a negotiated curriculum, this level of imposition was too much to bear. Although there would still be teacher assessment at Key Stage 3, with the teachers' judgement being given equal weighting alongside the test score, the overwhelming feeling was that for the purposes of league tables it would be the test result that would have far higher status in the eyes of those with an interest in ranking schools.

LATE was ideally positioned to lead the calls for a boycott on the SATs. As an organisation it was really a forum and network for colleagues to meet. Its organising committee was formed entirely of volunteers. It had no significant finances and it owned no property. It meant, in a sense, it had nothing to lose, and did not have to be cautious in the way that NATE might have to have been – the National Association owned property and employed staff meaning that it might have been vulnerable to legal challenge if it were to take the lead in organising direct protest action. LATE, in any case, had always been perceived as a more radical body than NATE; one description – in all probability inaccurate – caricatured the London branch at the time of the formation of NATE as 'militant dissenting incubus' (Ball, 1985, p. 68). LATE was in fact a broad church and the opposition to the SATs was not confined to those with particular left-wing ideologies, but it is nonetheless true to say that within LATE's steering committee there were many individuals with strong political convictions that made them happy to lead the fight.

The LATE Committee, reasoning that it would be unreasonable to expect individual schools to boycott the SATs, reckoned that a significant show of strength in numbers would empower English teachers and departments and bring a legitimacy to a call for collective action. Thus LATE wrote directly, and using the school directory known as the 'Yellow Book' sent a letter – these were pre digital communication times, of course – to 4,000 heads of English in secondary schools. In the letter, LATE said that if 1,000 or more schools replied in support then a boycott would be called. It was a phenomenal undertaking for a relatively few highly committed individuals and elicited a phenomenal response, with not one reply arguing in favour of the tests or the Anthology (and this included support from private and grammar schools). Selected impassioned responses were collected and published by LATE in *Enough is Enough* (LATE, 1993a), and later in *Voices from the Classroom* (LATE, 1993b). Responses came from across the country and it was particularly notable how many heads of English in independent schools wrote to express their support for LATE's stance, even given the fact that they themselves, standing outside the state sector, were not required to subject their pupils to the tests. One experienced head of English called the arrangements for the tests 'the most dreadful thing I have encountered in 33 years of teaching' (ibid., p. 11) whilst others used words like 'nightmare' or 'shambles' (ibid., p. 10) to describe the situation. If only a snapshot, *Voices from the Classroom* gave a striking picture of the anger felt by English teachers across Britain.

The title of that LATE publication, *Enough is Enough*, perfectly encapsulated the feeling of large parts of the profession; the level of central imposition emerging, the amount of political interference in curriculum and assessment, the destruction of 100 per cent coursework and the rubbishing of Cox had all led to a situation where the SATs, particularly the anthology, were the straw that broke the camel's back.

The LATE-led campaign gathered momentum at an astonishing rate. Support from schools was bolstered when Brian Cox spoke at a LATE conference in November 1992 and claimed that 'teaching to get high marks in the SATs will be bad teaching' and that there was a movement 'to a situation where a boycott may be necessary' (*The English and Media Magazine*, 1992a, p. 3). With the former editor of the *Black Papers* and architect of the National Curriculum on board, there was a sense that the campaign had heavyweight support, and not just from the usual suspects.

According to Wilks the number of responses was nearing the 1,000 mark when the game changed. No doubt sensing the momentum, the unions – initially the National Association for Schoolmasters and the Union of Women Teachers (NASUWT) – balloted their own members on a boycott of the English tests, using increased workload as the justifiable professional grounds for dispute. The National Union of Teachers (NUT) joined the campaign, in what the *English Magazine* called 'an unprecedented move on a subject-specific issue by a national union' (*The English and Media Magazine*, 1992b, p. 3) and, to all intents and purposes, the 1993 English SATs failed to happen. There were some valiant efforts to force the issue – one Conservative-led London local authority parachuting in cover staff to invigilate the tests, for example[8] – but the boycott campaign had been successful on more or less a national scale.

Subsequent changes to the assessment arrangements (the appointment of external markers, for example) meant that in the following years it was impossible to sustain the boycott on grounds of workload, and so consequently impossible for union support to be retained. The LATE-led protest, of course, was centred entirely on issues of teaching and learning and teacher professionalism; John Hickman, who was heavily involved along with Wilks in the LATE activism on the issue, considered that allowing the unions to take control of the boycott was 'the worst thing we ever did, it was inevitable, but it was the worst thing we did because they turned it into a workload issue'. It will never be known now whether the LATE drive for a boycott on those educational grounds could have withstood local authority or school management directives, or – if it came to it – a legal challenge. It's entirely possible that the LATE-led movement was simply a bluff that would have been called with teachers forced to comply or face disciplinary procedures – certainly the unions' refusal to take a stand on an educational argument indicated that these grounds would not be defensible in terms of teachers' conditions of service. In some ways, and John Wilks said as much, LATE was relieved that this wasn't itself put to the test, albeit the result was the ultimate demise of the boycott.

The English teachers' boycott was, then, short-lived, but it did have an effect; the Anthology, for example, disappeared in future iterations of the Key Stage 3 test. It's likely too that the furore around the Key Stage 3 tests played its part in the decision of John Marenbon, chairman of the English committee at SEAC and thus ultimately responsible for the SATs, to resign in the spring of 1993. In his resignation letter (*Times Educational Supplement*, 1993) he cited the problems with the Shakespeare paper and the fact that his own advice had been ignored. Marenbon had been the author of the right-wing think tank the Centre for Policy Studies' *English Our English: The New Orthodoxy Examined* (Marenbon, 1987), a withering attack on the progressive model of English and its associated focus on oracy, language in use and a child-centred pedagogy. Any sense that policy may have been influenced by the direct action of the so-called progressives would most certainly have been an anathema to such a man.

There was some sense of euphoria amongst significant numbers of English teachers in the wake of the 1993 boycott. John Wilks recalled unknown colleagues at the subsequent NATE conference shaking his hand and expressing their sense of collectively having achieved something. It was, for Wilks, an expression of 'English teachers feeling like they were a profession'. Any euphoria was frustratingly fleeting, however. When the Union-led boycott disappeared and SATs, certainly from 1995 onwards, became part of the cycle of the school year for the following decade, with their importance in the eyes of school managers ratcheted up by the use of results in school league tables, the sense that English teachers could act collectively on points of principle seemed to wither. There was certainly still a great deal of anger within the profession, though, and LATE tried to continue the fight. In the summer of 1995 they surveyed primary and secondary schools on the effects of SATs and published a selection of the responses in *The Real Cost of SATs* (LATE, 1995). The responses cited numerous problems – the loss of teaching time, the narrowing of the curriculum, the inaccuracy of results, the negative impact on teacher morale and additional workload chief amongst them. Two years on from *Voices in the Classroom*, the anger of many heads of English had not abated; one called the tests 'valueless, time-wasting and expensive' (LATE, 1995, p. 22) whilst another claimed that there was 'absolutely no justification on any front to test 14-year-old students in this way. It has done positive harm' (ibid., p. 16). Again the responses came from across the country, and now they were not alarmed at the prospect of the tests – they were reflections on the actual impact of the assessment regime on their teaching and on their pupils.

LATE called for 'a real debate about the purposes of testing and assessment' and condemned the 'consultation conferences and meetings at SCAA where the agenda is determined behind the scenes by ministerial diktat' (ibid., p. 4). Perhaps the desperate defiance of the tone conveyed not just continued anger, but also the frustration at realising the battle had probably already been lost.

Before the SATs boycott, English teachers had tried to accommodate the views of policymakers and actively engaged with consultations, and tried, in effect, to make the National Curriculum work. The increasing sense of a marginalisation of teachers' voices and a process of deprofessionalisation no doubt contributed to the mood at the time of the boycott, when English teachers felt that things had gone too far and that a line had to be drawn. Enough really was enough. Many of the heads of English would have had involvement – directly or not – with enterprises like the National Oracy Project or National Writing Project, and some would have been used to the workings of the Schools Council as part of a climate of teacher involvement in reform of curriculum and assessment. The sense of feeling that things were being done to them, things that went against their own professional judgement based on real experience, would have been intensified by the fact that any attempt at negotiation was not working; direct action was inevitable. The victory was real but short lived, and it could easily be argued that the lessons from this were learned not as much by English teachers as by the policymakers. In subsequent years, increasingly centralised intervention, with fewer and fewer nods to consultation and an ever-tightening accountability framework through Ofsted inspection and league tables, worked together to create a context where the spaces for opposition were closed down and the opportunities to raise dissenting voices were minimised. The future saw moments when collective action might again take place – there was the potential for revolt, for example, when a stand-alone grammar test was mooted later in the 1990s, though proposals for this were in fact withdrawn. More than a decade later a concerted attempt by unions, local authorities, NATE and pupils themselves brought a legal challenge concerning the grading of English GCSE papers (*The Guardian*, 2012), but this ultimately failed in the courts.

The boycott of Key Stage 3 testing demonstrated English teachers could still wield some collective power. This would not be allowed to happen again. The LATE-inspired campaign to boycott the SATs remains, however, the last teacher-led movement to effectively cause a change in policy. For that, if for nothing else, it should be celebrated.

Conclusion

The years of Conservative administration were certainly tempestuous and tumultuous for English teachers. The Tories governed the country for 18 years from 1979 to 1997, a period that saw the growth and demise of 100 per cent GCSE coursework assessment, three versions of the National Curriculum, and – in no small part thanks to the Ofsted report *Boys and English* (Ofsted, 1993) – an obsession around the achievement of boys in the subject that would continue to haunt English teachers for many years. It seemed a time when English teachers' own ability to influence policy steadily waned, as first the Schools Council was abolished and then as subsequent manifestations of policymaking groups became increasingly removed from the profession. There was undoubtedly a growing, and intensifying, sense of a deprofessionalisation; this was felt across the teaching profession but the intense nature of the battles around English meant it was felt most keenly by teachers of this subject.

However, the Conservative party itself was riven by internal divides and conflict – most notably over its position on Europe – and it was no surprise when they fell to a devastating election defeat in 1997 that would lead to a 13-year period in opposition. For many in the teaching profession there was optimism at the prospect of the new, New Labour administration. Certainly education seemed to figure highly on the list of the incoming administration's potential priorities. That fact, however, signalled the reality that central intervention into the domain of teachers would, to use the phrase of the time, be ratcheted up in the pursuit of ever higher standards. As ever, English would be the focal point for the pressure that would be exerted and, even if the assault became less ideologically driven, its intensity was undiminished. Advocates of the progressive, growth model of English – familiar with the attacks of the back-to-basics traditionalists – would confront a new challenge in the form of the champions of literacy.

Notes

1 Comments from Sue Horner come from an interview with the author. Horner was an English teacher in Sheffield for 13 years before becoming an English adviser. She was both secretary and treasurer of NATE, and a local coordinator for the National Writing Project before taking a position in the National Curriculum Council. She ultimately headed the English team within QCA and QCDA.

2 Chris Woodhead would subsequently become the head of Ofsted; in this role he had a particularly combative relationship with the teaching profession. Woodhead, in the late 1960s and early 1970s, had been a teacher of English and was reportedly in favour of the new progressive methods. By the time he arrived at Ofsted, via roles in teacher education and the National Curriculum Council and the School Curriculum and Assessment Authority, he was a vociferous critic of progressive teaching and an advocate of traditional methods.

3 SCAA – the School Curriculum and Assessment Authority – had been formed in 1993 as a result of a merger of the National Curriculum Council and the School Examinations and Assessment Council. SCAA rapidly morphed into the Qualifications and Curriculum Authority (QCA) in 1997 when it was joined with the National Council for Vocational

Qualifications (NCVQ), and then in 2007 a final change saw the body become the Qualifications and Curriculum Development Agency (QCDA). Ultimately QCDA was closed in 2012 and its work taken on by the Standards and Testing Agency – the new body's name giving a clear indication of where priorities lay.

4 John Hickman taught for over 20 years in Forest Gate Community School in East London and was a prominent member of LATE's committee for much of that time. On leaving Forest Gate, Hickman succeeded Alistair West as the English advisor for the London Borough of Redbridge.

5 Richmond told how his mother vowed to never again buy the *Daily Telegraph* following its treatment of her son in the wake of the LINC project.

6 Paul Black and Dylan Wiliam were the joint authors of *Inside the Black Box* (1998), a meta-analysis of global research projects on the use of formative assessment. It is generally credited as establishing assessment for learning (AfL) as fundamental to discussions about effective teaching and learning.

7 Furlong, a past chair of NATE and IFTE, and Barnes, once NATE's general secretary, had established track records in developing assessment in English. Furlong, who achieved some notoriety when he was widely quoted in the media for the claim in the early 1990s that the effect of the Key Stage 3 Shakespeare test was to make teaching of the Bard 'arse achingly boring', had been a strong advocate of both CSE and 100 per cent coursework GCSE as systems that allowed pupils to be assessed on a broad curriculum and a full range of skills.

8 The London Borough of Wandsworth, a Conservative-led local authority, did all it could to ensure that the government policies around Key Stage 3 testing would be enacted.

References

Ball, S. (1985). English for the English Since 1906. In Goodson, I. (Ed.), *Social Histories of the Secondary Curriculum*. Sussex: Falmer Press.

Black, P. and Wiliam, D. (1998). *Inside the Black Box*. London: King's College London.

Centre for Educational Studies. (1987). *National Curriculum Task Group on Assessment and Testing*. London: King's College London.

Centre for Educational Studies. (1988). *National Curriculum Task Group on Assessment and Testing: Three Supplementary Reports*. London: King's College London.

Coles, J. (1994). Enough was Enough: The Teachers' Boycott of National Curriculum Testing. *Changing English: Studies in Culture and Education*, 1(2), pp. 16–31.

Cox, B. (1991). *Cox on Cox: An English Curriculum for the 1990s*. London: Hodder and Stoughton.

Cox, B. (1995). *Cox on the Battle for the English Curriculum*. London: Hodder and Stoughton.

Department for Education. (1993). *English for Ages 5 to 16: Proposals of the Secretary of State for Education and the Secretary of State for Wales*. London: Her Majesty's Stationery Office.

Department of Education and Science. (1984). *English from 5 to 16: Curriculum Matters 1*. London: Her Majesty's Stationery Office.

Department of Education and Science. (1988a), *The Curriculum from 5 to 16: Curriculum Matters 2*. London: Her Majesty's Stationery Office.

Department of Education and Science. (1988b). *Report of the Committee of Inquiry into the Teaching of English Language (The Kingman Report)*. London: Her Majesty's Stationery Office.

Department of Education and Science. (1988c). *Response to the Kingman Report*. London: Her Majesty's Stationery Office.

Department of Education and Science. (1988d). *English for Ages 5 to 11: Proposals of the Secretary of State for Education and Science and the Secretary of State for Wales*. London: Her Majesty's Stationery Office.

Griffiths, Lord of Fforestfach. (1993). *A Matter for Us All: Testing English in the National Curriculum*. Text of speech given at SEAC conference, 19th January 1993 inLondon.

Johnson, J. (1992). Pondering the Project. *Talk: The Journal of the National Oracy Project*, (5), pp. 48–50.

Jones, K. (Ed.). (1992). *English and the National Curriculum: Cox's Revolution*. London: The Institute of Education.

LATE. (1993a). *Enough is Enough*. London: LATE.

LATE. (1993b). *Voices from the Classroom*. London: LATE.

LATE. (1995). *The Real Cost of SATs*. London: LATE.

Marenbon, J. (1987). *English Our English: The New Orthodoxy Examined*. London: Centre for Policy Studies.

Marshall, B. (2008). Brian Cox and English: From the Black Papers to the National Curriculum. *English Drama Media*, (12), pp. 38–41.

Myhill, J., Jones, S. and Bailey, T. (2011). *Grammar for Writing? The Impact of Contextualised Grammar Teaching on Pupils' Writing and Pupils' Metalinguistic Understanding ESRC End of Award Report, RES-062-23-0775*. Swindon: ESRC.

NAAE. (1994). *English in the National Curriculum: A Response to the Draft Proposals, Second Draft*. Birmingham: NAAE.

NATE. (1988). *A Response to the Committee of Inquiry into the Teaching of English Language*. Sheffield: NATE.

NATE. (1989). *A Response to the Proposals for the National Curriculum Orders for English*. Sheffield: NATE.

National Curriculum Council. (1992). *National Curriculum English: The Case for Revising the Order*. York: National Curriculum Council.

National Curriculum Council. (1993). *National Curriculum Council Consultation Report: English*. York: National Curriculum Council.

National Writing Project. (1989). About Writing. *The National Writing Project Newsletter* (10).

Ofsted. (1993). *Boys and English*. London: Department for Education Publications.

Pollard, A. (1969). O and A Level: Keeping up the Standards. In Cox, C.B. and Dyson, A. E. (Eds), *Black Paper 2: The Crisis in Education*. London: The Critical Quarterly Society.

Richmond, J. (1992). Unstable Materials. *The English and Media Magazine*, (26), pp. 13–18.

Stubbs, M. (1991). Educational Language Planning in England and Wales: Multicultural Rhetoric and Assimilationist Assumptions. In Coulmas, F. (Ed), *A Language Policy for the European Community: Prospects and Quandaries*. Berlin: Mouton de Gruyter.

Teaching London Kids. (1990). *Language, Culture and the National Curriculum: An Interview with Harold Rosen*. London: The English Centre.

The English and Media Magazine. (1992a). Enough is Enough – The SATs Campaign. *The English and Media Magazine*, (27), 3.

The English and Media Magazine. (1992b). Stop Press. *The English and Media Magazine*, (27), 3.

The Guardian. (2012, 11th October). GCSE English Marking Faces High Court Challenge. Available at http://www.theguardian.com/education/2012/oct/11/gcse-english-legal-challenge (accessed 24th April 2016).

The Telegraph. (2002, 11th June). Professor Arthur Pollard: Obituary. Available at http://www.telegraph.co.uk/news/obituaries/1396854/Professor-Arthur-Pollard.html (accessed on 1st June 2016).

Times Educational Supplement. (1993, 7th May). Letter from John Marenbon. *Times Educational Supplement*, p. 2.

Watts, R. (2011). *Language Myths and the History of English*. USA: Oxford University Press.

5

NEW LABOUR, NEW POLICIES: THE FOCUS ON LITERACY

Asked to recall two soundbites from Tony Blair's speeches in his time before election to prime minister, it's likely that one might first remember 'Tough on crime, tough on the causes of crime'[1] from his period as shadow home secretary, a phrase that set out his serious credentials as a future Labour prime minister. The second would very likely be from his 1996 conference speech on the eve of the general election, when Blair explained that his three priorities for government would be 'education, education and education'.[2]

Clearly economic competitiveness lay behind the focus on education – referring to England's place in international league tables, Blair went on to say in the same speech, adapting the commonly known Jesuit maxim, 'give me the education system that is 35th in the world today and I will give you the economy that is 35th in the world tomorrow'. However, that is not to say that there were not ideas around social justice in the would-be prime minister's words. Whatever history makes of the New Labour years, it is difficult not to believe that the focus on education was in part an attempt to address the huge underachievement of certain groups of children in England, most notably those from socially deprived backgrounds. Although the word class had long since been part of the rhetoric – New Labour certainly didn't want to evoke such concepts as it tried to harvest the votes of disillusioned conservatives in the home counties raised on Margaret Thatcher's notion of a classless society – there was a recognition, perhaps overtly for the first time, that the real scandal of the English education system was the huge tail of underachievement. The availability of increasingly sophisticated data on attainment was showing up the particular groups who were failing – or more likely being failed by – the system; and in English it was no longer good enough to point simply to boys' underachievement, which had for some years become a near obsession.

Ofsted's *Boys and English* report (Ofsted, 1993) had sparked an intense focus on the issue of gender and achievement in English. The report, which drew on inspection evidence gathered between 1988–91 and which considered public examination results over a ten-year period, highlighted what to many was obvious: girls did better than boys when it came to any measure of attainment in the subject. As the report had come from Ofsted, though, it suddenly became the most important question in many English departments – 'what are you doing about the boys?'.

Ofsted's report itself had some relatively bland central findings – boys like drama, the influence of the teacher is important, girls read more fiction, and so on – but the mere fact that it was clearly on Ofsted's agenda meant English departments felt impelled to respond. A brave head of English, it would have been, to face an Ofsted inspection without some ready answers about boy-friendly strategies and text choices; war poetry, if it were not already, became ubiquitous. In the wake of the Ofsted report a SCAA Boys and English working group was established which – when the organisation was rebranded as QCA – published a set of support papers in 1997. There followed the somewhat patronisingly titled *Can Do Better: Raising Boys' Achievement in English* (Qualifications and Curriculum Authority [QCA], 1998a) and later still Ofsted returned to the area in *Yes He Can: Schools Where Boys Write Well* (Ofsted, 2003a). Throughout these papers and reports – most strikingly in the earlier ones – boys tended to be treated as a homogeneous mass, with phrases like 'the average boy' – whatever that meant – being commonly employed. A less-than-benign view of the inspectorate and curriculum authorities would suggest that gender was a convenient area around which to focus the debate about underachievement. Effectively this placed the onus for remedial action in the hands of English teachers. Recognising socio-economic factors as contributory to underachievement might legitimately result in a call for government action, but there was nothing government could do about gender.

Gender, however, if it was indeed part of the attainment problem, was just that – a part; other factors – socio-economic in particular – were more important and this was increasingly recognised as data on differing groups of pupils' attainment became progressively sophisticated, and reports like *Mapping Race, Class and Gender* (Gillborn and Mirza, 2000) appeared. Thus it is fair to say that addressing the very real underachievement amongst certain groups was not simply about economic competitiveness, it was also about social cohesion as New Labour pointed to statistics around low levels of literacy and prison populations, and drew on reports such as that from the Basic Skills Agency (Bynner and Parsons, 1997) to illustrate the somewhat obvious link between poor educational attainment and restricted ability to take a full and productive part in society and the community. The links between low levels of literacy and a dysfunctional society did perhaps illustrate there was some element of a social, as well as economic, agenda in the New Labour programme for education.

The National Literacy Strategy

Nowhere was the New Labour focus on education more pronounced than in the domain of English. A radical shift in nomenclature was ushered in by the government as it came to power in 1997 as literacy came to replace English in the primary school. Reports like that from the Basic Skills Agency (ibid.) and the later Department for Education and Employment review (Bynner et al., 2001) may have highlighted the problems of poor literacy in adulthood and indicated that resources were needed to tackle the problem, but reaching and having an effect on that group has always been notoriously difficult and prohibitively expensive. Even if identifying individuals in this group were possible, addressing adult illiteracy can mean overcoming sometimes decades of negativity in terms of attitude to education, self-esteem and confidence even before any meaningful programme of literacy teaching can begin. In essence the approach of the New Labour government seemed to be that, though the problem of adult illiteracy was appalling, money would be better spent on early years and school education in the bid to ensure that future generations would not follow the same path as their ancestors.

The launch of the National Literacy Strategy (NLS) in 1998[3] was the main plank in the government's strategy to transform the teaching of reading and writing (speaking and listening was really not a focus) in primary schools. The NLS was in fact a product of both New Labour and Conservative policy; in opposition New Labour had set up a Literacy Task Force, but in launching the NLS in 1998 the work of the National Literacy Project (NLP), set up by the Tory administration in 1996, was heavily drawn upon.

The NLS in primary schools had a number of central features, a framework of almost innumerable objectives for the teaching of reading and writing across Reception to Year 6, a stipulation that there should be one dedicated 'Literacy Hour' in the classroom per day, and – in what was the major shift in central intervention – recommended teaching approaches. These recommendations included how the literacy hour should be split between different types of activity (whole class, group and independent work) and also a range of pedagogies – shared and guided reading and writing amongst them, as well as a model for the teaching of writing based on the notion that language could be considered at word, sentence and text level – in essence, a genre-based approach to the teaching of literacy.

The NLS was supported by an infrastructure that saw regional directors monitor local authorities who employed teams of literacy consultants who disseminated the core training to teachers and supported schools with implementation of the Strategy. It was, to echo John Richmond's words on the design of LINC, an exercise in educational pyramid selling, certainly the biggest in the history of education policy in the United Kingdom. The Strategy was non-statutory – thus allowing policymakers to defend a claim that they weren't forcing teachers to do something. However, in this exercise of pyramid selling, there was little option but to buy.

Challenging targets for the numbers of children expected to achieve Level 4 by the end of Key Stage 2 were set by the then education secretary, David Blunkett, who vowed to resign if the targets were not met by the NLS's fourth year in operation.[4] It was without doubt the largest centrally driven intervention into teaching in England, and it is difficult to say what the total cost was, given the numbers of staff and the volume of training material generated. Using the earlier

NLP as a guide, it was estimated that the cost of the initiative was £25 per pupil per year (Machin and McNally, 2004). There were something in the order of 4,000,000 children in primary schools during the period of the initiative.

It is difficult to say with any certainty how effective the NLS was. Certainly test results improved, and the government's own evaluation viewed the NLS in primary schools as a success on many fronts (Department for Education, 2011). Claims based on data from the SATs have always been disputable, of course, and such evidence may prove nothing more than teachers got better at preparing pupils for examinations and that 11 year olds got better at passing the tests. The reliability and validity of such tests has been questioned. Such points have been acknowledged, though questioned, even by those who took a generally positive view of the impact of the NLS (for example, Beard, 2011). The NLS did, however, have a profound impact on the nature of teaching of English in a large number of primary schools; of this there can be little doubt. A new vocabulary was added to the teacher's lexicon – starters, plenaries, text types, word level – and for many children, English was no longer what was taught in the primary schools, instead it was literacy.

The impact of the NLS was perhaps more profound than its senior leaders could have envisaged; whereas it might have been imagined, as with many centrally driven reforms, that the core messages would have been watered down by the time it came to enactment of the recommended strategies in the classroom, it actually appeared that many primary teachers were doing exactly as they were told, so to speak. There is a reliable report, for example, that one of the senior figures in the NLS, giving an after dinner conference speech, confessed to being astounded that the poster of the literacy hour clock showing how the lesson time should be divided up was actually on the wall of the classrooms he visited – apparently he didn't think for one minute that teachers would take the NLS quite so literally.[5]

However, it was not difficult to understand why primary teachers toed the line in ways beyond the imagination of the architects of the strategy. Test results were poor in many schools, or at least poor in relation to the new stringent targets, and in an age of ever-increasing accountability the pressure on primary schools was progressively being ratcheted up. The majority of primary teachers did not have English degrees, and though they would have been trained in aspects of language development and early reading, subject knowledge may well have been an issue, particularly in areas such as grammar; *Grammar for Writing*, with its pages of terminology, would have been challenging for all but the most confident linguists.[6] Without a strongly informed alternative view, and with increasing pressure from schools, local authorities, and central government, it is not difficult to see why the NLS had such impact at the primary level; if for whatever reason the children in your class were going to fail to reach the expected level in the SATs then at least if they failed following the prescribed advice then as a teacher you couldn't be entirely blamed. Although the NLS was never statutory, for a teacher to pursue an alternative vision for the teaching of reading and writing was to put herself in a position of huge vulnerability. There were teachers who had this strength of belief in their own knowledge, but they were in the minority. Thus it must be said that the NLS's impact on primary English teaching was huge and perhaps will prove to be longstanding.

The Key Stage 3 Framework for English

In 2000, the decision was made to extend the primary strategies into secondary schooling; there would be a Secondary National Strategy, with a specific English strand. In some ways the plans for the secondary English strategy mirrored the NLS; there would be a framework of objectives across the years of Key Stage 3, training material for English departments, and a veritable army of consultants employed by the Strategy and working through the local authorities to deliver training and offer support to schools. Also, pedagogies recommended through the NLS were extended to the secondary sector – particularly exploring texts at word, sentence and text level, and using shared, modelled and guided approaches in the teaching of reading and writing. There was not a literacy hour as such, but a recommended four-part lesson structure – beginning with a starter and ending with a plenary. There was much more explicit rhetoric about teaching, as opposed to learning, with whole-class teaching being strongly recommended as a central approach. Implicit was the suggestion that some of the failings of pupils in English resulted from the progressive methods of group work, investigation and explora-tory learning; there needed to be a re-emphasis on the teacher as the expert and a shift away from a child-centred pedagogy.

Unsurprisingly, the reaction to the secondary framework from English teachers was very different to that of primary teachers to the NLS. There were obvious reasons for this. First, despite the fact that in its secondary incarnation the title given was the *Key Stage 3 English Framework*, it was so closely allied to the primary strategy that for many English teachers this was turning the subject they loved and were passionate about into literacy. Literature, central to the concerns of so many English teachers, did not really play any meaningful part in the Framework. Sue Hackman,[7] who led the writing of the secondary Framework and accompanying training material, recalled that there was a conscious decision to focus in the first years of the secondary initiative on writing:

> In my own head I was thinking we do not have a pedagogy for teaching writing, we are a bit hopeful and too often writing takes place at home. We didn't teach it, we marked it and it struck me writing was often marked ret-rospectively. In my head that was the project at least for two years: to put writing at the top of the agenda and to try to harness grammar into writing.

This was the familiar criticism of the process approach to writing, an approach inspired by the work of Donald Graves;[8] teachers, in effect, did not actually teach writing – they let it happen and taught through correction – children learned through osmosis. It was a criticism based on a crude construct of the process approach, however, and not one that many English teachers were happy to hear;

process approaches to writing sat very neatly within the overall concept of a generally progressive, growth model of the subject.

The neglect of reading, and certainly literature, was, Hackman acknowledged, controversial within the profession, and the shift towards literacy meant a focus on some aspects of English teaching that were alien to the English teaching community. The teaching of grammar might have come under this heading – for though most English teachers were English graduates the majority of their degrees would have been literary in content – but perhaps the most obvious area was the teaching of spelling. Few secondary English teachers would have considered the explicit teaching of spelling to be part of their work; they would of course correct spellings or point out inaccuracies but it would have been very rare to find a lesson, or even part of a lesson, in a secondary English classroom devoted to the teaching of spelling rules or conventions. Drawing secondary English teachers' attention to the teaching of spelling was no bad thing in itself; the notion that by the age of 11 children are, and consider themselves to be, either good or bad spellers and that there is precious little that can be done about it is one that has always needed to be challenged. The *English Framework* did this, though the suspicion remains that many secondary English teachers still consider that the teaching of spelling is something that is done in the primary phase, and if children haven't grasped it by the time secondary schooling starts then the damage has been done.

Additionally, the implication of a new way of working and a recommended pedagogy was that English teachers had got it wrong – this was a big bang theory 'based on the premise that teachers' behaviours needed to be changed' (Ellis, 2011, p. 29). This is a message it is difficult for a professional group to hear – even if it happened to be true, or at least if there were statistics to support the position. What was true was that significant numbers of pupils who entered secondary school below the expected level of performance for 11 year olds – that is Level 4 – failed to catch up in terms of their final outcomes in GCSEs at age 16. According to the data many children – who came to be termed in the rhetoric of the Strategy as the stuck level 4s – failed to make good progress in the early years of secondary school. Also, according to Sue Hackman, significant numbers of high-attaining students were among the apparent 20 per cent of children failing to make good progress. Thus, for Hackman, even if the initial data available had suggested that the initiatives ought to be targeting certain underperforming groups – Turkish and African-Caribbean boys, for example – the focus for her was wider: 'We were interested in all children but once I realised there were slow progressors I wanted to target the slow progressors whatever their level of attainment.' The education secretary Alan Johnson, Hackman said, 'was very sympathetic to the notion that progress was an important way of looking at children and (he) did introduce progress into the accountability regime'.

There may have been many reasons to account for the lack of progress of significant numbers of students that the data revealed;[9] that there was something rotten in the state of English teaching was never really established. However, the implication of a top-down delivery of a new model of writing was that the approaches of the progressives – the child-centred process teaching of writing with its links to the growth model of English – were failing. The rhetoric of the Strategy talked of transforming teaching and learning.[10] It is not difficult to see that some English teachers, experienced professionals committed to a pedagogy informed by their own education, training and work, would consider that an assertion that their work needed transforming was an affront to their experience and professional identities.

The theoretical underpinning for the strategy

Understandably, many English teachers wanted to know what evidence informed the recommended teaching approaches in the *Key Stage 3 Framework for English*. A large proportion of English teachers, at least according to some studies (for example, Goodwyn (1992)), most closely associated their view of English with the personal growth model articulated by Cox. This model was a progressive one, with an emphasis on the student's own language development, autobiographical writing and the reading of relevant literature. It was decidedly child centred. The Strategy approach was markedly different; the emphasis in the *Framework for English* (Department for Education and Employment, 2001a) was on objective-focused, teacher-led lessons and an approach to reading and writing that forefronted non-fiction genres and prioritised technical aspects of language use rather than expression; playing with language and subverting genres could only come once the rules had been mastered.

In relation to the primary literacy strategy, Roger Beard of the University of Leeds had been engaged to present the research evidence base for the new policy directives (Beard, 1999; Beard, 2000). It was somewhat strange, then, that it was not until nearly two years after the Key Stage 3 pilot that the Department for Education published *Key Stage 3 English: Roots and Research* (Harrison, 2002), a document that presented the available evidence to support the approaches being recommended to secondary English teachers. In their account of the primary NLS, *The Literacy Game* (2007), John Stannard and Laura Huxford claimed that primary teachers tended to have only a 'passing interest in theories and tend to be more pragmatic' (p. 10). Contestable though such an assertion was, another assertion might be that secondary English teachers, given their specialist training and the history of the development of the subject in school, would be much more likely to have a grounding in theory governing the way they teach their subject. In 2001 the overwhelming majority of English teachers would have been trained through a university-based initial teacher training course, on which they would in all probability have explored contesting theories of effective English teaching and considered the underpinning rationales for these alternative approaches. Many would have engaged with the key thinkers in English – Barnes, Britton, Dixon, Rosen, Margaret Meek and others – and most would have known something of projects like the National Writing and National Oracy Projects and been aware of the debates around the National Curriculum and national assessment, even if their own careers had begun after the events. Few would have seen the teaching of English as in some way marooned from ideas about language, learning and development. Given this, it might have been in the Strategy's interest to publish *Roots and Research* at or around the launch of the policy, rather than wait two years in what to some looked like a post-hoc justification of ideas.

Roots and Research made for an interesting read, sometimes as much for what it omitted as for what it contained. Harrison broadly found theoretical support for the Strategy's proposed approach to lesson structure and to the teaching of reading, though struggled to find evidence to support the focus on grammar teaching. This was no surprise given that previous attempts to establish a link between grammar teaching and improvement in writing – the Strategy's reason for its explicit grammatical content – had failed to be convincing. A neat side step in *Roots and Research* claimed:

> It is difficult to link the findings of research in this area to the Strategy's recommendations for pedagogy. One reason for this, however, is the gap between the type of grammar teaching that has typically been researched (i.e. grammar taught as separate decontextualised knowledge) and the approach to grammar teaching in the Strategy.
>
> *(Harrison, 2002, p. 4)*

It's interesting that one of the central claims of policymakers at the time was that the NLS and Strategy were about implementing what is known to work. Clearly this was not the case with the approach to grammar, which still seemed only backed by the common-sense argument that if you know how a language works you will be able to use it more effectively. The evidence didn't exist then, and subsequent studies (for example, Andrews et al. (2006)) similarly failed to find such evidence. One eminent linguist – David Crystal – has likened the view to that which would suggest a mechanic ought to be a better driver because she knows the parts of an engine. There is of course no reason why she should be.[11] The grammar debate has long raged in English, and certainly many English teachers, with literature backgrounds, feel this is an area of deficit in their own subject knowledge. It is an area of acute sensitivity for many English teachers; the lack of strong evidence didn't help convince them of the Strategy's value.

Harrison's treatment of the Strategy's writing pedagogy was interesting too. He chose to devote considerable space to arguing with an earlier article by Mary Hilton (2001) in which she criticised the underpinning theory of writing in the Strategy, claiming that it misrepresented the work of the American George Hillocks. Harrison, whilst agreeing with the criticism to a point, did suggest that a rebalancing, rather than a restructuring, would be in order, and he pointed to the work of Maureen Lewis and David Wray on the EXEL[12] project – advocates of writing frames – and how they in turn drew on the genre theorists from Australia.[13] Not mentioned at all, however, or at least not explicitly, was the work of the New South Wales Disadvantaged Children's Project, detailed in Bill Cope and Mary Kalantzis' *The Powers of Literacy: A Genre Approach to the Teaching of Writing*

(1993a). This project, informed by the work of Jim Martin, would seem to have been mirrored in the Strategy approach, with the definition of text types, the linguistic analysis at word, sentence and text level and the modelled, shared and guided writing approaches leading to independent writing. If the Strategy took what worked from anywhere in terms of the approach to writing then it took it from this Australian project (for further on this view see Gibbons (2004)), and the evidence is that this project did work. Sue Hackman acknowledged the part of the Australian genre model in the strategy's pedagogy for writing, and it was writing that Hackman decided, given English teachers' predominantly literary backgrounds and the relative underperformance of pupils in writing as opposed to reading, should be the prime focus for the strategy roll out. The explicitness of a genre approach was, for Hackman, important particularly to certain groups of students:

> A sensible school teaches children how to write in different genres because they are not born knowing the social conventions. Some children pick them up quickly if they live in literate homes, but I don't believe that happens in homes that aren't reading, where parents don't have professional jobs.

Cope and Kalantzis' work drew on a project confined to non-fiction writing and directed at a particular group of disadvantaged children, those coming to school largely from socio-economically deprived areas with little home literacy. It was a project that looked explicitly at the types of writing pupils would need to master in order to access the curriculum in schools; it was not, however, primarily developed as a model for teaching English. This project was apparently successful in many ways, making explicit for less literate children the invisible rules governing writing types.[14] The Key Stage 3 strategy extended this genre-based approach to the teaching of fiction and creative writing – one training video featured a teacher writing the opening of a scary story following the Strategy's model for writing – and of course said that it should be for all children. If this was a research-informed approach then it may be another example – there are many within education[15] – of findings being taken from a particular, focused project and being over extended; they've probably never been asked, but Cope and Kalantzis would likely be nonplussed if their views on using the genre model to teach ghost stories were sought.

Perhaps most interesting about *Roots and Research* is the overall impression one gets from reading it. One doesn't come away with the impression that the research was done prior to the implementation of the Strategy and that the resulting policy decisions were informed with a strong, coherent, underpinning vision for English. Rather the document seems to treat each element of the Strategy in isolation and find snippets of research to back the approach in that particular area. This cherry picking, one might even say manipulation, of research was a feature of both the primary and secondary strategies. There was no acknowledgement in the document either that many of the recommended strategies and teaching approaches in the Framework may have been informed by such evidence that there was about what worked best with boys. Short-term targets, explicit objectives, non-fiction writing and plenaries – all central elements of the Framework approach – had been noted in documents such as *Boys and English* (Ofsted, 1993) to be techniques that particularly suited boys. Since it was boys' underachievement that lay at the heart of the depressing statistics on attainment, the *Framework* could well have been seen as part of the attempt to make English more boy-friendly. This was never explicitly conceded, however.

Roots and Research seemed to be an attempt, though the author explicitly said he was under no pressure to come to any findings or look at any particular research, to back up decisions that had already been made. For teachers of English who sub-scribed to a vision of English, an overarching pedagogy that would bring an overall coherence to the enterprise of teaching the subject they loved, *Roots and Research* failed to convince them that this was contained within the Strategy.

The reaction of the profession to the Key Stage 3 English Framework

Writing in *English Teachers at Work: Narratives, Counter Narratives and Arguments* (Doecke, Homer and Nixon, 2003), Andrew Goodwyn, who has long researched English teachers' views on their subject, reported the findings of his survey of experienced English teachers and their response to the Key Stage 3 English Strategy and its implementation. Although there were only 156 respondents to the survey, the views expressed may well offer an insight in to the way that the English subject community responded to the unprecedented central intervention into their way of working. As is perhaps inevitable with questionnaire research using a four-point scale, a lot of the views congregate around the middle, but the free-flow comments Goodwyn quoted revealed something more of the respondents' feelings. Typical of these comments were: 'Why is it that, all of a sudden, secondary English teachers need to be told how to teach English?'; 'I would simply like to be able to continue to teach what I have always done pretty well … The Teaching of English'; 'It is insulting rather than professional to be told both what to teach and how to teach it'; 'We strongly object to the presentation of the Strategy by the advisers. There is no open debate. At times it seems like 1984' (Goodwyn, 2003, pp. 124–125). And there was, of course, the inevitable remark, 'We teach English, not literacy' (ibid., p. 125).

The comments can appear to be somewhat arrogant; the views of experienced professionals protecting their vested interests, reacting predictably to outside attempts to shift their practices and to the assertions that hitherto their teaching had let children down. It's true, too, that surveys tend to elicit comments from those with the strongest feelings; satisfied customers are often silent. The comments were, however, indicative of fiercely felt beliefs about what good English teaching was, and these teachers would have included those who had been prepared to boycott testing a decade earlier to show the strength of these beliefs. The notion expressed that the central intervention was an undermining of professionalism and an affront to what they considered to be their own existing good practice, developed over time, may not have been representative of the entire English teaching community, but it is one that I recognise from my time as being one of those advisers delivering the Strategy, and one strongly articulated elsewhere (for example, Ellis (2011)). Particularly for teachers who had a notion of a progressive model of English, the new approaches seemed a particular affront; hardly surprising since its roots were in genre pedagogies in Australia and here the ideas were developed in response to a sense that progressive methods in that country's English classrooms were failing children from less literate family backgrounds. Somewhere in the genesis of this attempt to reframe English was an assault on progressive pedagogy.

I had the fortune of working as a English consultant in a relatively high-attaining borough, so in some ways could afford to mediate the *Framework* with a lighter touch than might have been possible elsewhere; there wasn't an ideological commitment from New Labour to change the way English was taught – they wanted improved progress and attainment, so where progress and attainment were already high there was no reason to impose a new model. Here the difference between the Conservative and New Labour education policies for English was clearly discernible.

Certainly local authorities that were perceived to be underachieving were dealt with more firmly; in such places the driving force of the Strategy – to enhance the performance of underachieving groups – was at its strongest. Nowhere would this have been more true than in the pilot authority of Tower Hamlets. As a pilot authority, Tower Hamlets was a testing ground for the Strategy in the year prior to its national roll out, so it was implemented in as unadulterated form as was possible. Statistically, attainment in reading and writing was not high in the borough, for reasons that would be obvious to anyone who had even a passing knowledge of the social, economic and cultural context of that part of East London.

John Wilks, a head of English in the borough, remembered the National Strategy training as being something he found totally unrecognisable from his experiences of continuing professional development at institutions such as the English and Media Centre and the Institute of Education. Wilks claimed that there was no space for discussion and debate in the Strategy training; the right way to teach – specifically focussing on text types in the teaching of writing – was laid out. When teachers had questions, these would be placed (in the increasingly ubiquitous style of management consultancy training) on post-it notes to be dealt with at the end of the day. Of course, after a full day's training, few were the teachers that wanted to extend the experience, so the questions were left unanswered. According to one account, those who did pursue their questions would be unceremoniously and ungraciously told to desist in what might be best described as agricultural language by 'someone important' (Ellis, 2011, p. 29).

There was an enormous amount of training on offer via the local authority English consultants when the *English Framework* was rolled out; the initial training for heads of English (or their representatives) was a minimum of two days being navigated through the collection of modules contained within the weighty A4 ring binder of materials (Department for Education and Employment, 2001b). These modules covered the teaching of reading, writing, speaking and listening and spelling but also inducted teachers into the use of the framework objectives to inform short-, medium- and long-term planning and urged the undertaking of a departmental self-audit to reveal the aspects of curriculum and teaching that needed to be addressed.

Almost simultaneously, a huge folder of *Literacy Across the Curriculum* materials was published (Department for Education and Employment, 2001c) and connected training around each of its modules offered. Then, it seemed almost monthly a new folder of materials for the English department would appear – grammar for writing, guided reading and writing, and so on – and further training was offered. Sue Hackman acknowledged that there was perhaps 'too much training, too many folders' and that time should have been left 'for it to settle and to be absorbed'. The speed at which such a high volume of training material was delivered and the pressure on English departments to quickly enact a whole series of new initiatives was satirised from the points of view of both a classroom teacher (Mallard, 2003) and a Key Stage 3 consultant (Anonymous, 2002). There was more than a hint of reality in both accounts which, in taking the form of diaries, showed how, almost daily, there was pressure on teachers and departments to ensure new planning was complete, new catch up units had been scheduled and sufficient attention had been given to starters and plenaries.

It was regrettable that some of the genuinely excellent material made available through the publications and the training may well have gone unnoticed in the deluge of packs arriving in school. The material on developing group talk contained within the literacy across the curriculum training, for example, led by Alan Howe, who had a distinguished history working in the area in initiatives like the National Oracy project, drew heavily on the work of Neil Mercer and promoted a model for developing oracy in the classroom that would have affirmed the practice of many progressive English teachers. How many actually engaged with this training – given the priority given to writing in the framework – is debatable. The very fact that the oracy materials drew on respected thinking and familiar good practice, whereas many of the writing and grammar materials were startlingly new to many English teachers, may have contributed to the problems the profession had with the Framework. It added to the sense that this was not an overarching formulation of subject English – rather it was a pick and mix of strategies that in themselves may have been evidenced to work, but when taken together formed a less-than-coherent whole that was not the sum of its parts.

For Wilks – and for those teachers quoted in Goodwyn's research and, it is probable, for many more experienced teachers who had entered the profession in a pre-National Curriculum context and developed a sense of professionalism and a way of teaching English forged through classroom experience, collaboration with colleagues and a democratic spirit – the interventionist nature of the Strategy was a direct affront. There was an obvious irony in the fact that a model for a subject built for many on effective oracy, discussion and debate was being delivered with minimal space offered for conversation. For Wilks, the whole basis of the Strategy was anti-intellectual and genre theory 'limiting' in the teaching of writing.

However, dissent, he claimed, was not merely discouraged, it called into question your integrity: 'There was an argument that if you are against this you are against working class children. This was a New Labour policy. That became the devious argument.' Just a few years later the phrase 'enemies of promise' would be used by a secretary of state to describe those who apparently stood in the way of reform. Though that phrase was not used at the time, a similar sentiment seemed to have been there; working-class children who didn't come from the middle-class literate backgrounds of the majority of their English teachers were being denied the chance to make progress by the progressive orthodoxy of their teachers who denied the power of literacy to those not fortunate enough to be born into households and communities where reading and writing were daily activities. There was, implicit at the very least, a moral crusade being waged with consultants acting as the missionaries; to stand in the way of this would not just be unprofessional, it would be unethical.

The legacy of the Strategy

The Strategy outlived its initial shelf life of three years, but in 2009 the curtain was brought down on what was the most heavily financed and resourced government-led education reform in history; a total of nearly £4 billion was finally said to have been spent across primary and secondary with more than a quarter of that on literacy and English (Ellis, 2011). In fact, prior to the Strategy's demise there was a rewritten – branded as renewed – *Framework for English* launched (Department for Children, Schools and Families, 2008), a much slimmer version that reverted to traditional organisation around the concepts of reading, writing and speaking and listening. This renewed framework broadened its reach to encompass Key Stage 4. Some questioned the purpose of this new version, and its relationship to the then recently rewritten National Curriculum (e.g. Gibbons (2008)) and the Assessing Pupil Progress[16] (APP) tools; it's likely, in any case, that it made little impact on English teachers given the withdrawal of the Strategy as a national initiative, and the fact that the profession was grappling with a new curriculum, imminent new GCSE specifications and a life in the wake of the abolition of Key Stage 3 national testing.

One would hope, at least one with a concern for the spending of public finances, that given the level of investment there was a lasting positive legacy from the initiative and that it wasn't in fact a notional rather than a national strategy. To an extent, this does seem to be the case, though to what extent it is a legacy that is a force for good in the teaching and learning of English is open to question. Over the past ten years I have visited dozens of English classrooms and seen hundreds of English lessons delivered by new entrants to the profession from a range of diverse backgrounds. Each of these individuals comes into teaching English full of a passion for the subject and its potential to transform the lives of children through the development of language and the experience of literature. When interviewed for a training place they almost unanimously allude – explicitly or implicitly – to a progressive growth model of English and use words like creativity and imagination. Though they often acknowledge the importance of developing literacy and of enabling children to access the curriculum, this is seldom their main motivation to become teachers of English. They almost inevitably prefer to talk about literature than literacy. They may, of course, be saying what they think their interviewers want to hear, but it's unlikely that this is the case across the board. These new entrants then experience teacher training, but they are not told there is a right way to teach English, and yet, almost across the board, certain features very quickly become part of their practice once they begin to teach in their school placements. Many of these features seem to derive from the years of the Strategy. A genre-based approach to the teaching of writing is certainly more dominant in English class-rooms than it was in the pre-Strategy era – the fact that this kind of approach was taken up in the writing triplets adopted for GCSE English was certainly a factor in it taking hold. Identifying the features of persuasive or argument writing through a shared reading of a text and then employing these conventions to construct a text of their own is, it appears, the default model for the teaching of writing. There is, too, certainly more teacher modelling of writing in the classroom. Few now are the lessons where learning objectives or lesson objectives are not dutifully copied by pupils at the start of the session – this seems to be a Strategy legacy, but one that might also derive from a misinterpretation of assessment for learning research where the rhetoric suggests explicit success criteria are key for children to know. And although it may always have been common to talk about lessons made up of different phases, the language of the three- or four-part lesson, introduced by the Strategy with the notions of starters and plenaries, is dominant in the discourse of lesson planning and observation feedback. There can be little doubt that in some significant ways the Strategy years changed at least the ways in which lessons are structured, organised and talked about and there are ways in which the pedagogy of English teaching, particularly around writing, have been shifted.

Other innovations of the Strategy, however, gained little traction in secondary classrooms. Guided group reading, heavily promoted in the primary sector and introduced in the later years of the Key Stage 3 Strategy, failed to seduce secondary English teachers for whom the twin concepts of the class reader and independent reading time were probably far too entrenched. This is perhaps to be regretted since there is certainly value in the guided group reading approach. Despite the quality of the material on talk made available through the Strategy, speaking and listening remains very often the least prioritised area of English – no doubt pre-dominantly as its assessment has always been problematic and its contribution to overall levels and GCSE grades has been progressively undermined. Based on his research, Goodwyn came to the conclusion that English teachers 'never developed a positive relationship with "The Strategies"' (Goodwyn, 2011).

When Sue Hackman reflected on what she felt were the lasting achievements of the English strategy, she pointed particularly to the narrowing of the gap in terms of pupils' achievement in writing. For her, adopting the genre approach to teach-ing was about making the 'invisible visible', particularly for those pupils whose background had not encultured them into valuing the written word. Hackman claimed 'a limited success' in this regard in a refreshingly frank appraisal. She pointed, too, to the work on group talk, and to the steps made on introducing grammar for writing – work that has since been developed by Debra Myhill and her colleagues from the University of Exeter.

However, if successive reports by Ofsted, culminating in 2015's *Key Stage 3: The Wasted Years?* (Ofsted, 2015), are any true measure then it appears that the lasting impact of the Key Stage 3 strategy has been negligible. In the Strategy's early years, Ofsted's evaluations of the impact of the initiative had been mixed, with positive impacts being seen on English department planning, but less evidence to suggest improvements in the quality of teaching and in pupil attainment (see, for example, Ofsted (2003b)). Triennial survey reports published in the first decade of the twenty-first century pointed to significant problems with Key Stage 3 English, particularly pointing to failure to articulate a vision for Key Stage 3 (Ofsted, 2009, 2012). By 2015, some years after the Strategy's demise, Ofsted's overall view on this age phase was almost unequivocal; Key Stage 3 still lacked clear direction in terms of an overall vision for English and there was a failure to adequately address the perennial issues of continuity and progression from Key Stage 2 and beyond to Key Stage 4. In the years of the Strategy it was not uncommon to hear those involved refer to Key Stage 3 as the Cinderella Key Stage; despite the best efforts of the Strategy's leaders and its army of consultants, and despite the vast amount of public money, little has changed. Hackman herself used the fairy-tale metaphor when she reflected on the direction of Key Stage 3 in 2015:

> I regret the loss of direction in KS3. It is not junior GCSE. It is not grown up pastoral primary. It is not a little holiday between 11 and 14. Some schools have found a purpose because some schools have a very strong ethos about what they are about and they use that to define KS3. It shouldn't be beyond the wit of a government to say what KS3 is for, to theorise its purpose, something suitable for in-between-agers …. We should be paying much more attention to KS3. It is the neglected, Cinderella curriculum and I think we've just gone back to the days before the National Strategies.

It would be natural for someone who invested so much of her own time and energy into the National Strategies to regret the fact that, in a sense, any ground that was gained in English teaching in Key Stage 3 has been subsequently lost. Critics of the Strategy – and there remain many of them – would probably see in Hackman's reflections something that to a large extent would, for them, reveal the biggest problem in New Labour's policy initiatives aimed at driving up attainment in English. It may not be 'beyond the wit of a government to say what KS3 is for', but if it is the government that decides this, and does so seemingly with little or no reference to the knowledge, belief and experience of the profession, then one view is that it will inevitably fail. Goodson's (2001) ideas about the importance of teachers' own passions to the sustainability of reform, and Friedman, Galligan, Albano and

O'Connor's (2009) argument that teachers need to be participants in, rather than enactors of, reform come back to mind. However passionately the New Labour policymakers held their views about the need to transform English teaching, however sincere they may have been in these views, and however vigorously the architects of the *Framework for English* tried to promote them, it is difficult, in the final analysis, to see how the policy initiatives took account of English teachers' own passions, or saw English teachers as much more than the enactors of the new methods.

Meanwhile, the National Curriculum

Through the Strategy's central years, it was difficult at times – given the levels of investment and training – to remember that it, and the *Framework for English*, were non-statutory initiatives. In reality, the only statutory regulation of what was taught in English was the National Curriculum. The curriculum had been revised in the early years of the New Labour administration and appeared in 1999. According to Sue Horner, when it came to the 1995 curriculum, three versions had been written – 'over my dead body, what we could live with and what we wanted'; the resulting orders had been, apparently 'something in between what we could live with and what we wanted'. It was certainly a more humane curriculum than the Pascal version it replaced, even if it shared many more of its features that those of the Cox version, and it is fair to say that the 1999 version showed continued improvement in terms of articulating a notion of English closer to the progressive model at the heart of many teachers' practice.

The 1999 rewrite began with a statement on the importance of English which included words such as 'creatively' and 'imaginatively' (Department for Education and Employment, 1999, p. 14), and there were some judiciously selected quotations from novelists and academics – Ian McEwan and Benjamin Zephaniah among them – to preface the orders themselves. Interestingly, in an attempt one assumes to foster a coherence across the secondary age phase, Key Stages 3 and 4 were presented for the first time as a single programme of study, and within the orders 'language structure' was used in preference to any explicit reference to grammar. Additionally, the amount of text dedicated to Standard English was significantly reduced. It was a curriculum that for many suggested a move in the right direction for English; Horner certainly felt it was 'an attempt to move the subject forward a bit' and represented, for her, 'some progress over time'. For oppositional English teachers, relatively fresh from the SATs boycott and the anger around the trashing of Cox's curriculum, QCA was still the them in a them-and-us binary positioning so reaction to the new curriculum was not overwhelmingly positive, but with hindsight it's difficult not to take a view that there were indeed people working within the organisation who had sound ideas about the subject and who did what they could to effect change, albeit that this was always going to be difficult in the political context and given the politically charged nature of English. In fact, through the years of the New Labour government the increasing contrast in the approaches of QCA and the National Strategy saw the former body viewed probably as increasingly more progressive and humane. Horner certainly looks back now on her time as leader of the English team at QCA and QCDA and considers that she was working on behalf of the profession, not at odds with them; this view was supported when John Hickman recalled his dealings with Horner as part of the consultations for the 1995 National Curriculum rewrite – without Horner's interventions and advice to members of the consultative group that curriculum, Hickman felt, would have been even worse.

As the Strategy became increasingly centrally driven, delivering a model of English pedagogy which, it was claimed, had proved to be effective and so needed no further discussion or consultation, QCA – perhaps because of this – adopted a far more consultative approach in working towards the revision of the National Curriculum which would be adopted in schools in 2008. QCA had in fact, for some time, been adopting what appeared to be a more discursive approach to the subject; where the Strategy had decided the best approach to the subject and the job of English teachers was to adopt this best practice, QCA, through a series of publications, had been inviting a debate about key aspects of English. This can be seen in the 1998 *The Grammar Papers* (QCA, 1998b), which offered some genuinely interesting perspectives on the perennial problem of language study, and in the follow up publication *Not Whether but How* (QCA, 1999), which explored approaches to grammar teaching and arose from a QCA conference which included contributions from some of the foremost thinkers in the field, including Ron Carter, Deborah Cameron, George Keith and Debra Myhill. There followed *New Perspectives on Spoken English in the Classroom* (QCA, 2003) and *Introducing the Grammar of Talk* (QCA, 2004), publications that – via contributions from Neil Mercer, Robin Alexander, Tony Edwards and others – explored what place spoken language study might have in the classroom, and how it might be best taught. Given the people involved, and the nature of the content, one could see a revisiting of the LINC project in QCA's work here. Ultimately this kind of work would lead to the very brief appearance of the study of spoken English in GCSEs.[17] All of these publications saw a shift in the work of QCA – the English team there seemed to want to genuinely engage in a debate about subject English. Perhaps this shift was an inevitable consequence of the National Strategy taking the ascendancy in terms of dictating what was actually going on in the area of curriculum and assessment.

QCA's shift in approach to English was most striking when it came to preparations for the second National Curriculum rewrite under the New Labour administration. An initiative called English 21 was launched in February 2005, as part of which the English team at QCA invited the profession into a discussion about what the subject should like, and do, for learners of the twenty-first century, those who would be leaving compulsory schooling in 2015. According to Sue Horner who devised the initiative, English 21 had the explicit endorsement of then education secretary Charles Clarke. Supported by the head of QCA, Ken Boston, Horner pitched English 21 to Clarke at an 8.00 a.m. meeting:

At the meeting there must have been 6 civil servants with Charles Clark. Ken said we've got this idea and Charles Clarke said off you go Sue … no softening me …. I did my 5 slides and my extremely succinct presentation and Charles Clarke said straightaway 'That's very good I think that's exactly the sort of thing we should be doing'.

Apparently this was much to the surprise of the civil servants present who were armed with their arguments as to why this attempt to engage the profession would be disastrous: 'you could see all their faces dropping as they were all ready with why you should not touch this with a bargepole'.

English 21 was an invitation to join an apparently big-picture discussion about the nature of the subject in a changing world and Horner saw it as a way to directly address the fact that English teachers had historically often proved difficult. The best way to avoid problems with a new curriculum would be to involve the profession in the discussions. QCA commissioned a number of think pieces from experts in various areas of English to stimulate debate including Gunther Kress, Eve Bearne and Neil Mercer and there did seem to be the beginnings of a genuinely discursive and consultative process.

Despite the many years of having their views ignored or rejected, English teachers demonstrated their indefatigable desire to positively influence the future of the subject by engaging in the debate by replying directly with written submissions to the consultation or by attending one of a large number of conferences and events organised to respond to English 21. These included events coordinated by societies such as the Royal Society of Literature, the Royal Society of the Arts, subject and professional associations like the United Kingdom Literacy Association, LATE and the National Union of Teachers, and universities including Keele, Sheffield and King's College London. The results of the conversations at these events, and the responses to English 21, were published as *English 21: Playback, A National Conversation on the Future of English* (QCA, 2005). This document indeed felt genuinely discursive; it highlighted a new emphasis on 'creative and arts aspects of English' and the importance of 'engaging pupils' imagination and commitment' (p. 6), the need to connect the English classroom to 'writers, actors, playwrights, journalists and others whose business is words' (p. 6) and argued that 'renewal of the English curriculum can only be achieved through collaboration and joint action' (p. 7). Though this may have been rhetoric, it was at least refreshing to hear rhetoric of this nature, so different as it was to the sort of language coming from the National Strategies. Sue Horner remembered this conscious attempt to bring about collaboration:

English 21 was definitely an attempt to get people out of their oppositional mode and into a 'come on, can't we think how we might deal with what we're all facing?' … [T]he government wasn't particularly pernicious at the time … it was about what can we do collectively which accepts some of the things in the curriculum and then does something positive with them.

The result of English 21 and Playback was an apparently radically reshaped English curriculum, using what were known as the four 'C's – Competence, Creativity, Cultural Understanding and Critical Understanding – as a lens to frame the traditional areas of speaking and listening, reading and writing. Although for some this was not a radical rethink but simply a repackaging (views expressed in Gibbons (2007)), and some things – Shakespeare's now immutable place in the document – were unchanged, the tone of the new curriculum was certainly more encouraging of teachers to become curriculum makers. There was a push to engage in cultural visits and to work with writers in the classroom, and a distinct creative edge that had been missing from the previous curriculums and was in many ways at odds with much that had been brought in under the umbrella of the National Strategies. In fact, the National Curriculum and the English Framework seemed further apart than ever by 2008 – despite the fact that Gerry Swain, then director of the Secondary English Strategy, claimed that the Renewed Framework for English 'captures the content and spirit of the new opportunities for youngsters that are available in the National Curriculum' (ibid., p. 45).

In some senses at least, QCA seemed to be trying to reinvent themselves as the good guys in the eyes of English teachers, launching a curriculum that was certainly more widely welcomed than any since the original Cox report. For Horner, there was scope within QCA – or QCDA as it had become by then as part of another reshuffling of departments that saw the 'D' for development removed from the Training and Development Agency (TDA) – to offer an independent view. In this way the organisation was very different from the National Strategy that sat within the DfE: 'At QCA I was able to give my independent advice. It may have been totally ignored but I was able to do that. Once the Strategies got into the Department it was very, very difficult to oppose.'

Conclusion

As New Labour's time in office drew to its inevitable conclusion, there were in fact many reasons for English teachers to be optimistic, if they could retain some sense of positivity given two decades of constant change and still having to function within an increasingly oppressive accountability framework. The new curriculum offered possibilities and placed the concept of creativity into its rightful place as a central strand of English, the Strategy had run its course, and – somewhat unexpectedly – secretary of state Ed Balls announced in the autumn of 2008 that there would be no more national testing in English at Key Stage 3. Many media reports at the time put this decision down to the marking problems of that summer's tests (for example, *The Guardian* (2008)) but the government insisted that this was a decision following reports on problems with the tests and a strategic rethink of how schools' performance would be judged. There certainly had been a number of independent reports – notably the Institute for Public Policy's report *Assessment and Testing: Making Space for Teaching and Learning* (Brooks and Tough, 2006) – that had documented the damaging consequences, even if they were unintended, of the national testing regime, but those arguments were far from new. Such arguments were rehearsed by the parliamentary education select committee report (House of Commons Children, Schools and Families Committee, 2008). However, if problems with the nature and effects of the tests were behind the removal of tests at 14, then it is difficult to see why the policy was not extended to encompass the tests at the end of Key Stage 2, at age 11, where the arguments about teaching to the test and the narrowing of the curriculum were even more striking than at Key Stage 3 given the peculiar importance of those scores in the ranking of a primary school's effectiveness. Whatever the genuine reason for the abolition of tests at 14 (there may even have been a financial one, given that the announcement came as the last great financial crash was just sparking into life), freed from external assessment, there was the opportunity to reshape at least the Key Stage 3 curriculum. However, even before the removal of the SATs I had expressed doubts as to whether such conditions would genuinely result in new, creative English curricula in schools. I suggested (Gibbons, 2007) that the effects of nearly 20 years of central reform had created not only a culture where only that which was tested was valued, but had deprofessionalised English teachers to the extent that freedom would be meaningless. Rather tongue in cheek, I drew an analogy to Stockholm Syndrome – English teachers, I suggested, had so long been under the tyranny of central imposition and central testing, that these had become their raison d'être; without them they would question their existence. The result would be simply starting GCSE content earlier and earlier, for without external assessment the curriculum would lack purpose and there would be no way to motivate a generation of children brought up in the world of high-stakes tests. I was being intentionally provocative, and hoped the effect – on those that read it at least – would be an act of defiance, a demonstration that English teachers welcomed the return of some power and were able to exploit it to make a curriculum that worked in the interests of their children and encompassed a genuine vision for the subject. Sadly, at least if the evidence of subsequent Ofsted reports (2009; 2012) was to be believed, my attempts at satire proved instead to be prophetic.

Perhaps it is not fair to be cynical. English teachers, particularly heads of English, had, by the end of New Labour's years in office, endured over 20 years of centrally imposed change, and there would have been understandable reluctance amongst many to suddenly grasp this apparent new freedom. Perhaps, too, there was a suspicion that subsequent change would be on the horizon so a conservative, rather than a radical, approach to curriculum development was advisable. This indeed proved to be sensible. Barely had the new National Curriculum been put in place, and barely had English departments begun to live in the reality of a world without SATs, than a general election ushered in a new administration, and it became clear, all too quickly, that English would be again the subject at the forefront of the politicians' desires to reform children's experience.

Notes

1 This phrase was used by Blair in his second speech as leader of New Labour at the annual conference in Brighton. He urged delegates to 'sweep away the dogma – tough

on crime, tough on the causes of crime' (full speech available at http://www.britishp oliticalspeech.org/speech-archive.htm?speech=201 accessed on 16th June 2016).

2 Often misquoted as simply 'education, education, education', Blair's words did – significantly or not, depending on one's views – include the conjunction 'and'. In the speech, Blair asserted that 'the first wonder of the world is the mind of a child', but along with the Romantic rhetoric there was a clear agenda set out for standards-based reform that would see Britain rise from 35th in a world league of standards in education so that the British economy would be globally competitive (full speech available at http://www.britishpoliticalspeech.org/speech-archive.htm?speech=202 accessed 16th June 2016).

3 The new policies on literacy, including the requirement for there to be one hour a day of dedicated literacy teaching in each year of primary schooling, were outlined in one of the government's first white papers – *Excellence in Schools* (Department for Education and Employment, 1997). In what many teachers saw as an attack on comprehensive ideals, this white paper also stated that setting in secondary schools should be the norm.

4 In 1998, Blunkett vowed to resign if fewer than 80 per cent of pupils in Year 6 reached Level 4 in English. In the event the target was missed by 5 per cent, but by that point Blunkett – as has been the way with education secretaries in recent decades – had already moved to become Home Secretary. By 2002, the year of Blunkett's target, the education secretary was Estelle Morris, and though she did resign in October of that year it was not specifically a move to enact her predecessor's pledge.

5 The author can testify to the validity of this reference, having been in the audience for the speech at an annual conference of the National Association for Advisers in English in the early 2000s.

6 The level of prescription and the intensity of intervention into primary pedagogy is perhaps most evident in the primary *Grammar for Writing* materials, which had, in effect, a series of scripted lessons, with speech bubbles advising teachers what to say at various points of each lesson (see, for example Department for Education and Employment (2000)).

7 Comments from Sue Hackman come from an interview with the author. Sue Hackman had been a teacher of English, beginning her career in the 1970s. She went on to become English advisor for Surrey before moving into the Department for Education, initially on a one year 'job swap' as part of Tony Blair's Future Strategy team. From there she moved into the National Strategies, initially leading the English strand before ultimately taking the lead on Primary and Secondary National Strategies. On leaving the Strategies she became a chief advisor at the DfE. In a varied career, she was also chief examiner on the Key Stage 3 SATs pilot and devised a 100 per cent coursework A level in English, though this was never fully developed.

8 The process approach to writing, characterised by high levels of pupil choice over topic, narrative and autobiography as predominant forms, writing for real audiences, and drafting and redrafting of material is often linked to the work of Donald Graves, for example *Writing: Children and Teachers at Work* (1983). The approach, associated with a 'whole language' model for teaching reading and writing, was highly popular in primary and secondary English classrooms, and certainly sat naturally with the overall progressive, growth model of English.

9 Failure to make progress in attainment in the move from primary to secondary school, and even regressing, is a well-researched phenomenon in the area of transfer and transition with many causes suggested and remedies proposed (see, for example, Galton, Gray, and Ruddock, (2003)).

10 The National Strategies in fact used the acronym EPET – standing for expectations, progression, engage and transform – which they even had printed on T-shirts to distribute to local authority consultants during annual conferences.

11 David Crystal made this analogy in a speech to a NATE/Buckinghamshire Local Authority conference on grammar in February 2013.

12 The Extending Literacy Project (EXEL) was funded by Nuffield between 1992 and 2000. Its aim was to develop teaching strategies in the reading and writing of non-fiction texts. It is probably most known for the introduction of writing frames (see, for example, Lewis and Wray (1997)). Popular with some teachers, others saw these scaffolds for young writers as overly constraining.

13 The genre approach to the teaching of literacy grew in Australia from the 1980s. Significant thinkers in the field included Jim Martin, Gunther Kress and Frances Christie. Although the genre approach is not a single entity, it is fair to say that the roots of the work are in the systemic functional grammar work of Michael Halliday.

14 For Cope and Kalantzis it was evident that groups of children from certain socio-economic and cultural backgrounds were marginalised from the literacy culture of schools. It was these sorts of children for whom a genre-based approach had most effect, for it is these children 'who need explicit teaching more than students who seem destined for a comfortable ride into the genres and cultures of power' (Cope and Kalantzis, 1993b, p. 11).

15 The classic example of over-extension of research findings cited by critics of phonics-based approaches to the teaching of reading is the Clackmannanshire research study (Johnson and Watson, 2005). A small study – in terms of number of subjects – this was apparently taken as enough evidence to recommend the teaching of systematic synthetic phonics as the first and only way to teach reading when the National Curriculum was rewritten in 2010.

16 Assessing Pupils' Progress, which evolved from the earlier Monitoring Pupils' Progress, was a system of assessing students reading and writing in English at Key Stage 3. Separating areas of English into discrete assessment focuses, APP was, according to its authors (see QCA (2009)), intended as a tool to enhance formative assessment by highlighting particular areas of improvement for a student, though it has been noted (Marshall, 2011) that its use was often more obviously for the purposes of summative assessment. It was viewed as the future for assessment at Key Stage 3 following the removal of national testing and it continues to be used by some schools even after the demise of levels in the wake of the most recent National Curriculum review.

17 The spoken language briefly formed a compulsory element of English GCSE until the significant changes to the specifications brought in following the election of the coalition government in 2010. Although an unfamiliar field to many English teachers, there was generally a welcoming of this area of study, given that it explicitly recognised the particular features of different types of talk and encouraged interesting explorations of language in use. It offered, too, a much clearer sense of continuity for any students going on to study English Language A level.

References

Andrews, R., Torgerson, C., Beverton, S., Freeman, A., Locke, T., Low, G., ... Zhu, D. (2006). The Effect of Grammar Teaching on Writing Development. *British Educational Research Journal*, 32(1), pp. 39–55.

Anonymous. (2002). Bronwyn Jones's Diary: The Cage of Reason. *English and Media Magazine*, (46), pp. 4–5.

Beard, R. (1999). *The National Literacy Strategy: Review of Research and Other Related Evidence*. London: Department for Education and Employment.

Beard, R. (2000). Research and the National Literacy Strategy. *Oxford Review of Education*, 26(3), pp. 421–436.

Beard, R. (2011). Origins, Evaluations and Implications of the NLS. In Goodwyn, A. and Fuller, C. (Eds), *The Great Literacy Debate: A Critical Response to the Literacy Strategy and Framework for English*. Oxford: Routledge.

Brooks, R. and Tough, S. (2006). *Assessment and Testing: Making Space for Teaching and Learning*. London: Institute for Public Policy Research.

Bynner, J. and Parsons, S. (1997). *It Doesn't Get Any Better: The Impact of Poor Basic Skills on the Lives of 37 Year Olds, a Summary*. London: The Basic Skills Agency.

Bynner, J., McInstosh, S., Vignoles, A., Dearden, L., Reed, H. and Van Reenen, J. (2001). *Improving Adult Basic Skills: Benefits to the Individual and to Society*. London: Her Majesty's Stationery Office.

Cope, B. and Kalantzis, M. (Eds) (1993a). *The Powers of Literacy: A Genre Approach to the Teaching of Writing*. Michigan: University of Pittsburgh Press

Cope, B. and Kalantzis, M. (1993b). Introduction: How a Genre Approach to Literacy Can Transform the Way Writing is Taught. In Cope, B. and Kalantzis, M. (Eds), *The Powers of Literacy: A Genre Approach to the Teaching of Writing*. Michigan: University of Pittsburgh Press.

Department for Children, Schools and Families. (2008). The Renewed Framework for English. Available at http://www.nationalarchives.gov.uk/webarchive/.

Department for Education. (2011). The National Strategies 1997–2011: A brief summary of the impact and effectiveness of the National Strategies. Available at https://www.gov.uk/government/uploads/system/uploads/attachment_data/file/175408/DFE-00032-2011.pdf (accessed on 1st March 2016).

Department for Education and Employment. (1997). *Excellence in Schools*. London: Her Majesty's Stationery Office.

Department for Education and Employment. (1999). *English: The National Curriculum for England*. London: DfEE.

Department for Education and Employment. (2000). *The National Literacy Strategy: Grammar for Writing*. London: DfEE.

Department for Education and Employment. (2001a). *Framework for Teaching English: Years 7, 8 and 9*. London: DfEE.

Department for Education and Employment. (2001b). *English Department Training Material 2001*. London: DfEE.

Department for Education and Employment. (2001c). *Literacy Across the Curriculum Training Material*. London: DfEE.

Doecke, B., Homer, D. and Nixon, H. (Eds). (2003). *English Teachers at Work: Narratives, Counter Narratives and Arguments*. South Australia: Wakefield Press.

Ellis, V. (2011). What Happened to Teachers' Knowledge When They Played the 'Literacy Game'. In Goodwyn, A. and Fuller, C. (Eds), *The Great Literacy Debate: A Critical Response to the Literacy Strategy and Framework for English*. Oxford: Routledge.

Friedman, A., Galligan, H., Albano, C. and O'Connor, K. (2009). Teacher Subcultures of Democratic Practice Amidst the Oppression of Educational Reform. *The Journal of Educational Reform*, (10), pp. 249–276.

Galton, M., Gray, J. and Ruddock, J. (2003). *Transfers and Transitions in the Middle Years of Schooling (7–14): Continuities and Discontinuities in Learning*. Nottingham: Department for Education and Science.

Gibbons, S. (2004). English Framed? Reassessing the Strategy Approach. *English Drama Media*, (2), pp. 34–38.

Gibbons, S. (2007). New Orders, Old Tests: The New English Orders in the Key Stage 3 National Curriculum Review. *English Drama Media*, (7), pp. 10–12.

Gibbons, S. (2008). Can Less Be More? The Renewed Framework for English. *English Drama Media*, (11), pp. 45–48.

Gillborn, D. and Mirza, H. (2000). *Mapping Race, Class and Gender: A Synthesis of Research Evidence*. London: Ofsted.

Goodson, I. (2001). Social Histories of Education Change. *The Journal of Educational Change*, (1), pp. 46–63.

Goodwyn, A. (1992). Theoretical Models of English Teaching. *English in Education*, 26(3), pp. 4–10.

Goodwyn, A. (2003). 'We Teach English Not Literacy': 'Growth' Pedagogy Under Siege in England. In Doecke, B., Homer, D. and Nixon, H. (Eds), *English Teachers at Work: Narratives, Counter Narratives and Arguments*. South Australia: Wakefield Press.

Goodwyn, A. (2011). The Impact of the Framework for English. In Goodwyn, A. and Fuller, C. (Eds), *The Great Literacy Debate: A Critical Response to the Literacy Strategy and Framework for English*. Oxford: Routledge.

Graves, D. (1983). *Writing: Teachers and Children at Work*. New Hampshire: Heinemann Educational Books.

Harrison, C. (2002). *Key Stage 3 English: Roots and Research*. London: Department for Education and Skills.

Hilton, M. (2001). Writing Process and Progress: Where Do We Go from Here? *English in Education*, 35(1), pp. 4–11.

House of Commons Children, Schools and FamiliesCommittee. (2008). *Testing and Assessment: Third Report of Session 2007–08*. London: The Stationery Office.

Johnson, R. and Watson, J. (2005). The Effects of Synthetic Phonics Teaching on Reading and Spelling Attainment: A Seven Year Longitudinal Study. Available at http://www.gov.scot/resource/doc/36496/0023582.pdf (accessed on 29th June 2016).

Lewis, M. and Wray, D. (1997). *Writing Frames*. Reading: University of Reading, Reading and Language Information Centre.

Machin, S. and McNally, S. (2004). *The Literacy Hour*. London: Centre for the Economics of Education.

Mallard, C. (2003). Rollercoasters and Rioja. In Doecke, B., Homer, D. and Nixon, H. (Eds), *English Teachers at Work: Narratives, Counter Narratives and Arguments*. South Australia: Wakefield Press.

Marshall, B. (2011). *Testing English: Formative and Summative Approaches to English Assessment*. London: Continuum.

Ofsted. (1993). *Boys and English*. London: Department for Education Publications.

Ofsted. (2003a) *Yes He Can: Schools Where Boys Write Well*. London: Ofsted.

Ofsted. (2003b). *The Key Stage 3 Strategy: Evaluation of the Second Year*. London: Ofsted.

Ofsted. (2009). *English at the Crossroads: An Evaluation of English in Primary and Secondary Schools, 2005/08*. London: Ofsted.

Ofsted. (2012). *Moving English Forward: Action to Raise Standards in English*. London: Ofsted.

Ofsted. (2015). Key Stage 3: The Wasted Years? Available at https://www.gov.uk/government/uploads/system/uploads/attachment_data/file/459830/Key_Stage_3_the_wasted_years.pdf (accessed on 1st May 2016).

Qualifications and Curriculum Authority. (1998a). *Can Do Better: Raising Boys' Achievement in English*. London: QCA Publications.

Qualifications and Curriculum Authority. (1998b). *The Grammar Papers*. London: QCA Publications.

Qualifications and Curriculum Authority. (1999). *Not Whether But How*. London: QCA Publications.

Qualifications and Curriculum Authority. (2003). *New Perspectives on Spoken English in the Classroom*. London: QCA Publications.

Qualifications and Curriculum Authority. (2004). *Introducing the Grammar of Talk*. London: QCA Publications.

Qualifications and Curriculum Authority. (2005). *English 21: Playback, A National Conversation on the future of English*. London: QCA Publications.

Qualifications and Curriculum Authority. (2009). *Assessing Pupils' Progress: Assessment at the Heart of Learning*. London: Her Majesty's Stationery Office.

Stannard, J. and Huxford, L. (2007). *The Literacy Game: The Story of the National Literacy Strategy*. Oxford: Routledge.

The Guardian. (2008, 14th October). SATs for Fourteen Year Olds Are Scrapped. Available at http://www.theguardian.com/education/2008/oct/14/sats-scrapped (accessed on 22nd January 2016).

6

TO COALITION AND BEYOND: BACK TO THE FUTURE?

The 2010 general election in the United Kingdom brought to an end 13 years of New Labour administration, but the equivocal outcome meant for the first time since the Second World War a coalition government took office following a deal struck between the Conservatives and the Liberal Democrats. As by far the largest party in this uneasy marriage of some inconvenience, major cabinet posts went to Tory members of parliament, and the choice of Secretary of State for Education was deeply significant for English and its teachers. Michael Gove, who had been the shadow secretary in opposition, was an English graduate, and whilst he had no experience of the world of education of which to speak (other than his own very particular school and university background), he had deeply and steadfastly held views on the nature of the subject and what should be taught in schools. He expressed these views in ways that left no room for debate, and which very quickly ensured he was at odds with large parts of the English teaching community, a community who, in the wake of the abolition of Key Stage 3 testing, the demise of the Strategies and the more liberal 2008 National Curriculum, perhaps should have felt some optimism about the potential future for the subject.

Any such optimism about a newly progressive refashioning of English was short lived. In his first Conservative conference speech as minister Gove very deliberately singled out English for specific comment in a speech, typically for a new secretary of state, generally bemoaning the failures of the policies of his predecessors. His comments, both on the place of the literary canon and the teaching of grammar, evoked Tory rhetoric of the 1980s, but was even more uncompromising:

> We need to reform English. The great tradition of our literature – Dryden, Pope, Swift, Byron, Keats, Shelley, Austen, Dickens and Hardy – should be at the heart of school life. Our literature is the best in the world – it is every child's birthright and we should be proud to teach it in every school.[1]

In one sense the apparent pick and mix from the English literary canon was laughable and echoed the infamous abandoned Anthology for the 1993 SATs; it would be difficult to find an English teacher anywhere – even one steeped in the Leavisite tradition – who would genuinely advocate the teaching of Dryden to secondary school children any more so than it would have been possible to find advocates for Johnson as part of the reading diet for 14 year olds 20 years earlier. It was a list that in all probability matched Gove's own experience of the subject as an undergraduate at Oxford University's Lady Margaret Hall.

However, to English teachers – once the laughs had subsided – the messages in these words were worrying. The implications were clear – English teachers were ignoring these great writers – in itself a fallacy given that for many years pre-twentieth century work had been a statutory element of the curriculum. The reference to 'our literature' being the 'best' simultaneously undermined the position of texts from other cultures and traditions that had become a central part of the diet for children in English, and so crucial in the drive for an inclusive culture in increasingly multicultural, multiethnic classrooms. The seemingly simple phrase 'our literature' was far from unproblematic in these sorts of classrooms. With words like 'birthright' and 'proud', Gove suggested English teachers were denying children their entitlement and there was more than the suggestion that English as a subject had an explicit job to do in establishing a culture of Britishness, however that most elusive of terms might have been defined. In a post-9/11, post-7/7 world, with the so-called war on terror in full swing, it was not difficult to see how a particular view of Britishness, or probably more accurately Englishness, was to be promoted through the revised English curriculum. Whereas progressive thinkers, embracing a concept of globalisation, would see English as a critical part of pupils' education into a liberal, democratic world, there was a clear sense of little England in the words of the new secretary of state. If New Labour policies designed to improve attainment in English seemed very heavily led by arguments about global competitiveness and economic prosperity, Gove's words suggested an explicit ideological reshaping of the subject.

Not that Gove utterly ignored the functional aspects of English and their assumed relationship to economics whilst exclusively extolling the value of the literary canon. On so-called basic skills he was equally reminiscent of earlier Tory spokespeople: thousands of children – including some of our very brightest – leave school unable to compose a proper sentence, ignorant of basic grammar, incapable of writing a clear and accurate letter.

The accuracy of this statement was difficult to establish, but Gove's pronouncements on education, and on English specifically, were not noted for their rigorously evidence-informed nature. In his speech, Gove took the opportunity to score political points by suggesting that it was the outgoing New Labour government that had presided over changes to the system that meant, in essence, a student who could not write accurately would still be able to obtain a 'C' grade pass at GCSE. In many ways, though, it was simply a reworking of the assertion so oft repeated through the decades by those who sought to establish a more traditional writing curriculum, that is, that in some distant golden age when children were taught grammar properly they could all write accurately and this had been destroyed by progressive methods.

There is no doubt Gove's views were deeply set, passionately held, and presented in such a way as to leave little space for questions of evidence-based robustness. Typically, critics of progressive English have drawn on voices from the business community in their pronouncements on the lack of basic standards in the English of school leavers. It's highly likely Gove did too, albeit that there is evidence from the business sector that it is actually the aptitude and attitude of school leavers that are real concerns along with a deficit in other sorts of soft skills, like teamworking and self-management.[2] Gove seemed a man quite at ease with statements and positions that he would have known would put him at odds with large swathes of the English teaching community, in fact he seemed to relish such tension.

Swiftly, Gove announced that there would be a reform of the National Curriculum, meaning the 2008 four 'Cs' curriculum would be obsolete almost before it had arrived in schools. The notion that English departments would be empowered to reshape their curriculums around creativity was swiftly quashed. At Twyford School in West London in autumn 2010, Gove launched the curriculum review alongside the expert panel he had appointed to lead the work. The panel, made up of notable academics Tim Oates, Mary James, Andrew Pollard and Dylan Wiliam,[3] would, it was claimed, lead an evidenced-based review of the curriculum, notably drawing on the evidence of so-called high-performing jurisdictions to inform proposals. High performing would be defined by rankings in the international tables such as PISA and PIRLs, another indication of the increasing dominance of these statistical comparisons in the marketisation of education more generally.

At the launch, the secretary of state again made specific reference to the English curriculum, lamenting the supposed fact that the only novel read by 95 per cent of GCSE students was Steinbeck's *Of Mice and Men*. Quite where this statistic came from, and – even if it were true – quite what was so awful about a novel held dear by so many teachers and students, were points that were never clarified, but the message was abundantly clear; there would be major reform of the English curriculum, and of the assessment system, with a focus on terminal examinations and a heavy weighting for the accurate use of spelling, punctuation and grammar. Gove's style was deliberately antagonistic, a style that reached its zenith when branding a group of leading academics who voiced objections to some of his proposals for curriculum reform as representative of 'the blob', a group of ivory-towered educationalists whose prime concern was politically motivated self-interest not the education of children.[4]

In fact, there was undoubtedly sympathy from some English teachers for aspects of Gove's suggested reforms. There have always been, of course, English teachers who incline towards the Cambridge/Leavisite tradition of English as literature, and for this group the proposed stronger emphasis on the literary canon would have been welcomed. However, more widely than this, it was becoming clear that GCSE was becoming an almost constant treadmill of controlled conditions assessments, with so many discrete assessed elements that it may well have been true that for the majority of students a single prose text was their lot over a two year period. Controlled assessments had been brought in on the back of popular media condemnation of coursework and accusations of cheating; internet plagiarism or certain types of middle-class parents doing their children's work for them were blamed, and though both claims lacked real evidence the final nail in the GCSE coursework coffin was hammered home. With controlled assessments and a modular system where students could retake individual components of the examination at different sittings, trying to wring out extra marks to push themselves over grade borders, it was not surprising that assessment, rather than teaching and learning, dominated many students' experience of the GCSE course. With the stakes so high in terms of accountability measures, the pressure on schools and on English teachers to do all they could to improve the A*–C percentage (often focussing resources on the group of students on the C/D borderline) was all but irresistible but it certainly narrowed many students' experience of English.

The narrowing of reading at GCSE highlighted by Mr Gove in his speeches was not only bad in itself, it was woeful preparation for further study in English and a common cry from literature A-level teachers was that students not only didn't, but didn't know how to, read books. Perhaps there would be benefits to reshaping English at GCSE level as a linear course with terminal examinations, and accompanied by proposed changes in the way that schools' effectiveness would be judged through the Progress 8 measure there might be a greater focus on the attainment of all.[5]

However, even if one possible outcome of the proposed reforms would be to encourage more reading in Key Stage 4, the concern raised for many teachers by Gove's words was that this would have to be more reading of a certain kind, rather than experience of a broad range of texts.

The Expert Panel report

The Expert Panel reached its conclusions the following year, and in the event many teachers welcomed aspects of its report. The criticism of the levelling culture – with children more concerned to know what level they were at rather than what they could do and needed to do to improve – was a refreshing public acknowl-edgement of what the profession knew to be the consequence of the assessment and accountability framework. English teachers in particular welcomed the report's chapter on 'Oral Language and its Development in the National Curriculum'. Referencing the work of Robin Alexander and Neil Mercer, and even giving a nod to *The Bullock Report*, the chapter made a strong case for effective speaking and listening teaching across the curriculum, and for a strong presence for oracy in English:

> An overarching statement could be introduced covering the whole English Programme of Study. Discrete 'speaking' and 'listening' strands could be retained (as in the 2007 and 1999 National Curriculum documents), or such

provision could be reorganised into new combinations of 'speaking and writing' and 'reading and listening'. Such provision must draw on well-evidenced content elements and progression in oral development.

(Department for Education, 2011, p. 53)

The emphasis placed on the development of speaking and listening skills was even supported by the insistence that all teachers should receive professional development training on how to effectively promote oracy within their subject areas. It is doubtful that any teacher reading the document believed that resources would be channelled into this always-overlooked aspect of learning; even in the relative boom economic times of the late 1990s and early 2000s, whilst millions of pounds was directed into improving the teaching of writing and, to an extent, reading, scant financial support was made available to develop oracy. In the age of austerity, the notion that profession-wide in-service training to promote expertise in the teaching of speaking and listening would be delivered was inconceivable.

The new, new National Curriculum

The report of the Expert Panel made even more curious the final documents that emerged as the new National Curriculum for English. The disparity between the recommendations of the Expert Panel and the curriculum – most notably in English, but evident in other subject areas too – prompted controversy, with two members of the panel – Mary James and Andrew Pollard – tendering their resignations to Michael Gove. Whilst their concerns centred fundamentally on drafts of the primary curriculum, they expressed too their feeling that consultations with teachers and subject experts had been largely ignored in the writing of the curriculum (*Times Educational Supplement*, 2012). Mary James had met many of those with interests in the English curriculum, including a number of representatives from NATE, having conversations that appeared to be genuinely open and constructive,[6] but it was hard to see anything of the content of these discussions emerging in the draft orders that followed. It emerged that the English draft orders had been written by a single consultant contracted by the Department for Education: Janet Brennan, a former member of Her Majesty's Inspectorate and expert in the primary sector, particularly the teaching of phonics. According to the DfE, a group had drafted the maths programmes of study, but a single author worked on the English orders. There had apparently been consultation; noted individuals included Robin Alexander, Ron Carter, Neil Mercer and the then director of NATE, Ian McNeilly, all of whom would certainly not have recommended much of the content that appeared.

The Guardian ran a story that intimated the real author – of the primary orders at least – was in fact Ruth Miskin, an educational consultant with a company that publishes phonic reading schemes which, at the time, were endorsed by the government with schools purchasing the material receiving £3,000 in match funding (*The Guardian*, 2012b). That a commercial writer, whose work was officially endorsed by the Department, may have been responsible for laying out statutory requirement for schools should have been a national scandal. Certainly many questioned the political interventions into the curriculum, with Dominic Wyse, a professor of early years and primary education at London's Institute of Education, quoted as saying 'Ministers seem to be picking the advisers who fit the political story they want to tell, rather than ensuring a wide range of views'. Wyse called this 'undemocratic' and in stark contrast to approaches in, for example, Scotland (ibid.).

Whatever the provenance of the earliest drafts of the new curriculum, one does not need to be overly cynical to agree with Wyse's views given the content. Speaking and listening merely got a mention, and though oracy was instated to a certain extent in final drafts, beyond a general statement of importance the focus was on performance and presentation and debate, not on developing language – nor on the links between oracy and learning which had figured so clearly in the Expert Panel report. The priorities of the English curriculum lay elsewhere. The primary curriculum was lengthy and extremely detailed (Department for Education, 2013a). In Key Stage 1, the teaching of reading through phonics was the central message, with the much-questioned Clackmannanshire research used to promote the use of systematic synthetic phonics as the method that should be used first, fast and only in the teaching of reading. At Key Stage 2 a heavy emphasis on the teaching of grammar dominated, with lengthy appendices and glossaries detailing terms that children should know and be able to use – again apparently the common-sense view that explicit grammatical knowledge would improve writing ability had been taken on wholesale.

When they finally appeared (after some suggestion that there might not actually be a secondary curriculum), the Key Stage 3 and 4 orders for English were, perhaps most strikingly, unfeasibly slim in comparison to their primary counterparts (Department for Education 2013b, 2014). Where primary orders had page upon page of explicit content, the secondary orders, with the exception of statutory reading, set down few requirements. As one might have predicted, the reading specified was heavily weighted to the English literary canon, with Shakespeare, nineteenth century prose and so-called representative Romantic poetry all included. Scant attention was paid to speaking and listening, and whole areas of study – the media and moving image, multicultural texts, drama, etc. – were either completely ignored or mentioned only in passing. Creativity – one of the four Cs of the previous curriculum, and something central to the work of so many English teachers – was essentially written out; the one mention of the word came in the primary orders when, in referring to the long list of grammatical terms to be taught to pupils, the document stated, with no hint of irony, 'This is not intended to constrain or restrict teachers' creativity, but simply to provide the structure on which they can construct exciting lessons' (Department for Education, 2013a, p. 5). Not a single mention of children's creativity across the whole 5–16 curriculum in English, and no mention of the word at all across Key Stages 3 and 4. The times had changed.

There were some interesting developments, too, for example in the requirement for author study in Key Stage 3, where students would be expected to study two writers per year, looking across their oeuvre rather than at individual works. This, allied with the instruction to study complete texts, certainly suggested a curriculum that was intended to encourage teachers to work with their classes on a broader and deeper range of texts, rather than studying one class novel a year as may have become the orthodox approach.

In itself, a curriculum light on content need not be a bad thing, and the argument around the new orders was that this was minimum core content. This in many ways reflected the direction of travel in the United States, where moves had for some time been towards a core standards curriculum. Clearly the Expert Panel members had been influenced by these ideas, and particularly by the work of American educationalist E.D. Hirsh. Hirsh advocated a core-knowledge, rather than a core-standards, curriculum and the influence of this could be seen across the proposed primary and secondary programmes of study for English. The central rhetoric that accompanied the production of the new orders had it that English departments and English teachers would build their own rich, broad and balanced programme embracing the few statutory elements. This would include a notion of a local curriculum with content paying attention to the particular communities in which schools were sited. The national, local and individual school curriculum would together create an overall broad and balanced diet of English for children. And, of course, in a secondary landscape dominated by schools holding academy status, and a growing number of free schools, the number of schools actually legally bound to offer the National Curriculum was dwindling by the term; in a sense the term National Curriculum was effectively losing whatever meaning it may once have had. Of course, English teachers and heads of department with a vision for the subject would ensure that the curriculum diet for their students exceeded the national orders and embraced those aspects of the subject that have made it so rich and diverse over the previous decades.

Freedom in itself, however, is not an unequivocal positive. The new National Curriculum may well have offered freedom, but conditions are needed to exploit such freedoms. In the first instance an English teacher or a head of department needs the necessary knowledge and experience to know that there are different ways to structure the curriculum in English, and then they must have the confidence (and in an ideal world the support of senior school managers) to demonstrate this confidence in devising a curriculum that the freedom allows. Over 20 years of heavily led central intervention calls into question the extent to which English teachers have had the opportunity to learn about their subject and about the different ways there may be to construct it in the classroom. It's arguable that successive, increasingly direct intervention into English effectively deprofessionalised teachers, putting them in no position to exercise the new-found freedoms. In this context, within a framework of high-stakes assessment and heavy accountability, what happens in the classroom runs the risk of being overly led by examination specifications, and these would, of course, reflect only the content laid down as statutory in the orders. The combined forces of a narrow, traditional curriculum on which external examination specifications would be based, a profession unused to being given the invitation to exercise its professional autonomy and the fear of failure in a world of league tables and performance management, undoubtedly influenced English in classrooms in the coalition years.

The ambiguous nature of the concept of freedom could perhaps be seen most strikingly in the decision, following the Expert Panel report, to do away with National Curriculum assessment levels. In English the levels had become part of the discourse of many classrooms, and with Assessing Pupils' Progress used widely – ostensibly as a tool for formative assessment, but more often than not simply to tell children whether they were a 5a or a 5b – the numbers from 1–8 had a prominent role. When introduced, the levels had drawn concern from many quarters – with good reasons. English was not a linear subject in which pupils could progress seamlessly up a ladder, and the broad nature of the levels meant that it was difficult to reconcile genuine assessments of performance with the need of many senior school leaders to have the kind of data that showed clear progress over the course of a term, or an even shorter period of time.

Over the course of time, most English teachers had been able to accept a broad notion of best fit levels as originally imagined in Cox, used at infrequent intervals to give an overall picture of a pupil's performance in the subject. APP had meant a much more prescriptive approach, however, and this – within a context that demanded frequent numerical indications of consistent progress of individuals – had undoubtedly created the kind of unhelpful levelling culture described by the Expert Panel. Naïvely – and perhaps the Department for Education themselves were naïve at the time – it might have been assumed that removing the levels would lead to a collective sigh of relief amongst English teachers and perhaps, just as when the Key Stage 3 SATs were abolished, this was an instinctive response. The response soon turned from relief to a sense of what do we do now? How do we show progress without levels? How will children and their parents know how they are doing? How will we be able to demonstrate progress has been made across years and Key Stages? How will we be able to demonstrate to Ofsted that we are teaching effectively without such data? These sorts of questions often dominated conferences and professional development events at which spokespersons from the DfE would – it seemed expecting a positive response – declare that it was now in the hands of individual schools to determine their own policies in these areas.[7] Such had become the hegemony of levels it seemed many English teachers – a large number of whom knew nothing else and had in fact had their own progress as school children measured in this way – were frightened by their removal, rather than inspired by it. By no means meant by way of criticism, this was an inevitable – intended or unintended – consequence of the policymakers' decisions for the preceding decades. The reality was that removing levels wouldn't of itself change the culture – since the accountability culture of performance measures, inspection, and league tables was still very much in force.

What happened was predictable. Rather than devise innovative and creative new ways of assessing, and drawing on the kind of assessment for learning research which had only ever been given lip service in official policy that in effect reduced a complex, evidence-based approach to assessment to a set of handy classroom tools and strategies, many departments sought more pragmatic solutions – ones that would continue to satisfy the multiple purposes made of classroom assessments. For some English departments this simply meant continuing to use the outgoing level system and APP, supported by the argument that, after having used them for years, pupils, parents and teachers had an understanding of what they meant – however flawed they might be. Some departments looked to the publication of the new 9–1 GCSE grading system[8] and devised ways of employing this from the very beginning of Key Stage 3. Again, the logic in such an approach is clear; in the absence of Key Stage tests the whole of the secondary phase is leading inexorably to the final GCSE grade so why not start in Year 7? It does present the problem as to whether you judge something to be, say, a 4 on the new system in terms of what you would expect of a pupil of a particular age, or whether you apply the new grades absolutely (in which case most year 7 pupils would have the dispiriting experience of receiving what appear to be very poor grades). Some English departments genuinely developed their own systems, sometimes drawing on ideas like those from Carol Dweck on growth mindsets to construct assessment practices encouraging progress and motivation, rather than a culture of levelling and capping expectations.

Of course, when the government effectively deregulates an assessment system the space is left open to the market to stake its claim and there was no shortage of commercial assessment packages appearing for schools to purchase. Commercially available systems included those that allowed schools to assess children and assign them to a flight path that would map their expected progress over the years of secondary schooling; data would then be generated to show how many pupils were performing in line with, above or below their flight path. Although there were doubtless meaningful conversations held in English departments across the country, what was notable from commercial offerings, and from debates about whether to use existing levels, GCSE grades or another numerical system, was the absence of the really important questions about what is valued in English, and how that is best assessed – the sorts of fundamental questions about assessment that LATE had been raising 60 years before but which were no longer really part of any detectable discourse. The conversations were about what kind of grading system would be most effective in demonstrating progress and generating data. If that is the conversation, of course, then levels just get replaced by something else (which may as well be called levels) and there is no hope of a change in culture.

Finally, there was some official guidance of a sort offered when the government commission set up to explore the area of assessment without levels made its final report (Department for Education, 2015). This report was an informed and reasonable evaluation of the culture of levels and made recommendations to schools for developments given the new context. It warned of the dangers of bought-in assessment systems, made clear that Ofsted had no particularly favoured form of assessment system or data and clearly argued for genuine formative assessment to be at the heart of school practice. The government's response (Standards and Testing Agency, 2015) fully endorsed the findings of the commission, though – predictably – it was somewhat non-committal over those recommendations that might actually require some form of central resources for their implementation.

Perhaps inevitably, the absence of any national external testing at Key Stage 3 meant that the changes that would be wrought to GCSE English and English Literature would undoubtedly weigh heavy on English departments' decisions about both assessment and curriculum in this supposed new age of freedom.

Reforms to English examinations

Reform to external examinations has been a constant for English teachers since the introduction of the National Curriculum, with each revision of the orders necessitating a revision of examination specifications. Moves to reduce coursework and then replace it with controlled conditions assessments also altered the shape of the qualifications in English through the 1990s and first decade of the new millennium. However, along with the sweeping changes to curriculum brought in by Michael Gove's strong reformist agenda came the promise of even more significant shifts in the way students would be examined at ages 16 and 18. Initially it was suggested that there would be a return to something that looked like O-level examinations and that these would be taken by the academically able, with another qualification available for those not up to the challenge. It was a return to the two-tier system of O level and CSE that had been swept away, to many English teachers' delight, and a return to a linear structure with all assessment resting on the performance in terminal examinations. With the content defined by the new National Curriculum, and with the decision to remove speaking and listening as part of student assessment in English at GCSE, the status of oracy was threatened, and the study of spoken language, a recent innovation, would disappear. English, as ever, would be among the first subjects to undergo the reforms. And in a new way of measuring school performance, with only certain core subjects counting in terms of the scores, there was the additional threat that English literature would again become the subject of the elite, with many students missing this area of English after Key Stage 3.

As it transpired, these plans, deeply unpopular across the profession, were not enacted. According to reports (for example, *The Guardian* (2012a)), it was the influence of the Liberal Democrats within the coalition that mitigated the proposed changes. Instead of a return to O level, GCSEs were retained, albeit with a revised grading system with numbers replacing letters. There was movement on the position of English Literature, too. Initially this didn't feature as a subject that would count as one of the big five in the new so-called EBacc (not a qualification in its own right, but something earned through achieving five GCSEs at Grade C in English, maths and a small selection of other subjects). The position of English Literature at GCSE was perceived to be at risk; although English Language GCSE would include the assessment of reading, and so students would still be exposed to text, the emphasis was on basic skills so that engaging with full texts from across the range of literature might be unlikely. Schools might return English Literature to the status of an optional, elite subject with the inevitable consequence that fewer students would study it and that those students would probably be of higher ability, from certain backgrounds and in certain types of school. Robert Eaglestone, a professor of English Literature and contemporary thought at Royal Holloway, suggested the result could ultimately be to 'send English – the most popular school and university humanities subject – into a rapid decline of the sort that has devastated modern languages and classics' (*The Guardian*, 2013). Author of *Doing English* (2000), Eaglestone was not simply an ivory-towered academic seeking to shore up his own position – he had consistently demonstrated his commitment to effective English teaching in secondary schools. Writers and actors, including former children's laureate Michael Morpurgo, wrote a letter to the *Sunday Times* expressing their anger at the reforms to GCSE that they, too, felt would reduce the access of all children to literature (*The Sunday Times*, 2013).

In the face of this criticism, and perhaps understanding what was undoubtedly an unintended threat to the status of literature, Gove – for whom such a threat sat very uneasily with his unequivocal statements about access to the canon as a birthright – revamped the progress measures for schools to ensure a pupil's best score in either English language or English literature would count double in the league tables provided both qualifications had been taken. This move seemed to assure that the long-established tradition of the vast majority of pupils following an integrated language and literature course at Key Stage 4 would remain in place.

Whilst the worst excesses of Gove's original plans were not implemented, significant change was introduced for pupils beginning their GCSE and A-level studies in the autumn of 2015, change that would prove challenging for English teachers. With the focus on the English canon, texts which had become GCSE stalwarts like *Of Mice and Men* and *To Kill a Mockingbird* would no longer be teachable – or at least not assessable, which in many cases amounted to the same thing. A standalone speaking and listening assessment was introduced, all coursework and controlled conditions removed, and an emphasis on unseen texts appearing in the terminal examinations was established. Concurrent changes at post 16 meant a decoupling of AS and A2 assessments, presenting difficulties in course structure and cohort management.

Changes of course brought challenges, but there were opportunities presented by the new arrangements for those with the confidence and energy to take a glass-half-full approach. The relative lack of content across Key Stages 3 and 4 meant that it might be possible to take a genuinely holistic view and put in place a vision of what English might look like for pupils from 11–16. Given that success in the exams would mean that students would need to be confident users and interpreters of language in a variety of forms and adept at bringing skills of analysis to unseen material from across time periods, it would make sense to devise a rich and diverse curriculum, one not governed by a narrow set of texts to be studied but by a vision of the subject and of its transformative power for students. The knock-on effect ought to be much more experienced readers and writers prepared for the challenges of studying English at Key Stage 5. However, as has been said, that confidence to take advantage of freedom may be in short supply given recent history, and certainly national reports on the state of English in recent years have seen that the grip of accountability and assessment have exercised a control over English teachers and their schools from which they have had difficulty liberating themselves.

Ofsted views

The consequence of a slimmed-down curriculum and two decades of increasing accountability had the potential to severely influence students' experience of the subject. Whilst the rhetoric may have talked of freedom in a post-SATs, post-levels, academy-dominated sector, the reality for secondary-aged students was not, in many cases, a sudden reinvigoration of a broad, balanced and enriching vision of English – certainly not if the picture emerging from Ofsted's English survey reports was anything like accurate. Two key Ofsted survey reports, *English at the Crossroads* and *Moving English Forward,* appeared in 2009 and 2012 respectively (Ofsted, 2009, 2012). These reports, authored by the then-chief inspector for English, Phillip Jarrett, drew on data gathered from the normal cycle of school inspections and offered thoughts on the state of English. Whilst acknowledging much good practice, there were worrying trends emerging in these documents, particularly with respect to the early years of secondary schooling. *English at the Crossroads* pointed to the lack of direction and organisation pupils perceived in Key Stage 3 – for many it seemed 'a random sequence of activities' (Ofsted, 2009, p. 22). By 2012, *Moving English Forward* ironically posited that the removal of testing had the effect of increasing the sense of confusion around Key Stage 3, reinforcing the notion that a culture had been created in which meaning and worth is only really bestowed on that which is assessed and measured – the product of 20 years of heavy accountability. According to the report,

> Too many schools in the survey offered no rationale to students for Key Stage 3 work, referring instead constantly to the GCSE examinations to be taken at some point in the distant future. This led to a narrow concentration on the skills tested at GCSE, experience of a limited range of texts, and too few opportunities for creative work in English. Year 7 students were not all motivated by appeals to the needs of an examination to be taken in five years' time.
>
> *(Ofsted, 2012, p. 23)*

Ofsted's reports gave little reason to anticipate innovation as Gove's National Curriculum reforms began to take effect. If such blatantly traditionalist reforms had been introduced 20 years earlier it is tempting to believe there might have been some mass rejection from English teachers as there had been to the SATs. By 2014, the fragmentation of the school landscape and the seemingly irresistible juggernaut of standards-based reform supported by the accountability stranglehold had probably made the notion of collective action unthinkable. However, whilst individual English teachers and departments may have continued to pursue a more progressive, humane version of the subject by acting under the radar, Gove's reforms were seen by some as so regressive that they felt impelled to respond publicly. In doing so, there was evidence that groups of English teachers felt compelled to fight back and reclaim both their subject and their sense of professional self.

Swimming against the centralist tide – three projects

1 Looking for the Heart of English

As the implications of Conservative reforms to curriculum and assessment were becoming clear, three projects gave English teachers a chance to exercise some agency of their own. These very different projects all to some extent sought to re-engage the profession in practising and promoting the kinds of work that had been legislated to the point of extinction. One significant project, led by the one-time head of the English team at QCDA, Sue Horner, was a genuine attempt to activate a debate about what English should really look like. In some ways, this project had echoes of the one Horner had led at QCDA – the English 21 initiative that sought views of the profession in the run up to the 2008 curriculum rewrite. The Looking for the Heart of English campaign, though, was not backed by the department or in receipt of any funding, rather it began as a personal project for Horner who was frustrated with the direction English had taken, believing that 'I'd rather have no curriculum than the one we've got now'. Aware that her own name – somewhat unfairly perhaps – was not an unambiguously welcome one amongst English teachers, Horner left it out when launching the project. She built alliances with the National Association for Advisers in English (NAAE) and the United Kingdom Literacy Association (UKLA), which led to a number of teacher conferences where members of the profession were invited to discuss what they felt English should look like. A collection of noted academics, educationalists and leaders of arts and cultural institutions were invited to write short pieces on various aspects of the curriculum, and these were published in part as a stimulus for discussion at the teacher conferences – *Meeting High Expectations: Will the New Primary Curriculum Be Good Enough for Our Children?* (Looking for the Heart of English, 2012). For Horner it was a project 'borne out of a sense of thinking that English had reached a point as far as it could go' and she 'wanted people to lift their eyes a bit'. Doubtless, too, given the amount of work she had put in to the 2008 curriculum that barely had time to find its feet in schools, there was a sense of anger and injustice that served as a motivation.

The Looking for the Heart of English project did generate some significant interest, with successful conferences held at venues including The Globe Theatre in London, but it was not sustainable as a venture. As with voluntary subject associations, such as NATE, that has seen a dwindling membership over the course of the past 20 years, organisations and initiatives like Looking for the Heart of English that seek to engage English teachers and encourage a sense of professionalism and agency have the legacy of two decades of deprofessionalisation to contend with. In this climate, it is difficult to encourage English teachers to give of their own free time and resources given that they probably believe little else than that the powers that be will do whatever they like anyway. With the severe pressure exerted by the accountability framework, performance management and the demands of the school inspection framework it is surprising that any English teachers have the time or energy to devote to projects that may seem ultimately to have little chance of impact.

Looking for the Heart of English was a brave attempt to engage the English teaching profession as a group in a rethinking of the curriculum. In part it was protest at the existing proposals for curriculum and assessment, but its main thrust was the desire to encourage English teachers to think for themselves, propose alternatives, and regain a sense of professionalism and agency. Ultimately, although it had some impact, and doubtless did have a positive effect on some teachers' sense of self, it had a relatively brief lifespan. It was not, however, the only concerted effort to propose an alternative model of English in the wake of Gove's revisions to the programmes of study.

2 John Richmond's alternative vision for English

By 2013, John Richmond, central to the Vauxhall Manor Talk Workshop Project and co-author of *Becoming Our Own Experts*, might well have been enjoying a well-earned retirement. He had had a wide and varied career; from working in London schools he moved to be an advisory teacher for ILEA in the early years of the 1980s, in what he described as 'a tremendous and carefree time'. He was then a project officer on the National Writing Project, helping to develop curriculum in the way he was absolutely committed to: 'find the interesting work that is being done, help them to develop it, then disseminate the work that's been done'. Then, after working as an English adviser and being a key regional lead in the LINC project, he moved into educational television, first with Channel 4 and then, between 2004 and 2010, as commissioning editor for Teachers TV. When Teachers TV – widely viewed as making a positive contribution to the profession and its status – was shelved after first being moved online, Richmond briefly worked as a consultant in the US where a similar venture was being launched, funded by the Gates Foundation. He then planned to retire to spend his time both relaxing and writing.

However, in 2013, such was Richmond's disquiet at the new curriculum proposals, he felt compelled to return to the subject of English. In 2013 he joined forces with Mike Raleigh, a former English adviser and HMI, and Peter Dougill, who had co-founded Owen Education, an independent educational consultancy. Viewing the new curriculum as an almighty backward step – for Richmond 'we are no further forward than we were half a century ago' – they set about offering an alternative vision for English. Beginning with taking on the hegemony of systematic synthetic phonics, the initial project grew until it became the production of 'a complete alternative curriculum' which for Richmond was 'part personal therapy' but also the 'important job of restating things that are true'. Like many of his colleagues who had personal experiences of the kinds of advances made through progressive versions of English in the 1970s and 1980s, and had strong views about the value of bottom-up teacher collaboration and classroom-based enquiry, Richmond was alarmed at the ways in which versions of English were seemingly being swept away. Some have referred to 1988 as Year Zero, but the description probably more aptly applies to 2010; when the coalition came to power things changed overnight.

Owen Education collaborated with the United Kingdom Literacy Association to publish ten booklets on various areas of the curriculum, each offering a critique of the new National Curriculum and offering an alternative model. Whilst others were involved – Andrew Burn from the Institute of Education, for example, penned the booklet on Media – the bulk of the material was written by Richmond himself, a huge undertaking and evidence of his depth of feeling. The opening summary booklet (Richmond, Dougill and Raleigh, 2015) outlined seven key principles, offering a devoutly progressive approach to the teaching of English rooted in the interests and desires of the learner, centred on the making of meaning and championing diversity. Answering their own question as to why these principles have not been self-evident and uncontroversial, the authors suggest:

> The reason why they haven't has something to do with the history of the contest for control of the teaching of English, language and literacy in our schools and colleges over the last five decades. It also has to do with the fact that worthwhile professional knowledge can sometimes be forgotten, get lost, in the welter of new initiatives and changes of course – often politically driven – affecting the curriculum.
>
> *(ibid., p. 4)*

The booklets were well received at NATE and NAAE conferences, and Richmond has said he has experienced gratitude from teachers who have expressed the thought that they hadn't realised that they 'could do it a different way'.

3 A new National Writing Project

Another example of a desire to return a sense of agency and professionalism to English teachers in the face of the decades of centralised policy and consequent deprofessionalisation came in the guise of a newly developed National Writing Project. This was not, however, a rebirth of the project of the same name from the 1980s, and nor was it a direct consequence of work done by Richard Andrews in the final years of the New Labour administration. In 2008, funded by CfBT, Richard Andrews, then of the London Institute for Education, produced *The Case for a National Writing Project* (Andrews, 2008). The document, which included a review of relevant research literature from 1974 and interviews with experts including the emeritus director of the National Writing Project, USA, Richard Sterling, gave a compelling argument for the development of a new writing project in the United Kingdom, which would develop teachers' expertise in writing teaching pedagogy, in part through teachers developing their own writing. This approach was central to the US project which had begun in the Bay Area in 1974 and grown to be a federally funded programme running in 200 sites across all states in the country. *The Case for a National Writing Project* suggested designing a project that would see teachers work in collaboration with each other and with colleagues from higher education institutions, which would involve an intensive ten-day summer institute and which would contribute to continuing professional development and allow those involved to obtain academic qualifications up to masters level. Two possible models for a pilot study were proposed and costed.

Sadly the Department for Children, Schools and Families took the decision not to fund the proposed pilot studies, and so a centrally funded national writing project failed to emerge from Andrews' work. The proposals came as the effects of the financial crisis were beginning to bite and in that context public money was unlikely to be forthcoming for a project that wasn't offering quick wins. The direct impact on standards – in the discourse of policymakers this meant writing levels as evidenced through external testing – of a project like this would not be felt immediately. The sort of writing project Andrews was advocating was one that would take time and investment before yielding the sorts of results that a minister might want; time and money were luxuries the government was rapidly running short on.

Andrews' work, however, did have the effect of sparking into life the ideas of two interested parties – Simon Wrigley, a local authority English adviser and past-chair of NATE, and Jeni Smith, from the University of East Anglia. Wrigley and Smith set up their own National Writing Project in 2009. With some support from NATE, Buckinghamshire local authority and UEA, and with Richard Andrews on board as a consultant for the first two years of the project, Wrigley and Smith set about the ambitious task of developing teachers' writers groups. Smith knew the value of teachers being writers through her work with new entrants to the profession at East Anglia, and for Wrigley the decision to kick start a project was the conclusion to work that had begun in 1992 when, at NATE national conference, he had taken part in a commission led by James Britton and Nancy Martin which, whilst focused on writing, had at its heart the notion of teachers as creative individuals with agency. Through his career as a classroom teacher, local authority adviser and chair of NATE, Wrigley had witnessed, in his view, systems of curriculum and assessment that were progressively 'inhibiting teachers' creative freedom', and for a man who joined teaching 'to be a professional, not merely an operative' the formation of the writing project – though he was of course interested in the process of writing – was as much about reinvigorating a sense of professionalism and agency amongst teachers as it was about promoting any particular pedagogy. He didn't want the writing project to become some form of CPD, recommending a model for teaching writing; he was interested not in 'helping teachers do the job they'd been asked to do', rather he was interested in 'helping teachers do the job they wanted to do'. For Wrigley this necessarily would involve teachers being creative – producers of ideas rather than receivers and communicators of the ideas of others.

Modelled on the Bay Area Project in the States, Wrigley and Smith's project's five key principles are stated on their website as 'teachers as agents of reform; professional development through collaboration; sustained partnership in research, analysis and experience; free and structured approaches in teaching writing; leading teachers collecting and disseminating evidence of effective practice' (National Writing Project, 2016). It's no accident that agency and professional development are forefronted in the principles – the projects' founders are passionate that this is a bottom-up initiative. Teachers involved in the project join local writing groups and meet at evenings and weekends in a variety of settings to write and develop their own writing. The argument of the project is that, by developing themselves as writers, and by developing a clearer understanding of the challenges of writing and what it means to be an effective writer, there will be a direct impact on the work of those involved as teachers of writing in the classroom. Teachers involved in the project do so not for any extrinsic reward – they are giving up their own time but do so not only to develop but to regain a sense of agency in an era of deprofessionalisation. It is this that makes the project so striking, and the fact that it is not really funded, and that no teachers involved are rewarded in any material sense, makes it all the more laudable that by 2016 the National Writing Project had managed to establish 24 writing groups from North Wales to Nottingham and from Cardiff to Camden. Some of these groups have more explicit focus on the pedagogy of writing; others are much more concerned with enabling teachers to engage in their own writing in the context of supportive peers. There is not a one-size-fits-all model but the groups share some central premises; for Wrigley these are that the writing process needs to be opened up, rather than made formulaic and commercial, and that – essentially – learning should come through creativity.

In 2015, Smith and Wrigley's book of the project, *Introducing Teachers' Writing Groups: Exploring the Theory and Practice,* offered an account of their experience in a publication that, according to its authors, 'emphasises the central importance of teacher agency. It is important to us that teachers' voices are very present throughout this book, through their words and through their actions' (National Writing Project, 2016). The book provides a historical context and theoretical framework for the approach of the project and includes practical suggestions and examples of writing and reflections from teachers involved in the various groups. With little or no funding, and reliant as it is on teachers' own energies and initiative when their day jobs are increasingly pressured and time consuming, it is perhaps over optimistic to imagine that the national writing project will ever be truly that. However, it is an important initiative in many ways. It does offer an alternative view of writing and its teaching to that proposed through curriculum- and National Strategy-recommended approaches, a wholly more progressive approach to writing pedagogy – simultaneously child centred but foregrounding the importance of the teacher as a writer herself. For this it should be praised. Beyond this, however, its existence says something to show that there are still many English teachers, who despite the decades of central intervention and despite the context of huge reform to curriculum and examinations in the most recent years of

Conservative administration, retain a sense that English is a subject that should be in their hands and developed in the best interests of the children they teach. These English teachers retain a spirit of collaboration and collective enterprise that allows them to see beyond the latest set of directives and specifications and take themselves as professionals and the craft of English teaching as something that cannot be reduced to a set of strategies. They are pursuing the kind of personal and professional development that typified the early work of subject associations like LATE, when English teachers genuinely felt that the subject needed to be changed, and they genuinely felt they had the power to change it for the better for their children. National change may not be on the agenda for those in the National Writing Project, but the project's work is testimony to the indomitable spirit of so many English teachers who continue to strive to create a humane, inclusive and engaging English experience for children.

A final word on the grammar question

Looking for the Heart of English, Richmond's alternative curriculum proposals and the National Writing Project shared one basic common denominator: they were all projects that benefited barely at all from any external funding, being driven by colleagues volunteering time and perhaps seeking to cover their costs through publications. This is perhaps indicative of the fact that it has been increasingly difficult for those wishing to research and advance English teaching to access any public or research funding – witness the failure of Andrews' proposals for a writing project to reach even a pilot phase via national funding. Historically, projects like the Development of Writing Abilities accessed government funding; LINC and the Writing and Oracy projects, which were essentially action-based research initiatives, similarly benefited from access to the public purse. However, in the two decades since the introduction of the National Curriculum, funding for English was predominantly spent on the implementation of reform. And whereas it has always been easier for those working in other subject areas – particularly maths and science subjects – to attract funding (either from government or from bodies like Royal Institutes or research funding councils) to pursue development projects, English has not been an area that has offered such rich opportunities.

One notable exception to this, a research project in English that attracted a relatively large grant of nearly £160,000 from the Economic and Social Research Council (ESRC), was The Production of School English, a project led by Professor Gunther Kress from the London Institute of Education between 2000 and 2003. Essentially this project aimed to explore the actuality of what happens in English inurban schools, against the context of what is supposed to happen in terms of curriculum and assessment policy, that is to say the researchers were interested in seeing how central policy was mediated at local level and what the reality of English was for students, specifically schools in challenging urban areas. It was not, in essence, a project that involved teachers in developing their practice, rather it was an analysis of what was happening in the context of increasing central intervention; thus its messages were potentially more directed towards policy-makers than at teachers. The fact that it attracted such a high level of funding, however, was significant, although it may be that the attraction for the funders was as much in the way that the researchers claimed to be innovative in their research design – developing a so-called 'multimodal' research strategy – as it was an interest in English as a subject itself. *English in Urban Classrooms* (Kress et al., 2003), the publication arising from the project, was certainly an interesting read, but in its central findings about the influence of external pressures on the experience of English for students probably didn't tell teachers a huge amount that, if they were honest, they weren't already aware of.

The Production of School English apart, research funding in English has always been difficult to secure; however, if there ever was one area of English that might attract money, one area where repeated research had tried and failed to show sig-nificant impact, but one area where evidence of such impact might be highly prized, then it was the area of grammar. Thus in some ways it was unsurprising that *Grammar for Writing? The Impact of Contextualised Grammar on Pupils' Writing and Pupils' Metalinguistic Understanding*, a project coordinated by Debra Myhill from the University of Exeter, managed to secure funding, but it was remarkable that it was able to attract almost a quarter of a million pounds – a highly unusual sum to be granted by a research council to a project concerning the teaching of English.

Grammar for Writing was a project that addressed the perennial question for English teachers – does the explicit teaching of grammar and its associated termi-nology have a positive impact on the quality of pupils' writing. The common-sense view, and one that supported those who argued for greater emphasis on grammar in the curriculum, was that it did, but evidence (see, for example, Andrews (2005)) had stubbornly refused to support such assertions. There had been some slight evidence of the effect of sentence combination work, but Myhill's project set about systematically trying to establish what sorts of explicit grammar teaching might, or might not, improve writing. The project leaders produced classroom resources in the forms of schemes of work that included explicit teaching of grammatical forms, functions and terminology within the context of units around, for example, the writing of argument. English teachers – whose own linguistic knowledge was tested as part of the research design – taught these units to some classes, whilst others were taught similar units but without the explicit focus on grammar; these were the control classes. Writing tests – carried out by Cambridge Assessment – before and after teaching, along with observation data and interviews with pupils and teachers, provided the project's data sets.

In fact, for Myhill herself, the title of the project was not really an adequate description of the content and aims of the work. It was a title in some ways forced upon the project at the bid stage, emerging from the work within the National Strategies on writing. Rather than simply grammar for writing, for Myhill 'the fundamental aspect of the work is about developing knowledge about language' and 'helping learners find out how that knowledge is working'. The fact that this was not, for its organisers, purely a grammar project was reflected in the question mark used in the title of the original bid; quite clearly, however, there would have been little chance of any project titled 'knowledge about language' receiving funding given the history of that phrase. Theoretically the project drew heavily on the work of Halliday – as the National Literacy Strategy had clearly done – although there was no real explicit laying out of the systemic functional model of grammar to teachers involved – and certainly not to the classes taught.

The findings of the project were disseminated widely in publications (see, for example, Myhill, Lines, Watson and Jones (2012)) and at national and international English conferences, with Myhill speaking at the annual conferences of NATE, NAAE and UKLA as well as presenting at IFTE in 2011. Follow-up funding meant that the units of work developed could be made available to all members of NATE free of charge and further work included a tie in with one of the major examination boards to produce linked material to support the teaching of writing in the GCSE specification. Further work with primary-aged children has followed, and in some places teachers involved had taken ownership of the work and used it to lead development sessions for colleagues, thus enabling the work to spread far beyond those schools and teachers that were originally participants.

The research did indicate that explicit teaching of grammar, within the context of meaningful work, did statistically speaking have a positive impact on pupils' writing, but it's fair to say that the findings were far from unequivocal; they certainly didn't strongly support a case for those who wished to argue for explicit grammar teaching across the board. Teachers' own knowledge was key, and where there were positive impacts these tended to be with those who were already more able writers, with the potential for negative impact on those who may have been struggling already (Myhill, Jones and Bailey, 2011). Myhill has been keen not to construct the issue of teacher knowledge within the framework of a deficit model – the aim of those who worked on the project was to develop teacher expertise in a supportive context.

When reflecting on the outcomes for more and less able writers, Myhill pointed to the fact that, in the control group, the more able writers didn't improve at all – suggesting that they were simply coasting – whereas in the intervention groups both able and less able writers improved; the issue with the less able writers, Myhill thought, was that 'weaker writers are more likely to be confused by too much terminology'. For the architects of the project the knowledge of terminology was not actually that important – though they were clear such terminology was simply the equivalent of literary criticism terms that teachers generally were utterly comfortable with. The terminology, if used, was there to talk about real texts and children's writing in ways that helped learners understand what language was doing – in fact Myhill claimed that in effect the project was more about developing a pedagogy for writing than a knowledge of grammar, and that such a pedagogy was wholly compatible with ideas about dialogic teaching and talk for learning.

Interestingly, when asked about the success of the project Myhill suggested that part of the problem was that the question about grammar teaching has always been 'does it work?', which is just too big a question. The fact that the project used controlled groups did produce positive results that stacked up statistically, meant that one could claim that there was 'firm evidence to say teaching writing using this approach can have a positive effect on children's writing', but not that 'the answer to the question "does teaching grammar in the context of writing improve writing?" is yes'. When asked about the link between being taught explicit grammar and knowing the terminology, Myhill was clear:

> The connection between knowing grammar and knowing and identifying terms and becoming a better writer ... that's what I think is the real problem. There's no connection between the two at all. And never has been. Being able to name a noun doesn't make you a better writer.

Notwithstanding the somewhat equivocal nature of the findings, and despite her views that chimed with all previous evidence about links between grammar knowledge and writing quality, unsurprisingly the DfE were keen to engage Myhill in the writing of the grammar elements of the new National Curriculum. One assumes so that they could present the model of grammar therein as being based on research, and hope to convince teachers that the extraordinarily heavy emphasis on grammatical terminology across Key Stage 2 and 3 was linked to improvement in writing. Myhill was involved in the team that wrote the National Curriculum grammar annexes, with their list of terms and definitions. She was perhaps, at best, ambivalent when asked her views on the document – a lot of the content had been predetermined and 'it wasn't where I would have started' – and unequivocal in her views on the Year 6 grammar test, which 'doesn't tell us any-thing about children as writers .... As a substitute for an assessment of writing it's a completely flawed assessment.'

Conclusion

The *Grammar for Writing* project is an unusual outlier in that it was a project, involving English teachers, that did attract significant external funding and threatened, at least, to have direct impact on policy. The volunteer projects – Looking for the Heart of English, Richmond's alternative curriculum and the National Writing Project – are unlikely in themselves to change policy. They were and are all significant projects in their own ways, however. Each had at its centre the notion that there exists a way of teaching English that is fundamentally progressive and that sees the absolute centre of the curriculum to be the child, not the language, nor the literature, nor the teacher – the core notion that English is about learning, not about teaching. In its broadest sense this is a continuation of the model of English that emerged in the post-war years, gained traction after Dartmouth, rose to prominence in the 1970s and 1980s and has – to a greater or lesser extent – been under assault for the decades of central policy intervention beginning in 1988. None of the projects advocated a simple return to the past – the golden-age rhetoric is best left to those on the right who evoke it, erroneously, in seeking to advocate a back-to-basics curriculum. Each project, however, in varying degrees acknowledged that there is a huge risk to the subject if advances from the past are simply erased. New English teachers need of course to forge their own way, and they have to deal with the particular circumstances and contexts in which they find themselves. They need to find new solutions – sometimes to new problems, sometimes to longstanding ones. As they do this, though, the architects of these projects, and the teachers that engaged with them, would advocate an understanding of that English progressive pedagogy that did so much to improve children's experience. And each of these projects fundamentally believes that English teachers are professionals, and that they should have agency in developing their curricula and assessment systems that best serve the needs of the children they teach. The severity of policymakers' assault on progressive English teaching, particularly in the Conservative attempts to impose such a traditional curriculum, served as a catalyst for these projects; the fight, for some at least, continues.

In reality it is difficult not to believe that a great deal of what goes on in English classrooms has been changed quite radically over the course of the years since the introduction of the first National Curriculum. Although it may be an idiotic pursuit to generalize, what follows is not, I believe, an inaccurate representation of much of what passes for secondary school English in the second decade of the twenty-first century. Learning objectives or learning outcomes – in one way or another – frame the lesson. These may be differentiated, and they may be closely or more loosely linked explicitly to one form of national or local assessment criteria or another. Speaking and listening, although undoubtedly still happening, is at the margins. It is seldom, unless part of a single standalone assessment for GCSE, the focus of the lesson – talk is rather used as a vehicle to transport pupils to the written work that is to be produced. Talk is a tool for the production of other types of learning, rather than viewed as learning in and of itself. Drama may still take place, but again this is rarely seen as an end in itself, rather as a precursor to writing or demonstration of comprehension. When writing occurs in the classroom, this is heavily prescribed by the teacher in terms of form and content, little time if any is given to free, creative writing or for pupils to choose their own topic. Though there may be attempts made to talk about audience, these are rarely real audiences and the focus is predominantly on purpose, and even more than that on the form that will enact that purpose. A model of writing instruction that is genre based prevails, with some ideas from a grammar for writing approach scaffolding pupils' efforts to write in a given form by a focus on particular types of word, phrase or rhetorical construction that a given form is seen to employ. Assessment criteria variously describe the types of forms and structures that typify achievement at incremental levels.

In the sphere of reading, there may be some time given to independent reading and individual choice, and pupils may occasionally be encouraged to offer a genuine personal response to a poem or story, but predominantly the text choice is the teacher's, governed ultimately by what are seen to be the demands of a GCSE examination, and responses to reading are highly controlled. Where there is personal response invited, this is ultimately sacrificed in the pursuit of a framed response governed by a point, evidence, explanation (PEE) model of one form or another that constricts pupils and insists – even implicitly – that they are searching for the right answer and that there is not only a right answer, there is, too, a correct way to express this. A successful lesson ends with a plenary in which pupils are invited to confirm they have indeed met the preformed objectives; that they may have learned other things – arguably more interesting or valuable – does not form part of the discourse. Pupils who haven't met the objective may be asked to say what they found difficult, or what they didn't get, and this may inform future work – but that work will be a return to ensure they do get it. There's not an invitation to explore what other things pupils might have wanted to discuss about a topic or text, or what else they might like to explore. The lesson is part of a sequence, and the sequence needs to be followed to ensure things are covered.

This is, as stated, a generalisation but it is one supported by observations of many hundreds of lessons, and one supported – to a large extent at least – by Ofsted's more extensive dataset.[9] It is not meant as a criticism of a teacher or teachers, more an indictment of what English has become for many teachers given the history of the past 30 years, and the effect that centralisation has had even on those who know in their hearts that there are preferable alternatives. This is sad for those teachers who have the ability and creativity to teach English in other ways; it is sadder still for those many who still have somewhere in their professional compass a sense that the most admirable model of the subject is a progressive, growth-inspired, child-centred model; but it is saddest for the pupils, whose experience of learning in English means that it seldom generates the passion and excitement that traditionally made it consistently one of the most enjoyable subjects on the curriculum for children.

However, in an age of academisation and free schools where, in theory, there is a notional freedom from the National Curriculum, teacher-driven projects such as NATE's National Writing Project and the Looking for the Heart of English initiative offer support for English teachers looking for another way and suggest that there are still significant numbers of English teachers – both new and experienced – who feel that the model of the subject that has evolved in the past 30 years, though at times they may enact elements of it, is far from satisfactory – there is, or should be, another way. There are certainly schools that are trying to forge different paths.[10] There will be, I hope, English teachers who read the description of practice above and feel that it is entirely unrepresentative of the kinds of creative work that they do. In all honesty, I'd be delighted if the response to the description were an indignant anger, rather than an acceptance, albeit sheepishly, of some truth. The progressive, humane, growth-based model of English that became so influential in England's schools has obviously not died, but it has been pushed aside, and its advocates have become, again, the profession's mavericks, who either practise subversively to avoid scrutiny or who involve themselves in projects outside of the mainstream of the kinds of professional development that find ways to manage and negotiate the system, rather than kick against it. They are the sorts of teachers who still regularly give their free time to attend subject association conferences and meetings and who try to develop and spread good practice through these professional networks.

Such activity, and such teachers, will not change the views of policymakers; they may even be seen as irrelevant sideshows by those who sit in DfE buildings, or perhaps less benignly as relics of the past or classroom-based examples of 'the blob' – the left-leaning enemies of promise. That is not, however, to deny the existence of such activities and such teachers, which do suggest that significant numbers of English teachers, despite hostile contexts, subscribe to a version of English, and a sense of themselves, that transcend political rhetoric.

The story of the age of intervention is one that has seen wave after wave of central intervention into curriculum, assessment and pedagogy in English. The policymakers have become smarter, or more ruthless, or both, in their methods – reducing to a minimum the profession's involvement in devising policy whilst making claims to consult, exploiting evidence to support dubious claims for the effectiveness of interventions, and publicly casting those that resist reform as unprofessional, self-interested, even immoral. The stakes have been raised and the deregulation of the school system has made teachers more vulnerable and thus less able to resist, even when offered supposed freedoms. Yet there are still English departments and teachers who have failed to fall into line and who remain stubbornly resolute in the face of the politicians. They suggest that English has a future, and one that can potentially learn from, and build upon, the best of the past.

Notes

1 For a full text of the speech – a wide ranging attack on the educational record of the former New Labour government and the so-called educational ideologues (that is to say educational academics and researchers) who had seen 'children condemned to a prison house of ignorance' – see http://conservative-speeches.sayit.mysociety.org/speech/601441 accessed on 16th June 2016.

2 The Confederation of British Industries (CBI) publishes an annual education and skills survey which offers a perspective on what business owners consider to be areas of concern with respect to the qualities of school leavers employed by their companies. Although these reports do indeed raise concern about literacy levels amongst school leavers, other skills emerge as, arguably, equally important. The 2011 survey, for example, in the year after the formation of the coalition government, pointed, even amongst graduates, to 'alarming weaknesses in skills around teamworking ... and problem-solving' (CBI, 2011, p. 6).

3 The expert panel was made up of an interesting team of very different backgrounds: Tim Oates was a career-long educational researcher who worked for Cambridge Assessment, having previously been head of research at QCA; Andrew Pollard had a background in the sociology of education and had written widely on reflective teaching; Mary James had been Deputy Director of the European Social Research Council's United Kingdom-wide Teaching and Learning Research Programme and had been Director of the TLRP's Learning to Learn project; Dylan Wiliam, originally a maths teacher, was at the heart of the work that came from King's College London on assessment for learning and by 2010 was Deputy Director of the Institute of Education. Although Mary James had taught English in schools for a short while, this was not her

specialist discipline and there was some disquiet amongst sections of the English teaching community as to how far the expert panel had the expertise to make informed decisions about the subject.

4   For a particularly vehement attack on 'the blob', or alternatively those he called 'enemies of promise', see Gove's article which brings university academics, trades unions and teachers into this group (MailOnline, 2013).

5   The Progress 8 measure is a measure of a student's progress across subjects from Key Stage 2 to Key Stage 4. Previously the key marker in school league tables was the measure of how many students in a school attained A*–C in five subjects, including English and maths. One intended consequence of the introduction of Progress 8 was to discourage schools from targeting their energies on only those students perceived to be around the C/D borderline.

6   I myself met Mary James as part of the review process along with then-NATE Director Ian McNeilly.

7   Speaking at a number of day conferences organised by independent professional development companies through 2012–2014, it was notable how many of the questions from the panel directed at DfE representatives sought explicit guidance on what to do in the absence of levels.

8   The new grading system to be introduced into English GCSE from 2015 would award a number rather than a grade – 9 being the highest, 1 the lowest. By replacing the A*–G system this effectively allows for the standard perceived to be a pass to be raised.

9   Ofsted's two triennial reports, *English at the Crossroads* (Ofsted, 2009) and *Moving EnglishForward* (Ofsted, 2012), as well as pointing to a lack of focus at Key Stage 3, also highlighted the way in which point, evidence, explanation responses to literature were dominating some students' experience of writing from the very beginning of secondary school. *Moving English On* included a section on common myths about good teaching, pointing out that relentless changes of activity, constant review of learning and the lack of time for independent work – amongst other things – were not things that Ofsted wanted to see. To what extent Ofsted have given mixed messages, or to what extent senior school leaders have misrepresented Ofsted – using them as the 'bogeyman' to enforce consistent practice – is unclear. The unequivocal impression gained from reading the reports – and, incidentally, the earlier report on poetry (Ofsted, 2007) – is that many English teachers reveal practice that seems to be not governed by their own sense of what is principled English teaching, or by a sense of what their learners need, rather it is overly influenced by assessment demands and the impact of the suffocating accountability framework (although the inspectorate would not phrase it in such stark terms, of course).

10   A notable example would be School 21, a free school in East London that has designed its curriculum and assessment around oracy, implementing a model called Voice 21, developed with experts such as Neil Mercer of Cambridge University. The school (according to its website, https://school21.org.uk/, accessed 1st June 2016) aims to give speaking the same status as reading, writing and maths. It's debatable whether only a free school could have the confidence to adopt such an innovative approach; there are attempts to roll out the Voice 21 curriculum and assessment frameworks but it will be interesting to see how far they gain traction in the wider secondary system that remains, all evidence would suggest, in thrall to the primacy of written assessments within the stringent accountability context.

References

Andrews, R. (2005). Knowledge About the Teaching of (Sentence) Grammar: The State of Play. *English Teaching Practice and Critique*, 4(3), pp. 69–76.

Andrews, R. (2008). *The Case for a National Writing Project*. Reading: CfBT Education Trust.

Confederation of British Industries. (2011). *Building for Growth: Business Priorities for Education and Skills*. London: CBI.

Department for Education. (2011). The Framework for the National Curriculum: A Report by the Expert Panel for the National Curriculum Review. Available at https://www.gov.uk/government/uploads/system/uploads/attachment_data/file/175439/NCR-Expert_Panel_Report.pdf (accessed on 12th June 2016).

Department for Education. (2013a). The National Curriculum in England: Key Stages 1 and 2 Framework Document. Available at https://www.gov.uk/government/uploads/system/uploads/attachment_data/file/425601/PRIMARY_national_curriculum.pdf (accessed on 1st July 2016).

Department for Education. (2013b). English Programmes of Study: Key Stage 3. Available at https://www.gov.uk/government/uploads/system/uploads/attachment_data/file/244215/SECONDARY_national_curriculum_-_English2.pdf (accessed on 12th May 2016).

Department for Education. (2014). English Programmes of Study: Key Stage 4. Available at https://www.gov.uk/government/uploads/system/uploads/attachment_data/file/331877/KS4_English_PoS_FINAL_170714.pdf (accessed on 12th May 2016).

Department for Education. (2015). Final Report of the Commission for Assessment without Levels. Available at https://www.gov.uk/government/uploads/system/uploads/attachment_data/file/461534/Commission_report_.pdf (accessed on 6th October 2015).

Eaglestone, R. (2000). *Doing English*. Oxford: Routledge.

Kress, J., Jewitt, C., Bourne, J., Franks, A., Hardcastle, J., Jones, K. and Reid, E. (2003). *English in Urban Classrooms: A Multimodal Perspective on Teaching and Learning*. Oxford: Routledge.

Looking for the Heart of English. (2012). Meeting High Expectations: Will the New Curriculum for Primary English Be Good Enough for Our Children? Available at https://heartofenglishblog.files.wordpress.com/2013/09/high-expectations.pdf (accessed on 1st July 2016).

MailOnline. (2013, 23rd March). I Refuse to Surrender to the Marxist Teachers Hell-Bent on Destroying Our Schools: Education Secretary Berates 'the New Enemies of Promise' for Opposing His Plans. Available at http://www.dailymail.co.uk/debate/article-2298146/I-refuse-surrender-Marxist-teachers-hell-bent-destroying-schools-Education-Secretary-berates-new-enemies-promise-opposing-plans.html (accessed on 12th June 2016).

Myhill, J., Jones, S. and Bailey, T. (2011). *Grammar for Writing? The Impact of Contextualised Grammar Teaching on Pupils' Writing and Pupils' Metalinguistic Understanding ESRC End of Award Report, RES-062-23-0775*. Swindon: ESRC.

Myhill, D., Lines, H., Watson, A. and Jones, S. (2012). Re-thinking Grammar: The Impact of Embedded Grammar Teaching on Students' Writing and Students' Metalinguistic Understanding. *Research Papers in Education*, 27(2), pp. 139–166.

National Writing Project. (2016). Available at http://www.nwp.org.uk/ (accessed on 1st March 2016).

Ofsted. (2007). *Poetry in Schools: A Survey of Practice, 2006/07*. London: Ofsted.

Ofsted. (2009). *English at the Crossroads: An Evaluation of English in Primary and Secondary Schools, 2005/08*. London: Ofsted.

Ofsted. (2012). *Moving English Forward: Action to Raise Standards in English*. London: Ofsted.

Richmond, J., Dougill, P. and Raleigh, M. (2015). *English, Language and Literacy 3–19: Summary*. Welshpool: Owen Education/UKLA.

Smith, J. and Wrigley, S. (2015). *Introducing Teachers' Writing Groups*. London: Routledge.

Standards and Testing Agency. (2015). Government Response: Commission on Assessment without Levels. Available at https://www.gov.uk/government/uploads/system/uploads/attachment_data/file/461311/Government-response-to-commission-on-assessment-without-levels-report.pdf (accessed on 6th October 2015).

The Guardian. (2012a, 21st June). Nick Clegg Vows to Block Michael Gove's Plan to Ditch GCSEs. Available at http://www.theguardian.com/politics/2012/jun/21/nick-clegg-michael-gove-exams (accessed on 14th January 2016).

The Guardian. (2012b, 12th November). The New National Curriculum: Made to Order? Available at http://www.theguardian.com/education/2012/nov/12/primary-national-curriculum-review (accessed on 14th January 2016).

The Guardian. (2013, 15th July). Do Michael Gove's GCSE Changes Pose a Threat to English Literature in Schools? Available at http://www.theguardian.com/education/2013/jul/15/michael-gove-gcse-changes-english-literature (accessed on 16th February 2016).

The Sunday Times. (2013, 3rd November). Authors Warn GCSE English Reforms Will Leave Literature on the Shelf. Available at http://www.thesundaytimes.co.uk/sto/news/uk_news/Education/article1335699.ece?CMP=OTH-gnws-standard-2013_11_02 (accessed on 3rd March 2016).

Times Educational Supplement. (2012, 22nd June). Experts Wanted to Quit Curriculum Panel Over 'Prescriptive' Proposals. Available at https://www.tes.com/article.aspx?storycode=6257908 (accessed on 8th January 2016).

PART III

Abroad and beyond

7

AN ENGLISH SUBJECT ABROAD

The central focus of this book has been a history of the development of secondary English in England's schools over the past half-century. The division into two sections marks – admittedly in an overly convenient way – the shift to central control. This move to central control has been, in essence, symptomatic of a move in the education systems of the western world, and indeed more globally, which is part of a standards-based reform agenda. Underpinning this – as was explicitly evident in the New Labour literacy initiatives, and similarly in Conservative policy (though here infused with other ideology) – is the belief that the core function of education is to contribute to a nation's economic competitiveness in the global market. The most obvious way to achieve this has been through the centralisation of curriculum and assessment, the introduction of the market into schooling and stringent accountability frameworks and performance measures to coerce the educational establishment into adopting an economic and functional view of schooling. The key marker for the success, or otherwise, of such reform is a nation's position in the PISA league tables.[1]

For many, one of the key effects of standards-based reform and centralisation has been the deprofessionalisation of teachers, so that they increasingly become enactors of policy reforms that seek to serve ends that may not be the teacher's primary objectives for schooling. If this is felt across the teaching profession, in no subject area is it felt more keenly than within English. Whilst acknowledging the essential skill of being literate as a necessary means to function in society and in the world of work, few teachers of the subject – whatever their own political beliefs – would see English as having a purely economic function. Thus the resistance to central reform has been strongest from English teachers, most obviously demonstrated by the boycott of the Key Stage 3 tests, a movement that had support from teachers in comprehensive, grammar and independent schools.

The move to central control can be seen, to greater or lesser extents, and at varying speeds, across the other major English-speaking nations of the world. A brief consideration of how subject English has developed in these nations can inform our understanding of what English is and throw further light on the ways in which the subject may be changing, and to what extent traditions and models of the subject are being supplanted. Equally, a comparative look at other major English-speaking jurisdictions can reveal if, where, and why ideas about English that have developed over the past 50 years have retained currency in spite of global reform agendas. Interesting in itself as it is to place English in England against English in other nations – as an exercise in seeing how visions of the subject have travelled and are shared – it may inform thinking of where the subject is headed.

English in the United Kingdom's other nations

When the Department for Education in England undertook its review of the National Curriculum in 2011, there was a commitment made for changes to be informed by intelligence from the curriculum policies of so-called high-performing jurisdictions. As evidenced in the *Report on Subject Breadth in International Jurisdictions* (Department for Education, 2011a) and the more specific report that focused purely on English, maths and science (Department for Education, 2011b), curriculums of the major Anglophone countries – Australia, Canada, the United States and New Zealand – were explored but there was apparently no consideration of the work of our nearest English-speaking neighbours, namely the other countries of the United Kingdom. This was presumably because these countries failed, by the measures of international comparison like the PISA data, to come into the category of high performing. However there have been sound arguments for the benefit of so-called home international comparison (for example, Raffe (1998) and Raffe, Brannen, Croxford and Martin (1999)), in part on the basis that the many similarities between the nations of the United Kingdom – socially, culturally and economically – mean that comparing education across them is potentially more valid than comparison with more distant cultures. It sounds like common sense; although a policymaker may look to somewhere like Singapore for inspiration for curriculum development given the high levels of the country's student performance, the vast difference in cultures between there and here at the very least suggests that there would be potential problems in attempting to import ideas and methods wholesale.

Central policy around the English curriculum in secondary schools in Wales, Northern Ireland and Scotland – how the subject is framed by the policymakers for the profession – has seen greater divergence from England in recent years, in particular since the devolution of powers under the New Labour government in the 1990s. Until then, the National Curriculum was one for both England and Wales, and the Northern Irish version differed only slightly (with, for example, speaking and listening being referred to as talking and listening); what has happened since is of interest when considering subject English.

A significant overhaul of the curriculum in Northern Ireland took place in 2007 following a lengthy period of review and consultation. The result was a very different curriculum model for English, which in the Key Stage 3 statutory orders became

English with media education. In this, albeit brief, curriculum, a model of English emerged that appears primarily designed to promote a cohesive society. Its prime objectives are developing pupils as 'individuals', 'Contributors to Society' and 'Contributors to the Economy and Environment' (Council for the Curriculum, Examinations and Assessment, 2007, p. 33). The details, such as they are, put emphases on creativity, curiosity and imagination, and there is a stress placed on exploring one's own emotions and the emotions, rights and needs of others. In what has been, historically, a very fractured community, English is to contribute to the building of a tolerant and empathetic nation. This is in somewhat stark contrast to developments in the National Curriculum in England, where the move to traditional orders with a heavy emphasis on the literary canon – in the context of an overarching educational priority to promote British values – appears to champion an insular outlook.

The English curriculum in Northern Ireland is certainly not a curriculum that bears the hallmarks of the centralist reform of England – either that of the New Labour administration or of their Conservative traditionalist successors. It is, in fact, an English curriculum to which many English teachers would very happily subscribe. The wholehearted embracing of media education as central to students' work in English again marks a stark contrast to the orders in England where all notions of media, moving image and multimodality have been purged.

In Wales, recent history in the teaching of English has been marked by change. When the National Curriculum was introduced in 1989, the Welsh version differed slightly to the English – this was necessary given the proportion of the population for whom English was in fact a second language. Significantly, when the new National Curriculum was introduced in 1995, 'Wales did not have a fixed canon to follow' (Marshall, 2011, p. 41). This can only have been galling to those on the consultation group, like John Hickman, who had protested in vain at the inclusion of prescribed authors for English teachers.

After devolution in 1999, there were more significant ways in which the teaching and learning of English differed in the two nations. Wales preceded England in scrapping Key Stage 3 testing in English, following announcements from the Welsh Education Secretary in 2004 (*The Guardian*, 2004). This move would potentially have the effect of liberating English teachers from the stranglehold of assessment, although the move was not unanimously welcomed, with some teaching unions fearing an increase in workload with a move towards portfolio assessment with sample external moderation.

Although assessment changed, the English curriculum in Wales remained relatively content heavy and in fact, most recently, central intervention has been intensified, with the introduction in 2014 of a National Literacy Framework to run across the primary and secondary phases. This introduction, along with a reintroduction of national testing, came primarily as a result of poor showing in successive PISA rankings. The reintroduction of annual national literacy testing for all students from the ages of 7 to 14 marked an end of a very brief SATs-free period. The speedy about turn demonstrated the influence that PISA and international rankings have over policymakers, and illustrated the apparent first response to a perceived fall in standards – more testing.

As a result of the introduction of the literacy initiative, the National Curriculum for English in Wales is a lengthy document that is a hybrid of both the English programmes of study and the objectives from the literacy framework. It is primarily a skills-based curriculum, with frequent references to Standard English and grammar, and with the word creativity mentioned only twice across both Key Stages 3 and 4 (Department for Education and Skills, 2015). Somewhat curiously, Wales seems to be following the approach adopted in England in the late 1990s and 2000s with a curriculum, framework and national testing system that must run the risks of having the same – perhaps unintended – consequences; a narrowing of curriculum, teaching to the test and a model of English that moves away from the humane, progressive version of the subject that lies at much of the profession's heart.

Whilst Northern Ireland and Wales joined England in the introduction of a statutory National Curriculum in 1989, successive administrations in Scotland have consistently opted for non-statutory guidance curriculum documents so that, whilst clearly public examinations and testing have exerted a central influence on content, there has been, throughout England's age of intervention, a contrasting freedom over curriculum offered to teachers north of the border; throughout the 1990s, for example, there was a non-statutory 5–14 curriculum for English language. Although there was mandatory testing during the period, teachers were permitted to enter students for the tests as and when they were ready. In reality, however, it has been claimed that, because the Scottish inspectorate made use of the results of these assessments, 'the tests began to dominate' (Marshall, 2011, p. 45).

Since 2002 the Curriculum for Excellence has emerged in Scotland, and within these advisory documents English has become 'Literacy and English'. However, the view of literacy differs markedly from the kind of reductive view that led so many teachers in England to reject the National Literacy Strategy. The principles and practice section of the curriculum begins with the kind of bold statements so absent from the most recent documents in England: 'Our ability to use language lies at the centre of the development and expression of our emotions, our thinking, our learning and our sense of personal identity' (Curriculum for Excellence, 2011, p. 1).

Although it has been claimed (for example, in McGonigal (2000)) that the tradition of rhetoric in Scottish education dating back to the eighteenth century, with its aim to ensure Scots were not linguistically – and therefore economically – inferior to the English, meant that the progressive model of English in the 1960s never took firm hold in Scotland, it is clearly the case that the guidance within the Curriculum for Excellence describes a model of English that draws far more heavily on the progressive model of the subject than does the curriculum south of the border. According to one account (Northcroft, 1990) it's possible to see that the recommendations for a new, progressive English were expressed by a Scottish Education Department report as far back as 1947 (Scottish Education Department, 1947). The report emphasised the fundamental importance of English, but proposed a new model for the subject 'in which pupils would write about their own experiences, develop the power of speech and read within its rich literature about matters of individual concern' (Northcroft, 1990, p. 40), though without changes to examination systems this vision for what reads like a version of growth English was not realised. Northcroft's account suggested that ideas such as those from Dartmouth, and from thinkers like Britton, Rosen, Dixon and Barnes, were slow to make the move north of the border and their impact, at least at the level of policy, was always affected by the demands of central assessment systems. This meant that when the Scottish Education Board published its English Arrangements (Scottish Education Board, 1987), the attempted balance between a skills and growth model for English was skewed.

If moves towards a progressive English model were neither rapid nor smooth, it is certainly the case that in the new Curriculum for Excellence the balance has shifted in a way that clearly differs from recent moves south of the border. For example, rather than marginalising the development of different types of text, Curriculum for Excellence attempts to make its definition of text future proof and so defines text as 'the medium through which ideas, experiences, opinions and information can be communicated' (Curriculum for Excellence, 2011, p. 4) and welcomes into its list of examples films, television programmes, games, blogs, social networking sites and text messages. Of the three areas of study, significant space is dedicated to 'Listening and Talking', giving it – in terms of word count at least – equal priority to 'Reading' and 'Writing'. 'Knowledge about language' is used in preference to 'grammar' and there is ample space given to writing from personal experience. Perhaps most striking about the way Curriculum for Excellence is written is the way in which the personal pronoun is used throughout; the document is expressed from the point of view of the learner – 'I can engage with…', ' I can listen to…', 'I can select ideas…' and so on. A rhetorical device, of course, but one which forefronts the idea that Curriculum for Excellence is a child-centred model of learning and which differs so markedly with documents like the Key Stage 3 Framework in which repeatedly there were instructions that children should be 'taught to' do certain things, without any explicit reference to their learning.

Despite the apparent progressive nature of the Curriculum of Excellence, however, the pressures of assessment and accountability seem to have caused another shift in policy which has the potential to impact on English teaching in Scotland. Under its National Improvement Framework (The Scottish Government, 2016) plans are in place to introduce national literacy tests for pupils in S3 (i.e. 14–15 year olds), as well as in the primary phase. If introduced, these tests have the potential to impact on curriculum in the same way as SATs in England and thus pose a threat to the relative autonomy that Scottish teachers of English have over what is taught. It seems to be a retrograde step in a country that managed to avoid the conflicts around curriculum and assessment in the 1990s and 2000s by approaching these areas in a seemingly more collaborative fashion. Again, it appears to be the case that in the face of pressures from international comparison data the tools of assessment and accountability are to be wielded in the bid to raise what is perceived to be children's attainment.

English in the United States

Arguments about what constitutes effective English teaching, and what the subject should look like, have been as fierce in the United States as in any other English-speaking nation. Given that no National Curriculum exists in the US, with education organised at State level, generalisations are fraught with difficulty, however it is possible to reflect on some of the key developments in subject English.

In *The Swinging Pendulum: Teaching English in the USA, 1945–87* (Simmons, Shafer and Shadow, 1990), the authors detailed how debates about the subject shifted over the post-war decades. Arguments about traditional language instruction were impacted by the work of Noam Chomsky and ideas about transformative generative grammars; the teaching of the literary canon had been challenged by champions of multicultural literature. Political and cultural contexts had their influence on the ways in which ideas shifted back and forth, so that by the eve of the Dartmouth conference in 1966, as we have seen, the metaphorical swinging pendulum was firmly on the side of a back-to-basics approach, with Project English having established a tripartite model for the subject.

Without question, events at Dartmouth shifted the ground, having significant impact on teacher educators, many of whom had their perspectives shifted by 'the force of the student-centred argument offered by the British' (ibid., p. 110). However whilst NCTE may have actively promoted the progressive, growth model of English emerging from Dartmouth, evidenced in the resolution passed at their 1972 annual convention on the right of students to use their own language,[2] the political mood was apparently still conservative with the back-to-basics movement gaining ground in the 1970s so that in terms of the direction of English policy and practice 'the road from Dartmouth was clearly the one less travelled' (ibid., p. 117).

If a back-to-basics, accountability-driven model gathered momentum in terms of the national policy discourse around curriculum and assessment through the 1970s in the United States, one notable project was important in the way that it promoted a different concept of how to improve the teaching of English, a model much more attuned to the bottom-up development of the progressive model of English. The Bay Area Writing Project began in 1974, in Berkeley, California, its aim to improve the teaching of writing but not through the top-down imposition of a curriculum or theory, but instead with three starting assumptions: that teachers should learn from other teachers, that all teachers of writing should be writers and that there was much research available to inform approaches to the teaching of writing, an area that had caused particular consternation in the public psyche in the United States in the mid-1970s.[3] Taking inspiration from various writers on writing, including Donald Graves and James Britton, the project was organised around summer schools for teachers at which they would share their practice, share their writing, and explore new approaches. The Bay Area project grew to become the National Writing Project, which – in part helped by endorsement and central government funding – has expanded to operate, according to its website, in sites across all 50 American states, as well as in Puerto Rico and the U.S. Virgin Islands.[4] It was important in informing Richard Andrews' attempts to launch a writing project in England, and although that failed to materialise, it has subsequently, to some extent, informed the work done by Simon Wrigley and Jeni Smith on NATE's National Writing Project in England (though clearly as a project with little or no funding it has to find alternative ways to operate). In some ways its essential principles, resting on teacher autonomy, teachers as researchers and teachers as agents of change, were at odds with the educational policy discourse of the States in the 1970s, and this disjunct has only become more pronounced. The United States National Writing Project's longevity, continued growth and success lends further weight to the argument that, for all the policymakers may try to intervene and impose, it is when teachers work together, using their own practice and concerns as a starting point, that meaningful change happens; English teachers as agents, rather than enactors, of change.

As in England, the 1980s was the decade that saw the most significant and far-reaching shifts in education in the United States, towards a more centralist, standards-based reform agenda. The publication of *A Nation at Risk: The Imperative for Educational Reform* (National Commission on Excellence in Education, 1983) was probably the start of this phase of the revolution. The report, or 'open letter to the American people' as it proclaimed to be, lamented the failings of the American education system over the past decade and more, citing statistics of adult illiteracy and pointing out the performance of the US in comparative educational datasets. Standards-based reform was designed to improve the performance of children and young people, ensure college-readiness, and ultimately secure the States' global competitiveness. In some senses the attempt to reframe the debates around education evoked the kinds of thinking the English delegates to Dartmouth saw in 1966 and was a reaffirmation of the fact that, in the United States, Dartmouth had failed to take a firm hold.

To achieve the aims set out in *A Nation at Risk*, it was asserted that explicit direction was needed from the centre on what students should know, more rigorous testing was required and more powerful frameworks for accountability needed to be in place. This set the policy discourse for the coming decades.

As with the move to the introduction of the National Curriculum in England, the move towards reform took time. In 1991, the respective presidents of the International Reading Association (IRA) and the National Council of Teachers of English (NCTE) wrote to the Secretary of State for Education proposing the development of a set of common standards for the English Language Arts. Supported by federal funding to the University of Illinois Center for the Study of Reading between 1992 and 1994, and subsequently self-funded, IRA and NCTE published their *Standards for the English Language Arts* in 1996 (IRA and NCTE, 1996). That the Standards took four years to produce reflected the aim that the content therein be generated through an 'open, inclusive' process (ibid., p. v). This involved the participation of thousands of classroom teachers in the writing, reviewing and drafting of the Standards so that what was produced was generated by the profession rather than by policymakers or an elite committee of experts. The length of time reflected, too, the arguments that any attempt to define English illicits both from within the profession and without. Whilst acknowledging that it would be impossible to reflect the specific concerns and interests of all, the document's stated goal was to 'define, as clearly and specifically as possible, the current consensus among literacy teachers and researchers about what students should learn in the English language arts' (ibid., p. 1).

The familiar disputes about the nature of English clearly surfaced through the consultative process, which 'revealed a series of divides within the English education professions, particularly between proponents of "literature" versus the integrated "English language arts" and between advocates of phonics versus whole language' (Brass, 2015, p. 246). Arguments over English as language or English as literature were familiar ones on both sides of the Atlantic, as were the debates about the teaching of early reading. There was also the inevitable feeling from within the profession that any attempt to define standards would be a threat to teacher autonomy and creativity. External criticism came as a result of the failure to list set texts and it was this that reportedly led to the withdrawal of public funds. Such was the level of dispute and delay caused by the seemingly endless revision process, it was in fact 'an un-named group' from IRA/NCTE that 'eventually circumvented their organizations' public review processes in 1996 to publish a "consensus" vision of what students should know and be able to do in the English language arts' (ibid., p. 246).

The document produced a broadly progressive view of English, and one that had its antecedents in Dartmouth – the learner was explicitly stated to be at the centre of the Standards – and the document strove to make clear that it was not intended in any way to be prescriptive:

> These standards are intended to serve as guidelines that provide ample room for the kinds of innovation and creativity that are essential to teaching and learning. They are not meant to be seen as prescriptions for particular curricula or instructional approaches.
>
> *(IRA and NCTE, 1996, p. 2)*

The twelve standards that the IRA and NCTE produced were broad and encompassing. They spoke of students building an understanding of themselves through their reading and of the value of literature in developing the understanding of human experience. A varied approach was recommended in the approach to development of reading abilities and text was used an all embracing term for print, non-print and visual artefacts. There was a call for an understanding and respect of language diversity and for the speakers of other first languages than English to be able to make use of their own language in the development of proficiency in English. Language was to be used by students for their own purposes, 'for learning, enjoyment, persuasion and the exchange of information' (ibid., p. 3). The chapter that elaborated on each of the 12 standards identified was not written in the bullet point style of so many subsequent curriculum documents around the world; the writing was in continuous prose, detailing the scope of each standard in very wide-ranging definition. As close as a curriculum document can get, it was philosophical in its approach, whilst further illustration of the standards in action was offered not by lists or notes, but by a series of genuine classroom vignettes designed to bring the standards to life and make them real for the reader. The IRA/NCTE standards document offered up a humane, progressive idea about English, whilst also disputing the popularly held claims made by educational reformers that standards had actually been on the slide at all. It was an optimistic vision of English for the future, building on the strengths of the past, rather than seeking to correct its inadequacies with a return to a skills or back-to-basics curriculum.

Recently, however, the moves in the United States have come again from the centre with attempts to introduce a set of nationwide common core standards in English and the Language Arts. The Common Core Standards Initiative created a central set of standards which, by 2016, had been adopted by the vast majority of states in the United States.[5] These core standards, which evolved from 2009, adopt a highly functional approach to both reading and writing: in reading there are calculations of text complexity that dictate the kinds of literature that should be read in particular years of schooling; in writing the focus is on non-fiction forms, particularly argument and persuasion. The goal of the standards is particularly to ensure college and career readiness, and according to polling by NCTE[6] the response from the profession on their introduction was mixed. As a body representing English teachers across the nation, NCTE has been politic in its response to the core standards, placing its emphasis on helping teachers work with central prescription. This is inevitably what a national body has to do – in the United Kingdom NATE has repeatedly made efforts to help teachers negotiate central policy rather than oppose it – but the vision of English in the core standards is vastly different to that articulated in NCTE's earlier version of standards.

An interesting side plot to the development of the Core Standards Initiative has been the work led by E.D. Hirsch on core knowledge. A core knowledge curriculum, though it may be compatible with core standards – as Hirsch claims[7] – has a distinct difference in that it rests on an assumption that there is in fact a distinct body of knowledge a young person needs to acquire in order to have the chance to participate fully in her society. Hirsch initially articulated his ideas in *Cultural Literacy: What Every American Needs to Know* (1987) and his Core Knowledge Foundation provides curriculum material for children up to the age of 14. Many schools in America have taken up the Core Knowledge approach, and a United Kingdom arm of the Core Knowledge Foundation now exists, though this currently only offers curriculum content for the primary school.[8] In the lead up to the rewrite of the primary National Curriculum in England, it was clear that both Michael Gove and his colleague in the education department, Nick Gibb, were firm supporters of an approach that seeks to define specific content that all children should know.[9]

An obvious criticism of the core knowledge approach would be that, although it aims to empower all children to have equal access to society, it does so by reinforcing existing structures and knowledge where power lies. In this way it does not open up society to those children from different cultures and backgrounds who may have other sorts of knowledge, nor does it challenge the assumptions of whose knowledge is important. Nonetheless the number of schools in the United States advocating a core knowledge programme, and the spread to the United Kingdom, suggests it has appeal to many. Taken together, the core standards and the core knowledge approaches to the teaching and learning of English clearly demonstrate that, in the current context at least, the legacies of the English promoted at Dartmouth are far from the minds of policymakers in the United States.

English in Canada

There are striking similarities but also very notable differences in the ways that English, or the language arts, have developed in the United States' closest neighbour, Canada. Education policy has traditionally operated at the level of province in Canada, which – given the vastly different demographics across the provinces in such a sprawling country – would appear to be the rational approach.

In their account of *Teaching English Language Arts in Canada: 1965–1985*, Robinson, Walker, Johnson and Gambell (1990) suggested that the ways in which the English curriculum developed – albeit that there were varieties across provinces – differed in the areas of language teaching, the teaching of writing and reading. In the area of language, the familiar arguments about the explicit teaching of grammar, and, indeed, what sort of grammar, reverberated as elsewhere, with reported public concern at levels of literacy linked to a lack of traditional grammar teaching in schools.[10] New ideas about language learning did have an impact at policy level, however, so that rather than simply a back-to-basics approach, by the 1980s the study of what was called language information 'was conceived of much more broadly in the English language arts curriculum' (ibid., p. 138). This involved secondary students exploring language variation, the origins of English, dialect and register.

In the teaching of writing in Canada there was a more definite sense of a 'concerted attempt being made to modify the traditional model for composition instruction in favour of teaching writing as a personal and social process' (ibid., p. 140). Here, then, the ideas from growth English emerging from Dartmouth and the work of James Britton influenced English teachers in Canada as they did elsewhere. Within the teaching of reading by the 1970s the psycholinguistic approach to reading instruction, advocated in the work of Frank Smith, came to the fore. Aligning this with the growth or process approaches to writing meant that, in general terms, Canada was moving towards a whole-language approach to the teaching of English.

Since the 1980s, Canada has certainly not been immune to the increasing influence of standards-based reform. The country has, however, taken a markedly different approach to their neighbours in the US or in England. Province-wide literacy testing exists, but these tests do not operate in the same high-stakes accountability framework as they do elsewhere. Although an individual student may need to pass the province test in order to secure graduation, the tests are not used to make judgements on individual teachers but on the schools as a whole. Where schools are judged to be underperforming, the response is to offer support rather than to make punitive judgements. When Canada's largest province, Ontario, introduced an equivalent to the National Literacy Strategy in its elementary schools, it sought to avoid the problems of top-down central initiatives. Hence, rather than adopting the idea of informed prescription the involvement of the profession was key, something made powerfully clear in comments from Michael Fullan in an OECD report on the success of Canada's system, when he said that the people in the centre were not in the business of telling teachers 'what to do', instead there would be partnership to 'identify good practices, consolidate those and spread them' – a process of 'jointly co-discovering' (OECD, 2010, p. 75). A markedly different approach to reform, and one reminiscent of England's National Writing and Oracy Projects of the late 1980s and early 1990s.

Avoiding a whole-scale embracing of standards-based reform, and avoiding the worst problems of top-down reform by involving the profession, has certainly been reflected in the various provinces' curricula for English or the Language Arts which generally reflect a broad and progressive model of the subject. For example, the curriculum for Ontario refers to the research that highlights the importance of students being able 'to choose what they read and write about' and which sees the overall purpose of an English curriculum as for students 'to better understand themselves and others, unlock their potential as human beings, find fulfilling careers, and become responsible world citizens' (Ministry of Education, 2007a, p. 5). As general principles for the teaching of English these seem admirable and reflect a notion of the subject that has increasingly been eschewed in other jurisdictions that have felt the full force of central intervention.

Similar sentiments can be seen in the approach of the Province of British Columbia to English, the stated aim of which is 'to provide students with opportunities for personal and intellectual growth through speaking, listening, reading, writing, viewing and representing' (Ministry of Education, 2007b, p. 2). In the British Columbia curriculum there is a lengthy section titled 'Considerations for Program Delivery' (ibid., pp. 13–40) that is an evidenced-based articulation to the approach taken. References are drawn widely, and the arguments are made explicit for teachers to engage with; for example, in the section on writing there is a discussion of process, genre and metacognitive approaches to the teaching and developing of writing and how a synthesis might be reached that could draw the best from what are described as 'complementary' approaches (ibid., p. 28). When discussing assessment, the work of Paul Black and Dylan Wiliam on assessment for learning is foregrounded. Whether or not every English teacher in the province read the section, it was clear that the profession was being engaged in a serious manner and invited to consider the debates about the subject and explore the rationale. Such an approach disappeared from England almost as soon as the Cox curriculum was revised.

Significant, too, was the explicit use of 'viewing' and 'representing' and this highlights how in each of Canada's states serious attention is given to media within the language arts curriculum. There has been a strong heritage of media education and media literacy work in Canada and this has been endorsed in provincial guidance.

Although there has been criticism of the province-wide literacy testing in Canada, both on the fronts that the tests assess a very narrow range of skills and that they potentially distort the teaching and learning experience of some students (particularly those, often from vulnerable groups, who may fail the test and have to retake it in conjunction with a specific literacy programme), it is clear from current province curricula that a broad and progressive model of English teaching still prevails in official discourse. There is certainly evidence, too, to suggest that for English teachers their practice is little influenced by the testing or by the broader idea of centrally driven reform agendas.[11] Whilst it has resisted full-blown, centrally driven, standards-based reform, Canada has in fact performed notably well in PISA comparisons.

English in Australia

There are clear parallels between the story of secondary English teaching in Australia and that in England, and influences on the development of the subject have flowed in both directions, with growth English exported from England in the 1960s whilst a new genre-based pedagogy moved in the opposite direction in the 1990s.

According to Reid (2003) and Homer (2003), English teaching in Australia – at least at the secondary level – was profoundly influenced by the work of those at the London Institute of Education and the personal growth English as language model. This was in part due to the influence of Australian teacher educators like Garth Boomer[12] who had spent a year at the Institute in the early 1970s and had been instrumental in bringing the ideas of Britton, Barnes and Rosen to his native country. A version of growth pedagogy was the 'supreme orthodoxy' (Reid, 2003, p. 99) in the 1970s in English across Australian secondary schools. Apparently Dixon's *Growth through English* had come at 'just at the right time to encourage those who were groping towards a new model of English teaching' (Davis and Watson, 1990, p. 158). When the six Australian states – each with autonomy in the absence of any national curriculum – began to generate new statements of what should happen in secondary English classrooms in the beginning of the 1970s, they moved away from the subject as content based to a growth model. Curriculum statements from Victoria in 1970, New South Wales and South Australia in 1971 and Queensland in 1973 ensured that 'Dixon's personal growth model had received official endorsement' (ibid., p. 159).

As in England, however, it did not take long for a backlash to the progressive model of the subject to be felt in Australia. The rhetoric in both countries was strikingly similar and, indeed, has been viewed as part of an international campaign around declining standards aimed at progressive education.[13] Key to this argument in Australia, advocating a back-to-basics curriculum was the Australian Council for Education Standards (ACES), whose main attacks apparently 'rested on unsupported claims that young Australians did not read and write as well as the young people of 30 years ago' (ibid., p. 162). Supporters of the back-to-basics approach in England had assumed positions of power in the realms of curriculum and assessment by the end of the 1980s, ushering in narrower statutory orders and national testing. This took longer to happen in Australia, perhaps given its sprawling size and the fact that education policy was delegated to state level. However, by 1990 state-wide literacy testing was introduced in New South Wales, and when looking at the direction of travel in English this caused some to observe that 'cultural cringe is alive and well' (ibid., p. 172).

There was, however, another model of development of English in Australia that took issue with both those who wanted a return to a traditional curriculum and those who advocated progressive approaches to the subject. This model, which went on to have influence beyond Australia's shores – particularly in England in the New Labour literacy initiatives – came from the work of the genre theorists. In a sense this work could be said to have had its roots back in England; it drew on the work of the architect of functional linguistics, Michael Halliday. He had connections to colleagues in LATE through the Nuffield Linguistics Project that ran in the 1960s and led to the Language in Use Publication.

The genre project began, it is claimed, as the progressive model for English that had grown in Australia in the 1970s and 1980s 'was not producing the goods' (Cope and Kalantzis, 1993, p. 1). The criticisms of progressive English from the genre theorists were numerous; rather than facilitating equality it played into the hands of middle-class children from child-centred backgrounds, it didn't work for children who weren't already knowledgeable about the power of reading and writing, and it reduced the teacher from professional to manager. Given that concerns about working-class children and the importance of teacher professionalism were central to advocates of progressive English, these criticisms struck at the very heart of the progressive orthodoxy.

Far from one fixed coherent theory, genre theory had different emphases to its different advocates. The model that gained traction in the teaching of English was that which came through the Disadvantaged Schools Project in Sydney. Here, the focus was on enabling those children for whom literacy was not already part of their culture to master the literacy skills needed across the school curriculum: through a combination of shared, guided and independent reading and writing and teacher modelling being able to produce the texts they needed for success. As we have seen, this model hugely influenced the Literacy and National Strategies in England in the late 1990s and early 2000s. Defenders of progressive approaches have suggested that a genre approach merely reinforces existing power structures and encourages children to reproduce; certainly in its worst incarnations this has happened, but many of the leading genre theorists – Bill Cope and Mary Kalantzis among them – made clear that real power in literacy came from being able to subvert conventions and produce new forms of text with new forms of power.

Genre approaches to the teaching of literacy and, by result, English more widely have had significant influence in Australia, as clearly detailed by Beverly Derewianka (2015) and, as she points out, influenced curriculums in 'Singapore, South Africa, USA, Hong Kong, UK, China, Canada, Sweden, Denmark and Thailand' (ibid., p. 84). In England, not only did the Literacy Strategy strongly promote the genre model, the rewrites of the National Curriculum in the 1990s, in particular, moved towards genre as an orthodox way to talk about the teaching and learning of reading and writing and this was, in a sense, reinforced when GCSE specifications began framing writing in terms of triplets of purposes. In one sense the genre approach sits much more easily in a wider context of assessment and measures of attainment; clearly it is much easier to construct marking criteria that focus on aspects of language use than it is to try to quantity the affective qualities of a piece of writing. Common sense would suggest that genre-based writing leads to more objective judgements about the quality of writing, though there may well be a problem if such judgements overlook affective qualities (D'Arcy (2000), strongly criticised the skewing of curriculum and assessment towards the genre model and the negative affects this would have on teaching and learning of writing[14]). Although the genre theorists were as critical of traditional English as of progressive English, their model was easier for those advocating a back-to-basics approach to appropriate and assimilate into curricula and forms of assessment that were actually designed with the intent to refocus the subject on Standard English, grammar and spelling.

Traditionally Australia had not had a National Curriculum, but the country and its educational policymakers were not immune to the standards-driven reform agenda that swept across many parts of the globe from the 1980s. Though Australia was some way behind the United States and England in this respect, by 2008 national literacy tests had been introduced for primary-aged pupils and for 14 year olds in the secondary sector.[15] Proposals for a National Curriculum were not far behind, made possible by the election of a government in 2008 which garnered significant support across the electorate for its promise to introduce one, thereby allowing it to 'reach agreements regarding the creation of national education policy, which were not possible under previous governments with less comprehensive support from states and territories' (Dilkes, Cunningham and Gray, 2014, p. 48). The Australian Curriculum, Assessment and Reporting Authority (ACARA) was established and by 2011 the Australian National Curriculum for English was being phased in.[16] In some ways it is ironic that, just as assessment and curriculum at Key Stage 3 were being loosened in England, the reverse was true on the other side of the globe, but it is indicative of the way that, even if a standards-based reform agenda is common across many parts of the world, there are shifts in emphasis about precisely which policies are most effective to deliver improvement.

The National Curriculum for English in Australia has four main areas: English, English as Additional Language or Dialect, Essential English and Literature. Across these four areas the ideas from genre theory are highly influential. There are references to personal response, but the overriding sense of the approach to reading and writing in the curriculum is genre based – with frequent references to style, register, mode and medium. What's also true, however, is that there was clearly a sense in the construction of the English curriculum to embrace new technologies, digital and multimodal texts; in these areas it is strikingly different to its modern counterpart in England which has wiped all references to such artefacts from its pages.

Conclusion

Accepting Canada as an unlikely outlier, and accepting, too, that these are brief sketches of English in countries that each have long and complex educational histories, if there is a theme that emerges in charting the development of English over the home countries and the major English-speaking nations of the world it is the way the subject, its curriculum, assessment and pedagogy have been impacted by the standards-driven reform agenda and its emphases on centralised curriculum, standardised assessments, and school and teacher accountability. To borrow the metaphor of the swinging pendulum, contrasts between these nations and their official approaches to subject English have varied as the pendulum has swung further to the side of central intervention, or away to collaboration with the profession and a notion of teacher autonomy. The default setting has often been that a response to a perceived falling in standards, perhaps revealed in the international comparison data, has meant government seeking to intervene more decisively, to more forcefully dictate what should be studied in English, and how this should be assessed. This was the case in England from 1989 until 2009 – and one could argue beyond – and in the United States from an even earlier period; Australia seems to have caught the fever most recently.

This wider political agenda has not only been at odds with the hearts and minds of many advocates of a progressive model of English, it has also provided a means by which advocates of a more traditional model of English have been able to exert influence on official policy. The overtly ideological moves of the National Curriculum in England in 2012 were unusual in the sense that the focus on Standard English and the focus on the canon were barely disguised as a return to a grammar school curriculum. Elsewhere, in the core standards and core-curriculum models of the United States and the heavily genre-based curriculum of Australia there is at least a more argued sense of how English as a subject should look. However, in all cases the threat of central policy has been to marginalise progressive, growth English and to impose – with varying degrees of force – a model of the subject that seems to be more about the curriculum and the assessment than it is about the learner. Progressive, growth English unashamedly put the learner at the centre of the thinking about what to teach and how to teach it; this has made it the point of attack for those that scorn what they see as the excesses of child-centred pedagogy, discovery learning and comprehensive education as a whole. Central policymakers almost invariably cast the learner as the object; the learner is to be taught what it has been decided is best for them, or rather best for the international standing and economic competitiveness of the nation, to know. The drive to ratchet up standards, expressed in the most simplistic of terms in test results, shows no sign of abating. The ultimate question is whether the kind of English that was conceived in the post-war years, was christened at Dartmouth and has grown – sometimes thriving – since has a future.

Notes

1 PISA is the Programme for International Student Assessment, a study that is run by the Organisation for Economic Co-operation and Development (OECD) and results in three-yearly international league tables of the performance of 15 year olds in reading, science and mathematics. Although the value of these tables is highly contestable, there appears to be a disproportionate emphasis placed on their importance by many govern-ments. In 2012, the United Kingdom were placed 23rd for reading, with Shanghai, Singapore, Hong Kong and Massachusetts (who took the tests as a separate entity to the United States as a whole) placed far above them. These were among the high-performing jurisdictions looked to in the 2010 rewrite of the National Curriculum in England.

2 According to Simmons, Shafer and Shadow (1990) the acknowledgement of the importance of students' own dialects in the classroom gathered momentum through the 1960s, particularly influenced by Labov's *The Study of Nonstandard English* (1969). Debates about the right of students to use their own language were fiercely contested amongst teachers, so that it was only a very narrow margin that carried the resolution at the 1972 NCTE convention which affirmed the importance of students' own dialects and condemned the 'myth of a standard American dialect' (Simmons, Shafer and Shadow, 1990, p. 115).

3 A lead article in Newsweek magazine in 1975 titled 'Why Johnny Can't Write' encap-sulated a popular view of the time that young people were not being taught to write properly in schools in the US.

4 The website of the US National Writing Project (http://www.nwp.org/ accessed on 15th June 2016) gives both a full account of the Project's history and details of the scope of its current work.

5 According to the Common Core Standards Initiative website (http://www.corestanda rds.org/ accessed on 15th June 2016), the Common Core Standards have been adopted by 42 states, along with the District of Columbia, four territories and the Department of Defense Education Activity.

6 See http://www.ncte.org/standards/common-core/kg_2-9-12 (accessed on 15th June 2016) for an open letter in 2012 from the then president of NCTE which includes details of its own polling of members on responses to the new core standards.

7 Hirsch's comments about the compatibility of Core Standards and Core Knowledge can be read on the website of the Core Knowledge Foundation (http://coreknowledge.org accessed on 1st June 2016).

8 The United Kingdom Core Knowledge website is http://www.coreknowledge.org.uk/ index.php accessed on 1st June 2016.

9 See, for example, *The Guardian* article of October 15th 2012, *US idea of 'cultural literacy' and key facts a child should know arrives in UK* (https://www.theguardian.com/education/ 2012/oct/15/hirsch-core-knowledge-curriculum-review accessed on 8th June 2016).

10 Robinson et al. cite, as an example, a 1975 report by the Canadian Chamber of Com-merce which led to schools being accused of 'failing to emphasise the teaching of basic skills, or avoiding drills, practice, repetition, and other forms of dull learning' (1990, p. 136).

11 There is currently a research project involving Bethan Marshall and Simon Gibbons from King's College London with colleagues from the University of Glasgow that is examining differences in secondary English teaching across England, Scotland and

Canada. Early indications from observations and interviews with teachers in Canada suggest they don't feel their practice to be impacted in the ways that English teachers in England do. Although a small case-study project, it's tempting to believe this opinion is not unusual in Canada given the relatively low levels of central reform and the comparatively light-touch accountability frameworks in operation.

12 A highly influential presence in the field of English teaching in Australia, Boomer became the English consultant for South Australia in 1968, a role that certainly helped to disseminate a view of growth English across the state.

13 Little (2004) cites Marginson (1997) in suggesting that the international campaign against progressive education was exemplified in the United States by the move to a skills curriculum in the 1950s and 1960s, in the United Kingdom by the *Black Papers* and in Australia by the founding of the Australian Council for Educational Standards.

14 D'Arcy's *Two Contrasting Paradigms for the Teaching and Assessment of Writing* (2000) is a deliberately polemic piece that essentially sets out the author's view that in England the National Curriculum, Literacy Strategy and national tests are constructed on a genre-based approach to writing, which values technical accuracy over affective aspects. Anyone subscribing to D'Arcy's view could easily form the impression that those in favour of a back-to-basics approach to English teaching were able to usher in traditional views about spelling, punctuation and grammar under the theoretically respectable guise of genre theory.

15 The National Assessment Programme – Literacy and Numeracy (NAPLAN) was introduced across Australia's six states and two territories in 2008. Previously individual states had been responsible for setting their own assessments and these were calibrated at a national level to give an overall picture of performance country wide. The introduction of common national testing was a logical, if not necessarily popular, next step.

16 The National Curriculum in Australia was not introduced across all states and territories simultaneously. Since its introduction there have been changes made to curriculum, so that by 2016 version 8.2 was published on the country's curriculum website (http://www.australiancurriculum.edu.au/).

References

Brass, J. (2015). Standards-Based Governance of English Teaching, Past, Present and Future? *English Teaching Practice and Critique*, 14(3), pp. 241–259.

Cope, B. and Kalantzis, M. (1993). Introduction: How a Genre Approach to Literacy Can Transform the Way Writing is Taught. In Cope, B. and Kalantzis, M. (Eds), *The Powers of Literacy: A Genre Approach to the Teaching of Writing*. Michigan: University of Pittsburgh Press.

Council for the Curriculum, Examinations and Assessment. (2007). *The Statutory Curriculum at Key Stage 3 Rationale and Detail*. Belfast: CCEA.

Curriculum for Excellence. (2011). Curriculum for Excellence, Literacy and English: Principles and Practice. Available at http://www.educationscotland.gov.uk/learningandtea ching/curriculumareas/languages/litandenglish/principlesandpractice/index.asp (accessed on 3rd May 2016).

D'Arcy, P. (2000). *Two Contrasting Paradigms for the Teaching and Assessment of Writing: A Critique of Current Approaches in the National Curriculum*. Sheffield: NATE.

Davis, D. and Watson, K. (1990). Teaching English in Australia: A Personal View. In Britton, J., Shafer, R., and Watson, K. (Eds), *Teaching and Learning English Worldwide*. Philadelphia: Multilingual Matters Ltd.

Department for Education. (2011a). *Report on Subject Breadth in International Jurisdictions*. Available at https://www.gov.uk/government/uploads/system/uploads/attachment_data/file/197636/DFE-RR178a.pdf (accessed on 12th June 2016).

Department for Education. (2011b). *Review of the National Curriculum in England: What Can We Learn from the English, Maths and Science Curricula of High-Performing Jurisdictions?* Available at https://www.gov.uk/government/uploads/system/uploads/attachment_data/file/184064/DFE-RR178.pdf (accessed on 1st June 2016).

Department for Education and Skills. (2015). *Curriculum for Wales: Programme of Study for English Key Stages 2–4.* Cardiff: Department for Education and Skills.

Derewianka, B. (2015). The Contribution of Genre Theory to Literacy Education in Australia. In Turbill, J., Barton, G. and Brock, C. (Eds), *Teaching Writing in Today's Classrooms: Looking Back to Look Forward.* Australia: Australian Literary Educators' Association.

Dilkes, J., Cunningham, C. and Gray, J. (2014). The New Australian Curriculum, Teachers and Change Fatigue. *Australian Journal of Teacher Education,* 39(11), pp. 45–64.

Hirsch, E.D. (1987). *Cultural Literacy: What Every American Needs to Know.* Boston: Houghton Mifflin.

Homer, D. (2003). Playing for the B Team: A Tale of the Eighties. In Doecke, B., Homer, D. and Nixon, H. (Eds), *English Teachers at Work: Narratives, Counter Narratives and Arguments.* South Australia: Wakefield Press.

IRA and NCTE. (1996). *Standards for the English Language Arts.* Illinois and Delaware: IRA/NCTE.

Labov, W. (1969). *The Study of Nonstandard English.* Washington, D.C.: Centre for Applied Linguistics.

Little, G. (2004). Introduction. In Sawyer, W. and Gold, E. (Eds), *Reviewing English in the 21st Century.* Melbourne, Australia: Phoenix Education.

Marginson, S. (1997). *Educating Australia: Government, Economy and Citizen Since 1960.* Cambridge: Cambridge University Press.

Marshall, B. (2011). *Testing English: Formative and Summative Approaches to English Assessment.* London: Continuum.

McGonigal, J. (2000). English Language Education. In Bryce, T. and Humes, W. (Eds), *Scottish Education.* Edinburgh: Edinburgh University Press.

Ministry of Education. (2007a). *The Ontario Curriculum Grades 9 and 10: English.* Ontario: Ministry of Education.

Ministry of Education. (2007b). *English Language Arts 8–12: Integrated Resource Package.* British Columbia: Ministry of Education.

National Commission on Excellence in Education. (1983). *A Nation at Risk: The Imperative for Educational Reform.* Washington, D.C.: U.S. Government Printing Office.

Northcroft, D. (1990). The Growth of Accountability and the Accountability of Growth: Secondary School English Teaching in Post-War Scotland. In Britton, J., Shafer, R., and Watson, K. (Eds), *Teaching and Learning English Worldwide.* Philadelphia: Multilingual Matters Ltd.

OECD. (2010). *Ontario, Canada: Reform to Support High Achievement in a Diverse Context in Strong Performers and Successful Reformers in Education: Lessons from PISA for the United States.* Available at http://www.oecd.org/pisa/pisaproducts/46580959.pdf (accessed on 1st July 2016).

Raffe, D. (1998). Does Learning Begin at Home? The Use of 'Home International' Comparisons in UK Policy Making. *Journal of Education Policy,* 13(5), pp. 591–602.

Raffe, D., Brannen, K., Croxford, L. and Martin, C. (1999). Comparing England, Scotland, Wales and Northern Ireland: The Case for 'Home Internationals'. *Comparative Research Comparative Education,* 35(1), pp. 9–25.

Reid, I. (2003). The Persistent Pedagogy of Growth. In Doecke, B., Homer, D. and Nixon, H. (Eds), *English Teachers at Work: Narratives, Counter Narratives and Arguments.* South Australia: Wakefield Press.

Robinson, S., Walker, L., Johnson, N. and Gambell, T. (1990) Teaching English Language Arts in Canada: 1965–1985. In Britton, J., Shafer, R., and Watson, K. (Eds), *Teaching and Learning English Worldwide*. Philadelphia: Multilingual Matters Ltd.

Scottish Education Board. (1987). *Standard Grade Arrangements in English*. Edinburgh: Scottish Education Board.

Scottish Education Department. (1947). *Report of the Advisory Council on Education in Scotland on Secondary Education*. Edinburgh: Her Majesty's Stationery Office.

Sheils, M. (1975, 8th December). Why Johnny Can't Write. *Newsweek, pp. 58–63*.

Simmons, J., Shafer, R. and Shadiow, L. (1990). The Swinging Pendulum: Teaching English in the USA, 1945–1987. In Britton, J., Shafer, R., and Watson, K. (Eds), *Teaching and Learning English Worldwide*. Philadelphia: Multilingual Matters Ltd.

The Guardian. (2004, 10th November). Wales Abolished Compulsory Tests. Available at https://www.theguardian.com/uk/2004/nov/10/schools.sats (accessed on 1st June 2016).

The Scottish Government. (2016). *National Improvement Framework for Scottish Education: Achieving Excellence and Equity*. Edinburgh: The Scottish Government.

8

CONCLUSION

The futures of English?

What then of the future, or futures, for secondary English in English schools? If the past five decades are any indication of the future then it seems the only safe thing to predict is yet more change, as successive governments seek to make their mark on education, and in making that mark acknowledge that, above all other subjects, English has a fundamental role to play in how individuals, communities and societies may be shaped. At a time of huge political turmoil in the wake of the European referendum, what will it mean in the future to be English or British, and how might education policymakers see the subject's role in this? Forecasting the future is fraught with pitfalls, and it is impossible to say how changes in culture, society and technology may impact on schools generally. However, a consideration of the history of the development of subject English may give some insight into what may be to come.

It's tempting to believe that, given the fundamental shifts in the school landscape since the introduction of academies, central intervention, at least at the level of curriculum, may increasingly be a thing of the past. The statistics showed that by 2015 over 60 per cent of secondary schools in England were already academies (Department for Education, 2015). This figure included a significant and growing number of free schools. All these institutions have been given the freedom to ignore the National Curriculum, and short of a wholesale process of bringing these schools back into local authority control – which seems almost implausible even in the unlikely event that there was a political will for it to happen – it is difficult to see how the freedoms offered could be wrested away. In fact, with the publication of its education white paper *Educational Excellence Everywhere* (Department for Education, 2016), the Conservative government announced its intention that every school would be an academy by 2022. Subsequent protests – some from within their own party, including those from Conservative-led councils who were concerned at the removal of any role for local authorities in education – meant the government swiftly backtracked on this proposal, with the Education Secretary Nicky Morgan claiming that, whilst forced academisation for all would no longer be within legislation, the aim remained that all schools would convert to that status but that now the government would 'change the path to reaching that goal' (*The Guardian*, 2016). Changing that path might perhaps mean manipulating funds to sixth forms, for example, to effectively make it impossible for secondary schools to exist outside of academy chains or multi-academy trusts. Time will of course tell whether the goal of full academisation is indeed achieved; with or without legislation, by direct means or by stealth, it is clearly the desire of the Conservative government to reach full academy status. The government, however, in the light of the referendum has other priorities and, with a change of education secretary in the wake of David Cameron's resignation, the further reforms promised in *Educational Excellence Everywhere* may well be in doubt.[1]

One's view on a move to full academisation of state schools will depend on whether one believes the rhetoric about the value of academies having freedom from local bureaucracy or whether one is suspicious of a policy that effectively makes schools answerable only to the minister and subverts any local democracy. It is certainly difficult to sustain an argument for academies on the basis of their success in terms of examination results or outcomes of school inspections, as the evidence is far from straightforward (see, for example, NFER (2015)).

What is laid down as statutory for the purposes of external examinations and qualifications in English and literature will of course in reality dictate content for the upper ages of secondary schooling, but it is increasingly likely that a National Curriculum covering all secondary years will become a thing of the past. It is perhaps more likely that the increasing number of multi-academy trusts and academy chains will mean that schools that are linked together will develop a shared curriculum and pedagogy and an agreed means of assessment. If the current trend to entrust schools with the training of entrants to the profession continues or is even extended – as *Educational Excellence Everywhere* proposed – it is perhaps even more likely that versions of English will be formed that are the domain of a group of schools. For argument's sake it could be said that an academy chain – 'Chain X' – adopts a particular form of English curriculum and assessment and promotes a particular pedagogy, and trains its own staff to enact this version of English – which may be in some way home grown, or it might be an import like Hirsch's core knowledge curriculum. In a worst-case scenario English teachers in such schools may only know one model of English and see it simply as the way English is done. Even if a curriculum were adopted by a group of schools that could be seen as progressive, humane and in the tradition of growth English, it would still be a shame if its enactors considered this simply as the way the subject is done.

Arguments about what effective English teaching is keep the subject alive and dynamic. Knowledge of the development of English over time, of the debates of Dartmouth, the contested nature of the National Curriculum and the protests over assessment – the sorts of knowledge primarily developed through the kinds of subject teaching accessed by new entrants to the profession through initial teacher training in universities – are all central to the arguments. Such knowledge, though, might well be deemed irrelevant in the pursuit of an English teaching that works. In a fully academised world, it's likely that there would be little, if any, role for local authorities and so those that have strived to maintain some form of advisory service in the years following the demise of National Strategy would see funding fall away even more sharply. Peer-to-peer support, collaboration and networking would happen not at local authority level, nor at independently organised professional development events – which in the years of centralisation have focused their content, more and more mechanistically, on implementation of new exam specifications and strategies to boost achievement of target groups (typically boys, or C/D grade borderline students). Nor, for the vast majority of English teachers, would professional development come through subject association conferences; even at the height of NATE's popularity attendance at annual conference was only ever a small proportion of the membership. Professional development would come increasingly from school-to-school support within multi-academy trusts sharing a common vision of the subject. The wider context of the seemingly unstoppable standards reform agenda and its links to international comparison, accountability and marketisation also have a potentially deadening effect on genuine development, innovation and risk taking.

It would be a sad future for the subject if the ongoing debates about curriculum, assessment and pedagogy were to be closed down as a result of national policy and the global market in education, and given the turbulent history of the subject it is perhaps unlikely that this would actually happen. The fragmentation of the school landscape and the increasing move to an apprenticeship model for teacher education[2] may work against teacher professionalism and collaboration, but it is difficult to believe that English as a subject could be depoliticised, and all the time the subject retains its political dimension it will be the case that new and existing teachers will hold differing views of what English should be. And even if a future central curriculum attempted to pin down the literary canon and reduce English language to a set of fixed rules, the reality is that new literature continues to appear, the language refuses to stagnate, societies become increasingly multilingual and modes of communication evolve at a pace. To try and fix English in the classroom, hermetically sealed from the outside reality of a dynamic, changing language in an increasingly complex, globalised world, would be a foolish task and certainly one doomed to failure. History has proved this to be so. Even in the face of the strongest central intervention, the story of secondary English has been one of notions of the subject – some complementary, some conflicting – co-existing.

It's been suggested that the future of English ought to see the subject undergo a change of name – a rebranding that would more accurately frame the scope of what many try to achieve through the discipline. In his article 'Curriculum, "English" and Cultural Studies; or, changing the scene of English teaching' (2004), the Australian academic Bill Green, neatly pointed out some of the complexities of the term 'English' given its increasing multi-use, referring to it as 'increasingly unstable' (Green, 2004, p. 299). As Green grappled with the uses of the term English and the changes being wrought on the subject by new technologies and the rise of 'literacy', whilst seeking to see some continuity with the best traditions in the subject, he suggested that the term English could not be jettisoned, but that there should be a 're-positioning' that 'lies in tracing the movement from "English" to "Cultural Studies"' (ibid., p. 300). Although Green wasn't simply suggesting a renaming, his thinking does inevitably lead us to consider the question of whether English is a suitable title for a subject that attempts to embrace literature, language and literacy whilst promoting growth, citizenship, an understanding of self, others, cultures, societies and histories, and strives to equip students to become experts of language in all the modes and forms it takes in the twenty-first century. Andrews (2001) suggested rhetoric might be a more apt title for such a broad subject. The question of whether English is no longer suitable as a title for what happens in English classrooms has been the subject of debate at a NATE annual conference,[3] and although the motion for a name change was defeated by the delegates' votes, the arguments – although at times tongue in cheek – were strong.

Optimistically, given English teachers' traditional desire to argue over the nature of the subject and how it should be experienced by young people, it might be the case that a gradual eroding of a National Curriculum gives rise to innovation and development in the subject, and perhaps even to a reassessment of the subject's evolution.[4] Such a reassessment will inevitably focus to a large extent on the growth of the progressive post-Second World War English.

The Cox curriculum may well have given the official seal of approval to personal growth English among its five models of the subject, but in doing so was only vindicating a broader progressive model of English that was already firmly established in the hearts and minds of many in the profession. This model, much wider than a narrow version of personal growth, had grown from the work of innovative teachers and academics, collaborating in classroom-based research and projects and led to the cementing of the student's place at the heart of the vision for the subject. What can generally be termed this progressive model of the subject made orthodox what – despite policy intervention – remains central to much of that that is good in good English teaching: the primacy of oral work; productive and exploratory group discussion; the celebration of linguistic diversity; the importance of relevance of English to the student's own experience and background; the exploration of language in all its modes; exploration of media; the breadth of literature to be enjoyed – traditional and contemporary, national and international. The work of LATE and NATE, the Schools Council's projects on Language in Use and the Development of Writing Abilities, the Talk Workshop enterprise, the National Writing Project and the National Oracy Project, and the Language in the National Curriculum projects have all – sometimes in the face of centralist opposition – been instrumental in developing this version of English, and all share, to a greater or lesser extent, the fundamental belief that in developing English teaching it is of critical importance that this development work actively involves those enacting the subject and those who are learning it.

It seems highly likely that some notion of personal growth will remain central to the English teacher's project. That may well be since, it has been claimed, 'it can mean different things to different people' (Reid, 2003, p. 104). In *The Persistent Pedagogy of Growth*, the Australian academic Reid – in many ways a critic of growth English – traced the roots of the personal growth model to the work of Words-worth, and viewed Dixon's articulation of the idea in *Growth through English* as heavily influenced by the author's own reading of *The Prelude* which, at the time of Dartmouth, he was using in training teachers at Bretton Hall in South Yorkshire. Reid stressed, however, that personal growth should not become 'personalism', something Dixon himself acknowledged when he made amendments to the 1975 version of *Growth through English, Set in the Perspective of the Seventies* (Dixon, 1975). The criticism of personal growth as having something of the cult of the self has dogged this vision of English, but such a criticism is to do a disservice to Dixon and to the many English teachers who view it as central to their own pedagogy. It misses the point that for Dixon the title personal growth was never satisfactory and that the model, even that articulated in the original publication of *Growth through English*, was always a much broader progressive, indeed radical, view of the subject. Dixon's political views and his work at Walworth developing *Reflections* cannot be ignored in an evaluation of growth English.

For Reid, Dixon's personal growth was 'neither doctrinaire nor merely personalist' (Reid, 2003, p. 103); even if it had its roots in *The Prelude* this poem itself was more than merely autobiography as it also 'testified powerfully to the widespread changes wrought by political and industrial revolution' (ibid.). Most would agree with the assertion made by Reid that 'inviting students to bring their own experience into the English classroom in their own language, to discuss their emotional responses to what they read, and to explore their attitudes in what they write, is always legitimate' (ibid., p. 104). For teachers who are passionate about English, the subject for them is simultaneously personal, political and social; we find ourselves moved by texts we encounter that touch on our own experiences, we share our interests in these texts with friends and colleagues through our talk and writing, in doing so we are shaping our views of ourselves and of the world. This is simply what happens; how could the subject ever become simply the transmission of knowledge of certain discrete forms of literature and language when it doesn't exist like that for us, in the real world?

Writing as I am in the year of the 50th anniversary of Dartmouth then perhaps what is needed for the future of English is a far-reaching and critical re-evaluation of growth pedagogy, and a full rearticulation of what a progressive model of the subject is or should be in an English classroom in a twenty-first century, globalised, multicultural, multimodal environment. Such a rearticulation would be mindful of tradition without being enslaved to it, and clear about the construction of self as something that takes place within and alongside the growth and development of friends, families, communities and societies.

The case for such a rearticulation has been made by Andrew Goodwyn, who is known for his research into the significance of personal growth to the English teaching profession over the past 20 years and more. Goodwyn's work, sometimes in collaboration with international colleagues, has repeatedly shown the pre-eminent place in English teachers' thinking of the growth model (see, for example, Goodwyn (1992, 2005) and Goodwyn and Findlay (1999)). This pre-eminence is seen not only in England, but in the United States, Australia, Canada and beyond. Goodwyn conducted a survey of delegates at the 2015 IFTE conference in New York, asking the 260 present to review the relative importance to their work of five models of English – four of these were first articulated in Cox's National Curriculum (the cross-curricular model was omitted), the fifth was critical literacy. According to that survey – completed by about 40 per cent of those present – 'most commentators acknowledged all the models as still relevant and important and felt that PG (personal growth) was still at the heart of English. There were critiques of its limitations but few of its salience' (Goodwyn, 2016, p. 18), leading to the conclusion that 'the work of Dixon and colleagues in the sixties and seventies deserves much more respect for its importance and for its robustness than it is frequently afforded, it has stood at least one test of time' (ibid., p. 19), and to the powerful claim that 'the Personal Growth model, certainly in England but also internationally, retains its pre-eminence as the preferred ideology of the majority of the teachers of English' (ibid.). Of course, delegates at an IFTE conference may well be predisposed to the growth model so the claim that these findings are generalisable is debatable, but it is not far-fetched to assume that the broad notion of a child-centred, progressive pedagogy is indeed important to many teachers.

In revisiting *Growth through English* – notably the 1975 second edition *Set in the Perspectives of the Seventies* (Dixon, 1975) – and reassessing its continued importance, Goodwyn goes on to suggest that two other models of English deserve to be in some way combined with personal growth in the attempt to articulate a notion of English for the future. Drawing from his IFTE survey data, Goodwyn proposes that personal growth, what he terms 'the affective model' of English teaching, might be combined with two other models that garnered support from the respondents: cultural analysis (CA) and critical literacy (CL). He suggests:

> PG [1] is the affective, emancipatory heart of English. CA [2] is concerned, as is Critical Literacy [3], with the cognitive, economic and cultural forces of the twenty-first century. These models are all concerned with the individual's agency formed by experiences and education and by the social and cultural materials available to teachers and students. Perhaps, then, a combination might be, something like, *Personal and Social Agency*?
>
> *(Goodwyn, 2016, p. 19)*

Inexact as he accepts this title may be, Goodwyn offers it as a point for further debate, and it seems a not unreasonable suggestion. It's arguable that this is a model of English that is already widely practised – Cox himself declared that his five models of the subject were not mutually exclusive and, though Goodwyn's research has highlighted the pre-eminence of growth, those respondents who point to it are likely to have a diverse range of views. Amongst these respondents would be those who would place more or less emphasis on media and multimodality within English, those who would have differing views on the teaching of grammar or knowledge about language, those who would have contrasting ideas about appropriate literature for the classroom, and so on. It's difficult to conceive of a teacher of English who didn't in some way practise forms of cultural and critical literacy through their classes' consumption and production of texts. In selecting personal growth as a preferred model when given a choice of discrete categories, it is probably more likely the case that what this reveals is a shared commitment to a broadly progressive model – one that places the student, rather than subject content, at the centre of thinking. This, more than anything, is the legacy of the work that led to the consensus from Dartmouth. Maybe it is time to jettison once and for all 'personal' given the unhelpful connotations the word attracts. Catchy or not, 'Critical, cultural, social and creative agency' would be the title for a model of English that may well accommodate most teachers' conception of the subject.

Where this rethinking or reconceptualising of a progressive view of the subject will happen is questionable. Both NATE and the English Association continue to hold conferences and publish their journals, *English in Education* and *The Use of English*. The United Kingdom Literacy Association, too, though primarily a group for primary teachers, convenes events and publishes its research journals *Literacy* and *Research in Reading*. Through these events and conferences, and in the pages of the journals *Changing English* and *English Teaching Practice and Critique*, the debates about the future of English will continue, but it must be acknowledged that the current trend is for subject association membership to be on the wane, and in reality few are the practising English teachers who actively read research. Whether these facts are explained by the effects of nearly 30 years of top-down reform on the sense of teachers as professionals with some form of autonomy and agency, or by the pressure brought to bear of standards-based reform and accountability frameworks, or by the sheer overload of work that a teacher currently has to shoulder, is questionable. The reality is probably that a combination of all these things has created a climate in which debates about the future of English inevitably take place at the margins and involve relatively few people. They do, however, continue to take place.

There are, of course, growing numbers of Teachmeets taking place, though these tend to be events to swap top tips rather than debate fundamentals of the subject, and there is no shortage of self-appointed experts blogging their views on the right way to teach English. It's hard to see such things playing a significant part in reshaping the subject through the twenty-first century.

If anything is clear from the history of English as a school subject it is that, though central policy intervention has had its undoubted influence, the truly transformative moves in pedagogy and curriculum – those that have captured hearts and minds and stood the test of time – have come from the bottom up, rather than the top down, something powerfully shown by Dixon's personal reflections on his involvement in the profession for over 50 years (Dixon, 2015). This is the most important lesson from the past: an appreciation of the history of English should empower English teachers of the future to know that their collective agency is the most powerful shaper of the subject. This work has shown how, after decades of profession-led change, the policymakers repeatedly sought to intervene to control English, primarily to make the subject play its part in a system that contributes to global economic competitiveness, but also to shape a notion of Englishness. That enterprise has necessarily involved sidelining much of the profession and the attempt to shut down intellectual arguments about the subject. It is an enterprise that has not, however, fully succeeded. At least, not yet.

The political context will change, it may even become more hospitable for educators. If English is a subject that looks to engender agency, its learners, its teachers must believe what they preach. The future will see more historical accounts of English as a discipline; if the sense of professional agency can be recaptured then those accounts will tell of a subject and its teachers that work, whether helped or hindered by policy, for the fullest possible growth of their learners.

Notes

1 Justine Greening replaced Nicky Morgan as Secretary of State for Education in the Conservative cabinet reshuffle of July 2016. Greening is the first person to attend a state comprehensive school to fill this post. Whilst it's tempting to believe this would make her sympathetic to the comprehensive ideal, early reports have suggested she is not averse to the ideas of the new Prime Minister, Theresa May, who is said to favour an increase in selective schools in the state system (see, for example, *The Independent* (2016) at http://www.independent.co.uk/news/uk/politics/grammar-schools-return-theresa-may-justine-greening-bring-back-selective-education-uk-a7141271.html accessed on 20th July 2016).

2 Increasingly, particularly since 2010, policy around initial teacher education has seen a huge emphasis on school-based teacher training, with university-based teacher education increasingly under pressure. New School Direct routes have been favoured in the annual allocation of trainee numbers to providers. The official line given for this is the policymakers' belief that the best way to learn how to teach is to do so by watching experienced professionals and engaging in professional practice – in effect, an apprenticeship model. In *Educational Excellence Everywhere* (Department for Education, 2016), the rhetoric simultaneously calls for research-based and evidence-informed teaching and champions the involvement of the best universities in the process. It is difficult to reconcile this apparent contradiction and much easier to subscribe to the view that the Conservatives' ideological pursuit is to take university academics – Gove's 'enemies of promise' – out of teacher education altogether. The proposals in the white paper to take the authority to award Qualified Teacher Status from accredited providers, like universities, and hand it to schools makes this entirely possible.

3 The debate – 'English is no longer a suitable name for the subject we teach' – took place at NATE's annual conference in 2006.

4 There does seem to have been a recent increase in interest in histories of English teaching. A good example would be *English Teachers in a Postwar Democracy: Emerging Choice in London Schools 1945–1965* (Medway, Hardcastle, Brewis and Crook, 2014), a book following a funded research project into the teaching of English in three London schools in the post-war decades. Along with the account of the evolution of LATE (Gibbons, 2014), it throws light on the emergence of an alternative English. 2016 saw a LATE conference

attended by over 100 English teachers that offered a retrospective evaluation of the work of James Britton and a NATE symposium to consider the ongoing impact of the Dartmouth Seminar on the 50th anniversary of the event. John Richmond's proposals for an alternative curriculum are, in many ways, a revisiting of the best ideas of the past. It seems one positive effect of centralisation since the late 1980s is that some teachers and researchers feel impelled to ensure that 1989 is not viewed as year zero, that the history is not forgotten, and they even carry the hope that history has the potential to inform the future.

References

Andrews, R. (2001). *Teaching and Learning English: A Guide to Recent Research and it Applications.* London: Continuum.

Department for Education. (2015). Schools, Pupils and their Characteristics. Available at https://www.gov.uk/government/uploads/system/uploads/attachment_data/file/433680/SFR16_2015_Main_Text.pdf (accessed on 8th March 2015).

Department for Education. (2016). Educational Excellence Everywhere. Available at https://www.gov.uk/government/uploads/system/uploads/attachment_data/file/508550/Educational_excellence_everywhere__print_ready_.pdf (accessed on 1st July 2016).

Dixon, J. (1975). *Growth through English: Set in the Perspective of the Seventies.* London: Penguin.

Dixon, J. (2015) Developing English. *English Teaching Practice and Critique*, 14(3), pp. 427–434.

Gibbons, S. (2014). *The London Association for the Teaching of English 1947–67: A History.* London: Institute of Education/Trentham Press.

Goodwyn, A. (1992). Theoretical Models of English. *English in Education*, 26(3), pp. 4–10.

Goodwyn, A. (2005). A Framework for English? Or a Vehicle for Literacy? English Teaching in England in the Age of the Strategy. *English Teaching Practice and Critique*, 3(3), pp. 16–28.

Goodwyn, A. (2016). Still Growing After All These Years? The Resilience of the Personal Growth Model of English in England and Also Internationally. *English Teaching Practice and Critique*, 15(1), pp. 7–21.

Goodwyn, A. and Findlay, K. (1999). The Cox Models Revisited: English Teachers' Views of Their Subject and the National Curriculum. *English in Education*, 33(2), pp. 19–31.

Green, B. (2004). Curriculum, 'English' and Cultural Studies: Or, Changing the Scene of English Teaching. *Changing English*, 11(2), pp. 291–305.

Medway, P., Hardcastle, J., Brewis, G. and Crook, D. (2014). *English Teachers in a Postwar Democracy: Emerging Choice in London Schools, 1945–1965.* New York: Palgrave Macmillan.

NFER. (2015). Academies and Maintained Schools: What Do We Know? NFER Election Factsheet. Available at https://www.nfer.ac.uk/publications/FFEE02/FFEE02.pdf (accessed on 9th May 2016).

Reid, I. (2003). The Persistent Pedagogy of Growth. In Doecke, B., Homer, D. and Nixon, H. (Eds), *English Teachers at Work: Narratives, Counter Narratives and Arguments.* South Australia: Wakefield Press.

The Guardian. (2016, 6th May). Government Backs Down Over Plan to Make All Schools in England Academies. Available at http://www.theguardian.com/education/2016/may/06/government-backs-down-over-plan-to-make-all-schools-academies (accessed on 6th May 2016).

INDEX

100% coursework A level 104n7
100% coursework GCSE 49–51, 54, 74, 75, 77, 78, 81, 82n7

academies 115, 120, 158, 159
action research 46, 54
adult literacy issues 43, 44, 86, 145
Alexander, R. 100, 112, 113
And When You Are Young 23
Assessing Pupils' Progress (APP) 96, 105n16, 116, 117
assessment 1, 5, 9, 21, 46, 62, 100, 102, 111, 117, 118, 121, 124, 126, 127, 130; assessment for learning 75, 82, 97, 116, 117; controlled conditions assessment 111–12, 118, 119; coursework 112, 118, 119; high stakes assessment and accountability 2, 3, 7, 61, 80, 115, 120, 122; modular assessment 112, National Curriculum levels 67, 97, 105n16, 116, 117, 120, 133n7; report on *Assessment without Levels* 117–18; speaking and listening assessment 97, 119, 130; terminal examinations 51, 76, 112, 118, 119
Australian Association for the Teaching of English (AATE) 30
Australian Council for Education Standards (ACES) 151
Australian Curriculum, Assessment and Reporting Authority (ACARA) 152

Baker, K. 63, 68, 75
Balls, E. 102

Barber, M. 7
Barnes, A. 75, 82n7
Barnes, Dorothy 9
Barnes, Douglas 9, 16, 19, 20, 21, 22, 23, 27, 28, 33, 34, 36n6, 45, 48, 52, 53, 55n1, 55n6, 90, 143, 150
Basic Skills Agency 85–6
basic skills in English 1, 33, 43, 44, 110, 118, 154n10
Bay Area Writing Project 124–5, 144
Beard, R. 87, 90
Bearne, E. 101
Beloe Report 55n5
Berstein, B. 26
bilingualism 71
Birmingham University School of Education 53
Black, P. 75, 82n6, 149
Black Papers, the 33–4, 43–4, 65, 71, 78, 155n13

Blair, T. 84, 103n1
'blob, the' 111, 133n4; *see also* 'enemies of promise'
Blunkett, D. 86, 104n4
Boston, K. 100
bottom-up curriculum development 15, 19, 46, 65, 67, 123, 125, 144
Brennan, J. 113
British Council 18
British Film Institute 41
Britishness 6, 110

Britton, J. 28, 36n11, 90, 124, 142, 144, 148, 150, 166n4; contribution to the Bullock Report 44–5; at Dartmouth Seminar 21; Language and Learning 26–7; in LATE 4, 16, 21, 45; in NATE 4, 20, 31, 34, 45; theorizing English teaching 26–7, 33, 34, 44–5, 47
Bruner, J. 26
Bullock Report (*A Language for Life*) 9, 27, 43–5, 46, 47, 54, 63, 66, 112
Burgess, T. 9, 15, 24, 25, 26, 30, 31, 36n7, 36n11, 46, 47, 55n4
Burn, A. 123
Butler Act 15, 36n1

Callaghan, J. 46, 62
Cambridge English 20, 22, 23, 24, 35
Cameron, David 158
Cameron, Deborah 100
Caribbean Teachers' Exchange 42
Carnegie Foundation 21
Carter, R. 73, 100, 113
Cassier, E. 26
Centre for British Teachers (CfBT) 123
Centre for Contemporary Cultural Studies, Birmingham University 41
Centre for Policy Studies 50, 68, 79
Certificate of Secondary Education (CSE) 42, 49, 50, 55n3, 118
child-centred approaches to English 8, 26, 31, 33, 34, 42, 43, 46, 50, 62, 79, 88, 90, 131, 143, 153, 163
Chomsky, N. 144
Circular 10/65 15
Clackmannanshire 105n15, 114
Clark, U. 6
Clarke, C. 100–1
Clarke, K. 76
classroom resources for English teaching 18, 42, 48
Clements, S. 9, 18, 26, 37n12, 41, 55n9
Clissold Park School 42
cognitive development 2, 35
cognitive science 26
Cold War 21
Coles, J. 77
combining document and oral data in research 10
Commission 7 (seven) 31, 55n4
common core curriculum 153
Common Core Standards Initiative 147
Communist Party 32
comprehensive schools 139, 165n1; criticism of 8, 33–4, 43, 65, 104n3, 153; the emergence of comprehensive schools 2,

15, 19; English in the comprehensive school 15–17, 18, 35, 47; moves away from comprehensive system 2; London schools 15–17, 18, 36n2, 71
Confederation of British Industries (CBI) 132n
Consortium for Assessment and Testing in Schools (CATS) 75–6
continuing professional development 44, 50, 53, 94, 113, 116, 124, 125, 126, 131, 133n7, 160
Cope, B. 91–2, 105n14, 151
core standards 115, 147, 148, 154n5
Cox, B. 71, 78, 89, 99, 102, 116, 149, 161; *Black Papers* 34, 65; five models of English teaching 22, 66, 161, 163; role in National Curriculum for English 65–9; views on aspects of English
creativity 8, 22, 33, 49, 97, 101, 102, 111, 114, 125, 141, 142, 146
critical literacy 162–3, 164
Crystal, D. 91, 104n11
Curriculum Matters series 62–3, 64, 70

Dartmouth Seminar 9, 20–5, 30, 34, 159, 162; background to 20–1, 26, 144; influence and legacy 4, 7, 8, 23–4, 25, 26, 34, 35, 44, 65, 129, 143, 144, 145, 146, 148, 154, 164, 166n4; perspectives on 21–2, 23, 24, 36n8, 56n12; outcomes from 16, 22–3;
Dearing, R. 69–70
Department for Children, Schools and Families (DCSF) 96, 124
Department for Education 69, 90, 112, 113, 116, 117, 140, 142, 158, 165n2
Department of Education and Science 64, 73
Derewianka, B. 152
Development of Writing Abilities, The 27, 46–7, 126, 161
devolution 140, 142
Dixon, J. 4, 9, 15–16, 20, 21, 22–5, 27, 28, 32, 36n3, 41–2, 48, 54, 55n9, 90, 142, 150, 162, 163, 165
document data 9
Dougill, P. 122–3
drama in English 17, 22, 28, 85, 114, 130
Dweck, C. 117

Eaglestone, R. 118
Eagleton, T. 35
East London and Macmillan Assessment Group (ELMAG) 75–6
Ebacc 118

economic competitiveness 84, 85, 139, 153, 165
Economic and Social Research Council (ESRC) 126
Education Reform Act 1988, the 7, 51
Edwards, T. 100
Ellis, V. 98, 94, 96
'enemies of promise' 96, 132, 133n4, 165n
English 21 100–2, 121
English Association 18, 20, 164
English in Australia 20, 150–3
English in Canada 20, 148–50
English Centre *see* English and Media Centre
English as language 8, 16, 17, 18, 20, 24, 26, 28, 35, 146, 150; *see also* London English
English as literature 24, 35, 111, 146 *see also* Cambridge English
English and Media Centre (formerly the English Centre) 31, 41, 46, 48–9, 54, 94
English in Northern Ireland 140–1
English in Scotland 142–3
English in the United States 20, 21, 43, 115, 144–8
English in Wales 141–2
Englishness 77, 110, 165
ethnicity 30, 31, 42, 43, 54
examination reform 117, 118–20, 133n8
EXEL Project 91, 105n12

film, use in English classes 41, 143
Ford, B. 19
formative assessment' *see* assessment
Froome, S. 44
Furlong, T. 75, 82n7

Gardner, P. 10
gender 2, 8, 30, 31, 41, 48: boys and English 84–5, 93; gender and attainment 84–5, 93; gender issues in the classroom 41, 43, 54, 55n3
General Certificate of Secondary Education (GCSE) 49, 54, 80, 96, 97, 98, 100, 103, 105n17, 110, 111, 112, 120, 128, 130, 152; *see also* 100% coursework GCSE
genre approaches to the teaching of English 28, 86, 91–2, 94, 95, 97, 105n13, 130, 150, 151–2, 153, 155n14
Globe Theatre, the 121
Goodwyn, A. 6, 8, 23, 90, 93, 95, 97, 163, 164
Goody, J. 9, 42
Gove, M. 113, 133n; education 109; National Curriculum reform 111–12,

120, 122, 147, 165n2; speech to party conference 109–10; views on English teaching 109, 111; views on examinations 118–19
grammar 4; approaches to teaching 18, 28–9, 43–4, 63, 88, 155; debates 33, 43, 64, 71, 91, 104n6, 148, 164; in the *Framework for English* 89, 91, 95; *The Grammar Papers* 100; *Grammar for Writing* 87, 98, 104n6; in Kingman Report 64; Language in the National Curriculum Project 73; in the National Curriculum 66, 68, 69, 70, 99, 114, 129, 142; *Not Whether but How* 100; research 28, 91, 98, 126–9; systemic functional grammar 28, 105n13; tests 80, 129; traditional grammar teaching 33, 43, 65, 110, 152
grammar school English 9, 16, 153
Graves, D. 88, 104n8
Green, B. 160–1
growth mindsets 117
Growth through English 16, 20, 22–5, 26, 27, 28, 29, 34, 35, 36n3, 54, 55n12, 150, 162

Hackman, S. 9, 88, 89, 92, 95, 97–8, 104n7
Hall, S. 41
Halliday, M. 28, 33, 34, 105n13, 128, 151
Harding, D.W. 37n14, 45
Harris, R. 9, 37n16, 41
Harrison, C. 90, 91
Her Majesty's Inspectorate (HMI) 62, 64, 74, 122
Hickman, J. 9, 71, 79, 82n4, 100, 141
Hilliard, G. 35
Hillocks, G. 91
Hilton, M. 91
Hirsh, E.D. 147, 154n7, 159
historical accounts of English teachers and teaching 4–6
historical research, importance of 3–4
Hoggart, R. 41, 42
Holbrook, D. 36n9
Holloway School 15, 36n3, 41
home international comparisons 140
Horner, S. 9, 52, 70, 71, 81n1, 99, 100, 101, 102, 121
Howe, A. 95
Huxford, L. 90

imagination 8, 97, 101, 141
Inglis, F. 35
initial teacher training 16, 26, 43, 54, 64, 73, 90, 96–7, 160, 165n2
Inner London Education Authority (ILEA) 31, 41, 46, 48, 122

international accounts of English teaching 6–7
International Reading Association (IRA) 145–7
interview data 9–10

James, M. 113, 132n3, 133n6
Johnson, A. 89
Johnson, J. 52–3, 67
Jones, K. 68
Joseph, K. 36n7, 50, 63

Kalantzis, M. 91, 92, 151
Keith, G. 100
Kelly, G. 26
Key Stage 2 tests 87, 103, 104n4
Key Stage 3 English Anthology 76–7, 78, 79, 110
Key Stage 3 Framework for English: content 88; development 88; impact and legacy 96–9; renewed Framework, teachers' responses to 88–90, 93–4; theoretical underpinning 90–3; training 94–5
Key Stage 3 tests and boycott 51, 69, 70, 75–80, 99, 103, 104n7, 110, 116, 120, 139, 141, 143, 152
Kidbrooke School 36n4
Kingman Report 64–5, 66, 72, 73
Kress, G. 101, 105n13, 126

La Rose, J. 43, 55n2
La Rose, S. 43, 55n2
Labour Teachers 32
language across the curriculum 45, 46, 47, 55n7
language arts (English as) 145, 146, 147, 148, 149, 150
language development 1, 54, 87, 91
Language, the Learner and the School 45, 46, 55n7
Language and Learning 26–7, 29, 45, 47
Language in the National Curriculum project (LINC) 29, 55n8, 64, 65, 72–4, 82n5, 100, 122, 126, 161
Language in Use project 27–9, 35, 161
Lawlor, S. 68
learning objectives see lesson objectives
Leavis, F.R. 16, 23, 24, 25, 35, 36n9, 40, 47, 110, 111
lesson objectives 92, 97, 130, 131
Lewis, M. 91, 105n12
linguistic and language diversity 29, 146, 161
literacy 9, 43, 54, 85, 86, 88, 92, 93, 96, 97, 105n14, 123, 132n2, 142, 145, 148–50,

152, 161; see also literacy across the curriculum; National Literacy Strategy; Key Stage 3 Framework for English
literacy across the curriculum 54, 95
literature 1, 8, 27, 30, 35, 73, 88, 96, 97, 112, 129, 133n9, 146, 160, 161, 162, 164; A level literature 47–8; in Australian curriculum 152; the canon 23, 25, 33, 43, 65, 109–10, 111, 114, 119; GCSE Literature 49, 50, 118, 119, 159; O level literature 27, 49, 55n11; prescribed authors in the National Curriculum 66, 69, 114, 141, 147; in Scottish curriculum 142–3; in United States curriculum 21, 144, 146
Lloyd, M. 51, 75
local authorities 2, 15, 43, 52, 53, 62, 75; role in the LINC project 72, 73; role in National Strategies 80, 86, 87, 88, 94; reduced role of/threats to 159, 160
local curriculum 115
Local Schools Network 36n5
London Association for the Teaching of English (LATE) 21, 22, 23, 25, 26, 28, 30, 31, 36n6, 44, 45, 46, 47, 53, 55n7, 55n9, 55n10, 67, 82n4, 101, 117, 151, 161, 165n4; early development and work 15–16, 17; publications 17–19, 78, 79, 80; role in boycott of national testing 76–80; working practices 17, 19, 53, 126
London County Council, the 36n2
London English 8, 15–19, 20, 21, 24, 26, 28, 34; see also English as language
London Plan 36n2
Looking for the Heart of English 121–2, 126, 131

Marenbon, J. 68. 79
Marks, J. 68
Marshall, B. 154n11
Martin, J. 92, 105n13
Martin, N. 4, 16, 36n11, 124
Massachusetts Institute of Technology 27
Mathieson, M. 5–6
McCulloch, G. 3
McEwan, I 99
McLeod, A. 46, 55n9
McNeilly, I. 113, 133n6
media studies in English 2, 8, 17, 18, 41–2, 48, 54, 73, 114, 123, 141, 150, 161, 164
Medway, P. 9, 29, 31, 37n15, 55n1, 55n4, 55n9
Meek, M. 52, 90
Mercer, N. 37n13, 95, 100, 101, 112, 113, 133n10

Miskin, R. 113
Mittins, B. 20
mixed-ability grouping 34, 43, 44, 49
Morpurgo, M. 119
multicultural literature 2, 42, 55n2,
    114, 144,
Myhill, D. 9, 98, 100, 127–9

*Nation at Risk: The Imperative for Educational
    Reform, A* 145
National Association for Advisors in English
    (NAAE) 69, 70, 104n5, 121, 123, 128
National Association for Schoolmasters and
    the Union of Women Teachers
    (NASUWT) 76, 78
National Association for the Teaching of
    English (NATE) 24, 28, 34, 36n, 48, 71,
    75, 80, 113, 121, 128, 133n6, 160, 161,
    165n3, 166n4; 1971 national conference
    30–1, 35, 45, 47; contribution to
    Dartmouth Seminar 21, 24; English in
    Education 28, 164; formation 19–20;
    membership 19; National Oracy Project
    53; National Writing Project 52, 53,
    124–6, 131, 145, 161; relationship to
    LATE; response to Kingman report 64–5;
    response to National Curriculum 67–8,
    69; working practices 30, 42, 53, 77,
    147, 164
National Council of Teachers of English
    (NCTE) 21, 30, 36n8, 144, 145–7,
    154n2
National Curriculum in Australia 150,
    152–3
National Curriculum Council (NCC) 51,
    52, 68, 69, 72, 81n1, 81n3
National Curriculum in England: 2, 3, 5, 7,
    8, 9, 40, 52, 118, 120, 123, 126, 129,
    130, 131, 140, 141, 145, 147, 152,
    155n14, 158, 159, 161; 1989 (Cox)
    version and responses to it 22, 34, 42, 61,
    62–3, 65–8, 161, 163; 1992 (Pascall)
    version 68–9; 1995 version and responses
    to it 69–72; 1999 version 99–100; 2008
    version and its development through
    English 21 100–2; 2012 version and its
    development 111, 112–15, 153, 154n9;
    attainment targets 66; origins of the
    National Curriculum 62–3; primary
    National Curriculum 114; Warwick
    University review of the Cox
    curriculum 68
National Curriculum Expert Panel:
    background 111; members 111, 132n3;
    report 112–13, 115, 116; resignations

from 113; views on language across the
    curriculum 112–13
National Curriculum in Northern Ireland
    140–1
National Curriculum in Scotland 142–3
National Curriculum in Wales 141–2
National Literacy Project (NLP) 86
National Literacy Strategy (NLS) 28, 85–8,
    128, 142, 149
National Oracy Project 51–3, 54, 72, 80,
    90, 95, 161
National Strategy 88, 100, 102, 160
National Union of Teachers (NUT) 76,
    78, 101
National Writing Project (in the United
    Kingdom): original project in England
    51–2, 55n8, 64, 66, 72, 80, 81n1, 122;
    Richard Andrews' project 123–4, 145;
    NATE project 123–6, 145, 161
National Writing Project (in the United
    States) 124, 125, 144–5
New Beacon Books 42, 55n2
New South Wales Disadvantaged Children
    Project 91
new technologies in English 2, 8, 40,
    153, 161
New Zealand Association for the Teaching
    of English 30
Newbolt Report, the 5, 43, 44, 53
Nuffield Programme in Linguistics and
    English Teaching 28, 151

O level 17, 26, 33, 49, 50, 55n5, 118
Ofsted 61, 71, 80, 81n2, 85, 116, 117; *Boys
    and English* 81, 84–5, 93; inspection 61,
    80, 84, 85, 116, 120, 122, 159; Key Stage
    3 report 98; triennial English reports 98,
    103, 120–1, 131, 133n9
Ogborn, J. 9, 55n1
oracy *see* speaking and listening
oral history 10
Owen Education 122–3

participant and spectator roles 27, 37n14,
    45, 47
Pascall, D. 68, 69, 70, 74
Patten, J. 68, 69, 76
personal growth English 8, 18, 20, 22–5, 29,
    54, 61, 66, 90, 150, 161, 162–4
phonics 105n, 113, 114, 122, 146
Piaget, J. 26
plenaries 87, 93, 95, 97
point, evidence, explanation (PEE) 131,
    133n9
Pollard, Andrew 111, 113, 132n3

Pollard, Arthur 33, 71
popular culture in English 17, 30, 41
post-16 English 47–8
Prentice, R. 43
Production of School English, the 126–7
Programme for International Student
   Assessment (PISA) 111, 139, 140, 141,
   150, 154n1
Progress 8 (eight) 112, 133n5
Progress in International Reading Literacy
   Study (PIRLS) 111
progressive English 48, 51, 65, 69, 120,
   129–30, 142, 159; attacks on/backlash
   against 4, 32–4, 43, 61, 63, 79, 81n2, 88,
   89–90, 94, 96, 110–11, 153; in Australia
   150, 151–2, 155n13; in the Bullock
   Report 44, 46, 47; in Canada 148, 149,
   150; development of 2, 4, 8, 15–19, 20,
   25, 30, 34–5,41–2, 48, 54, 62, 66, 67,
   123, 161, 162; future of 162–4; and the
   National Curriculum 66–7, 99; political
   dimensions 30–2; in Scotland 142, 143;
   theorising of 25–7, 29; in the United
   States 144, 146–7
progressive growth English; see personal
   growth English; progressive English
Project English 21, 144
pupil voice 31–2
psychology 2, 17, 24, 26, 29, 34, 35

Qualifications and Curriculum Authority
   (QCA) 52, 81n1, 85, 99–102, 132n3
Qualifications, Curriculum and
   Development Authority (QCDA) 81n1,
   82n3, 100, 102, 121

race 2, 31, 41, 42, 43, 54, 55n4, 85
reading 42, 43, 44, 94, 96, 97, 105n8,
   113, 130, 143, 146, 147, 148, 151, 152;
   in GCSE 111–12, 118, 152; guided
   group reading 88, 97, 92, 95, 151; in the
   Key Stage 3 English Framework 28, 88,
   89, 90, 91, 92, 94–5, 96, 97; in the
   National Curriculum 66, 68, 69, 70, 102,
   114; in the National Literacy Strategy 86,
   87; see also literature; multicultural
   literature
Reflections 18, 23, 37, 41, 162
rhetoric 142
Richmond, J. 9, 55n8; alternative English
   curriculum 122–3, 127, 129, 166n4;
   involvement in the LINC project 72–4,
   82n5; involvement in the National
   Writing Project 52; Vauxhall Manor Talk
   Workshop 45–6

Roots and Research 90–3
Rosen, H. 4, 16, 28, 32, 34, 45, 55n9, 65,
   67, 90, 143, 150
Rosen, M. 16, 36n5
Royal Society of the Arts 101
Royal Society of Literature 101

Sapir, E. 26
Sarland, C. 46
Save English Coursework campaign 51
Savva, H. 52
School 21 133n10
School Curriculum and Assessment
   Authority (SCAA) 70, 71, 80, 81n3, 85
School Curriculum Development
   Committee (SCDC) 51, 72
School Examinations and Assessment
   Council (SEAC) 68, 75, 76, 79
Schools Council 21, 27, 28, 29, 30, 36n7,
   40, 42, 44, 46–8, 49, 51, 62, 63, 80,
   81, 161
Scottish Education Board 143
Scottish Education Department 142
Searle, C. 31–2
Second World War 15, 26, 36n1, 36n2, 54,
   109, 161
setting and streaming 22, 104n3
Shakespeare, W. 16; in the National
   Curriculum 66, 71, 102, 114; in national
   tests 76, 77, 79, 82n7
Shayer, D. 4–6
Simon, B. 4
Simons, M. 41, 48
Smith, F. 148
Smith, J. 124–5, 145
social class 2, 5, 16, 17, 30, 31, 33, 42, 43,
   50, 54, 67, 84, 85, 96, 112, 151
soft skills 111
space race 21
speaking and listening 22, 27, 36n6, 46, 53,
   62, 79, 112–13, 130, 133n10, 140; in the
   GCSE 118, 119, 130 in the Key Stage 3
   English Framework 94, 95, 96, 97; in the
   National Curriculum 66, 69, 70, 102,
   114; in the National Literacy Strategy 86;
   see also National Oracy Project; Vauxhall
   Manor Talk Workshop
spelling, teaching and assessment of 33, 43,
   70, 89, 94, 111, 152, 155n10
spiral curriculum 67
Standard English 44, 63, 64, 65, 66, 67,
   68, 69, 70, 71, 72, 73, 99, 142,
   152, 153
standards-based reform 2, 3, 21, 104n2, 120,
   139, 145, 148, 149, 150, 152, 164

Stannard, J. 90
starters 87, 95, 97
Stepney school strike 31–2
Stepney Words 32
Stockholm Syndrome 103
Stratta, L. 41, 55n9
Summerfield, G. 22
Swain, G. 102

Task Group on Assessment and Testing
    (TGAT) 75
Tate, N. 71
Teaching London Kids 31, 68
teacher modelling 88, 92, 97, 151
teacher professionalism 7–8, 17, 53, 69, 74,
    76, 79, 93, 95, 103, 115, 121, 122, 123,
    124, 151, 160
Teachers TV 55n8, 122
teachers as writers *see* National Writing
    Project (in the United Kingdom);
    National Writing Project (in the United
    States)
Teachmeets 164
television, use in English teaching
    41, 143
Thatcher, M. 32, 36n7, 43, 62, 84
Top of the Pops 41
Tower Hamlets Local Authority 94, 55n
Training and Development Agency (TDA)
    102
Twyford School 111

underachievement in English 87, 89, 94;
    boys 84–5, 93; ethnic groups 89;
    socio-economic groups 84, 85
United Kingdom Literacy Association
    (UKLA) 101, 121, 128, 164
Universities and Left Review 41, 42
University of East Anglia 124
University of Exeter 127
University of Leeds 90

University of London, Institute of
    Education 22, 25, 26, 36n11, 46, 47,
    94, 114, 123, 126, 132n3, 150
Use of English, The 20, 35, 164

Vauxhall Manor Talk Workshop 45–6, 122
Vygotsky, L. 27, 37n13

Waddell Committee 49
Walworth School 16, 18, 22, 36n3, 37n12,
    37n15, 55n9, 162
Watts, R. 73, 74
West, A. 71, 82n4
Whannel, P. 41
Whitehead, F. 19–20, 22, 23, 24, 35
Wiliam, D. 75, 82n6, 111, 132n3, 149
Wilks, J. 9, 49, 50, 55n10, 76, 78, 79, 94, 95
Williams, R. 41, 42
Woodhead, C. 71, 81n2
Wray, D. 91, 105n12
Wrigley, S. 9, 70, 124–6, 145
writing 23, 44–5, 73, 94, 110, 113, 130,
    133n, 143, 147, 162; children's writing
    22–3, 29, 36n10; genre approaches to
    teaching writing 91–2, 97, 130, 151–2;
    guided writing 86, 88, 92, 95, 151;
    imaginative/creative writing 22, 92, 130;
    in the Key Stage 3 English Framework
    89–90, 91–2, 94, 95, 96; in the National
    Curriculum 66, 67, 69, 70, 102; in the
    National Literacy Strategy 86, 87; process
    approaches to teaching writing 104n8,
    148, 149; research into teaching writing
    46–7, 126–9, 161; writing triplets 97,
    152; *see also Development of Writing
    Abilities, The*; National Writing Project
    (in the United Kingdom), National
    Writing Project (in the United States)
Wyse, D. 114

Zephaniah, B. 99